The Meillassoux Dictionary

Edited by Peter Gratton and Paul J. Ennis

EDINBURGH
University Press

Edinburgh University Press Ltd
The Tun - Holyrood Road, 12(2f) Jackson's Entry, Edinburgh EH8 8PJ

www.euppublishing.com

Typeset in 11/13 Ehrhardt by
Servis Filmsetting Ltd, Stockport, Cheshire,
and printed and bound in Great Britain by
CPI Group (UK) Ltd, Croydon CR0 4YY

A CIP record for this book is available from the British Library

ISBN 978 0 7486 9555 3 (hardback)
ISBN 978 0 7486 9558 4 (webready PDF)
ISBN 978 0 7486 9556 0 (paperback)
ISBN 978 0 7486 9557 7 (epub)

Contents

Acknowledgements

We would like to begin by thanking all the contributors to this volume. Their efforts have allowed this work to become the rich resource we hoped it would be. It has been a pleasure to work with people we have known in various capacities through the years.

We also wish to extend our thanks to Carol Macdonald and the team at Edinburgh University Press for taking on this project and helping it come to fruition.

List of Abbreviations for Works by Quentin Meillassoux

AF   *After Finitude: An Essay on the Necessity of Contingency*, trans. Ray Brassier, London: Continuum, 2008.

AOTF   '"Archaeology of the Future": Interview with Quentin Meillassoux', *Paletten 1–2* 291/292 (2013), pp. 86–97.

BM   'Badiou and Mallarmé: The Event and the Perhaps', *Parrhesia*, 16 (2013), pp. 35–47.

CBI   '"There is contingent being independent of us, and this contingent being has no reason to be of a subjective nature": Interview with Quentin Meillassoux', in Iris van der Tuin and Rick Dolphjin (eds), *New Materialism: Interviews and Cartographies*, Michigan: Open Humanities Press, 2012, pp. 71–81.

(*CLN*) 'The Contingency of the Laws of Nature', *Environment and Planning D: Society and Space*, 30:2 (2012), pp. 322–34.

DI   'Appendix: Excerpts from *L'Inexistence divine*', in Graham Harman, *Quentin Meillassoux: Philosophy in the Making*, Edinburgh: Edinburgh University Press, 2011, pp. 175–238.

DI2   *L'Inexistence divine*, Doctoral Disseration, Université de Paris, 1997, available at <http:// www. scribd. com/ doc/127 012496/Quentin-Meillassoux-L-Inexistence-Divine> (accessed 1 September 2013).

IQM   'Interview with Quentin Meillassoux (August 2010)', in Graham Harman, *Quentin Meillassoux: Philosophy in the Making*, Edinburgh: Edinburgh University Press, 2011, pp. 159–74.

IRR   'Iteration, Reiteration, Repetition: A Speculative Analysis of the Meaningless Sign', Paper presented at the Freie Universität, Berlin, Germany, 20 April 2012, available at <oursecret-blog.com/txt/QMpaperApr12.pdf> (accessed 1 September 2013).

IWB   'The Immanence of the World Beyond', in Connor Cunningham and Peter Candler (eds), *The Grandeur of Reason: Religion, Tradition, and Universalism*, London: SCM Press, 2010, pp. 444–78.

MSC   'Metaphysics, Speculation, Correlation', *Pli: The Warwick Journal of Philosophy*, 22, (2011), pp. 1–26.

NS   *The Number and the Siren: A Decipherment of Mallarmé's Coup de Dés*, trans. Robin Mackay, Falmouth: Urbanomic, 2012.

PV   'Potentiality and Virtuality', in Robin Mackay (ed.), *Collapse Volume II: Speculative Realism*, Oxford: Urbanomic, 2007, pp. 55–81.

SC   'Subtraction and Contraction: Deleuze, Immanence and *Matter and Memory*', in Robin Mackay (ed.), *Collapse Volume III: Unknown Deleuze [+Speculative Realism]*, Falmouth: Urbanomic, 2007, pp. 63–107.

SD   'Spectral Dilemma', in Robin Mackay (ed.), *Collapse Volume IV: Concept Horror*, Falmouth: Urbanomic, 2008, pp. 261–75.

SR   'Speculative Realism', in Robin Mackay (ed.), *Collapse Volume III: Unknown Deleuze [+Speculative Realism]*, Falmouth: Urbanomic, 2008, pp. 408–99.

TWB   'Time without Becoming', Paper presented at the Centre for Research in Modern European Philosophy, Middlesex University, London, United Kingdom, 8 May 2008, available at <http://speculativeheresy.files.wordpress.com/2008/07/3729-time_without_becoming.pdf> (accessed 1 September 2013).

Introduction: From a Speculative Materialism to a Speculative Ethics

The French philosopher Quentin Meillassoux, born in 1967, has already had a remarkable impact on the direction of contemporary Continental philosophy. He has been the subject of an introductory text (Harman 2011a) and helped inaugurate a speculative revival in Continental philosophy (see Bryant et al. 2011). Whilst it is true that his thinking is a work-in-progress, he has by now sketched the outlines of his long-term project in two works: *After Finitude: An Essay on the Necessity of Contingency* (2008) and *Divine Inexistence* (in excerpted form in Harman 2011a). Alongside these two principal texts, a number of English language articles and a monograph on Stéphane Mallarmé, *The Number and the Siren* (2012), have appeared that paint various aspects of his project in further detail. Despite this, the sceptical reader may ask whether a dictionary devoted to his work is premature. This may be a legitimate concern, but there are sound reasons to begin this project sooner rather than later. In particular, Meillassoux's concepts are well suited to the format of a dictionary. More importantly, this dictionary acts as a site for scholars to carry forward the most important debates from the last ten years in Continental philosophy. Finally, in these pages critics and supporters have provided straightforward definitions of key terms while being clear about any problems they find in Meillassoux's presentation of his ideas.

Anyone familiar with Meillassoux will know that his system is structured in such a way that new readers often feel overwhelmed. There are a number of reasons for this. First, his language is often formal and his writing is stylistically closer to traditional rationalism or even Anglo-American philosophy. This is a virtue in terms of rigour, ambition, and directness, but at times Meillassoux can be overly compact when it comes to context. For instance, in *After Finitude* there are oblique references to the virtual, but this is only properly expanded upon in the article 'Potentiality and Virtuality'. The same is true for problems dealt with in chapters such as 'Hume's Revenge' that are given more detailed treatment in the article 'The Contingency of the Laws of Nature'. The reader exposed to the full range of these texts will discover not just new additions to Meillassoux's project, but, in some cases, the precise motivations for certain arguments and their roots in long-standing debates in rationalism and empiricism, the philosophy of set theory, and more besides. Moreover, the definitions of key terms in *After Finitude* provided here will reveal the ethical import of even his most abstract metaphysical considerations.

It should be noted that there is a further complication regarding his recption arising from the chronology of the texts as they are appearing in English. It is easily overlooked that *Divine Inexistence* precedes *After Finitude* by almost a decade. Although the 2003 revision surely improved the text, it remains the less rounded of the two. While the same confidence is evident in both it is clear that *After Finitude* is the more mature text. This perhaps explains why Meillassoux has been so hesitant to publish an updated version of *Divine Inexistence*. The published articles reveal that there is a consistency to his thinking going back to his dissertation, but it is difficult to know whether publishing it now would best serve his overall project. *The Number and the Siren* is something of an outlier within his thinking, but it speaks to his commitment, found throughout his works, to imaginative rationalism. In a recent interview with Sinziana Ravini, he says there is much more to come and that he is working on topics as varied as science fiction, Nietzsche, Duchamp, Hegel, and another engagement with Mallarmé (*AOTF*, 96). In an interview with Harman, he also mentions Darwinism and Pyrrho as future topics (*IQM*, 174). Nevertheless, it is a fair wager that these specific contributions will supplement rather than radically alter Meillassoux's architectonic.

Readers of Meillassoux will quickly notice certain tendencies when it comes to his argumentative strategy. In almost all his texts the same series of foundational arguments are repeated in condensed form. The reiterations are often based on accounts provided in *After Finitude*. On occasion this comes at the cost of clarity. This is also an issue when it comes to the background his system presupposes. Although rarely engaged outside of allusive footnotes, he takes it that his reader has a firm grip on everyone from Immanuel Kant to Martin Heidegger to his mentor Alain Badiou. This is why we have dedicated a number of entries to key figures in the Continental tradition. For many commentators, the chief defect in Meillassoux's system is that it oversimplifies the complex commitments of his interlocutors until they become mere caricatures. Here we hope to have provided the space for defenders of these thinkers to respond, which is but another way to expand the readers' context for reading Meillassoux. Finally it should be said that any critical engagement here comes from some of the best scholars in the field and thus the reader will have a front seat to the important debates Meillassoux's oeuvre raises.

Flowing from this is the related issue of Meillassoux's influences. Again, he is often enigmatic. What is certain is that he is a heterodox disciple of Badiou in as much as his mathematical ontology is clearly modelled on, but distinct from, that of his mentor. His evocation of Georg Cantor's set theory to solve Hume's problem of causal connection is the most direct example of Badiou's mentorship. Descartes is another clear influence and *After Finitude* is explicitly posited as an attempt to access the in–itself from a Cartesian rather than Kantian framework. His depiction of hyper–chaos as the primary absolute that founds a derivative mathematical absolute is modelled on Descartes' argument for extended substance, but with major surgery allowing for this adaptation. Finally, it is arguable that Gilles Deleuze is a strong influence since Meillassoux deploys rebooted versions of immanence and virtuality in his arguments. However, he is careful to ensure that he renders these distinct enough that his challenge to the prevalence of Deleuze's philosophy is clear. This is cemented by Meillassoux's bracketing of Deleuze under the category of subjectivist metaphysician in *After Finitude* (see also 'Subtraction and Contraction' where both Deleuze and Bergson are engaged indirectly).

On the flipside it is unmistakable that Meillassoux has certain philosophical targets in mind. The critique of correlationism is aimed squarely at the post-Kantian tradition of Continental philosophy. The term 'correlation' evokes everything from Kantian transcendental idealism to phenomenology/post-phenomenology, structuralism/post-structuralism, postmodernism, and deconstruction. Meillassoux directs especial ire at the thinkers of the theological turn in French phenomenology since he believes they have abandoned reason and revised the Kantian in–itself for their own quasi-religious ends. It is possible to get the impression that Meillassoux intends to develop a system broadly free from the traditional problems of post-Kantian philosophy. However, his project does not disavow the Critical project. Rather the Critical project is critiqued for its slow disengagement from attempts to think the absolute such that the forces of dogmatism, fanaticism and ideology have been given free reign over it. This is the problem of fideism by which philosophers provide cover for any belief about the absolute because it is a space untouchable by human reason. This gives his project, which at first seems to be nothing more than a defence of the natural sciences, a concrete edge.

In what follows we present Meillassoux's thinking in a twofold manner. We first provide an account of his ontology as developed chiefly in *After Finitude* and rounded out in the English-language articles such as 'Potentiality and Virtuality' and 'The Contingency of the Laws of Nature'. We then explain his ethical project as developed in *Divine Inexistence* and expanded upon in articles such as 'Spectral Dilemma' and 'The Immanence of the World Beyond'.

The central text of Meillassoux's system is *After Finitude: An Essay on the Necessity of Contingency*. It does not deal with the full range of his thinking and the reader unfamiliar with his others works may miss the

motivation behind it. We will come to see how this essay has a foundational role in his system, providing a set of ontological commitments in
order that we might build an ethics upon them. His belief is that a rational
ethics requires an ontological grounding to motivate one to live ethically.
By this he does not mean that ethics is impossible without rationalism, but
that a rational ethics would be immune to all manner of cynical, despair-
ing, or fanatical impulses following in the wake of the so-called Death of
God. It can even seem, at first, as if his arguments are indifferent to the
status of the human. This is a major error and the central aim in what
follows demonstrates that before all else Meillassoux is concerned with
human dignity.

The fundamental ontological principles guiding Meillassoux's work
are as follows: being is independent of thought and thought can think
being. This seems uncontroversial, but the crux of his argument will be
that philosophers are in practice forced to deny both principles due to
other foundational principles they hold. The first principle reveals to us
Meillassoux's general commitment to materialism. Being is matter independent of us. The second principle is evidence of his rationalism, and we
will come to see that being can be thought using formal languages such as
logic and mathematics.[1] There is also an important hint that this theory
will lead us to address 'the nature of thought's relation to the absolute'
(*AF*, 1). He aims to think this relation by way of the distinction between
primary and secondary qualities. Primary qualities are said to belong to
an object as properties independent of one's relation to it. They subsist
whether one is there or not. Secondary qualities are those sensual qualities
that exist only in one's relation to the thing and they disappear outside that
relation. After Kant, this distinction fell under suspicion for its naivety.[2]
We cannot claim to think primary qualities outside the entangled poles of
subjectivity and objectivity (and their avatars). Meillassoux will argue that
the attention in post-Kantian philosophy shifts toward the co-constitutive
bond between these poles, but he wishes to reintegrate primary qualities
according to the Cartesian variation where they are considered intrinsic to
the mathematical properties of the object.

Before we can grasp the nuances of his positive commitments in detail
we need to look at his critique of correlationism. He defines it as 'the idea

---

1 It is worth mentioning here, given how tempting this critique is, that Meillassoux is
   not going to say that being is mathematical in nature: 'This is not to "Pythagorize,"
   or to assert that Being is inherently mathematical: it is rather to explain how it is that
   a formal language manages to capture, from contingent-Being, properties that a ver-
   nacular language fails at restituting' (*CBI*, 80).

2 Meillassoux names Berkeley as a precursor to this position (*AF*, 3). Elsewhere, Berkeley
   is given a more central role as the founder of the era of correlation (see *IRR*, 3).

according to which we only ever have access to the correlation between thinking and being, and never to either term considered apart from the other' (*AF*, 5). There are two principal arguments used by correlationists: the correlationist circle and the correlationist 'two-step', the argument that what matters is the relation of the correlation rather than that which is related (*AF*, 5). The circle stresses the pragmatic contradiction faced by realists: 'when you claim to think any X, you must posit this X, which cannot then be separated from this special act of positing, of conception' (*SR*, 409). The implication of the circle is that one cannot, under pain of contradiction, claim to think an independent reality. Thus the correlationist affirms a 'correlational facticity' as a limit around which thinking cannot hope to get (*IRR*, 1). The true cost of correlationism is said to be our inability to think a non-relative outside: 'the *great outdoors*, the *absolute* outside of pre-critical thinkers' (*AF*, 7). To force an examination of the principles of correlationism he focuses on statements that require objects to subsist outside our thinking them. He does not mean subsisting outside our relation to them in the present, but at a time when there was no human relation to objects at all: ancestral time.

This brings us to Meillassoux's scientifically realist account of ancestral statements meaning those which refer to any reality prior to the emergence of consciousness, such as the statement that the date of the origin of the universe is approximately 13.5 billion years ago. The correlationist will normally accept what science tells us about ancestral realities, but not literally. The principles of correlationism undermine the literal sense of scientific statements and, more importantly, Meillassoux will claim this equates to undermining their sense altogether. Ancestral statements are said to be based on arche-fossils, which are defined as materials 'indicating the existence of an ancestral reality or event' (*AF*, 10). The correlationist tends to focus on how these exist in the present and so are 'contemporaneous' with us (*AF*, 12). Meillassoux calls this the 'codicil of modernity', which appends the adage '*for humans*' to all scientific statements (*AF*, 13). This seemingly innocuous point about arche-fossils has, however, significant consequences. Firstly, it distances the philosopher from the literal and directly realist sense of the ancestral statement. Secondly, it generates a new level of meaning that is said to be deeper than the scientific one: a 'more originary correlationist meaning' (*AF*, 14).

This deeper meaning does not render scientific knowledge impossible in terms of intersubjective verifiability by a contemporary community of scientists. Meillassoux however is not simply interested in verification in the present, but in how the sciences aim at concrete determination concerning, in this case, ancestral realities. He claims that science 'carries out repeatable experiments with a view to external referents which endow these experiments with meaning' (*AF*, 17). Meillassoux is concerned with how this more originary meaning, that to be is to be a correlate, directly undermines this necessity of having the capacity to speak in a register of signification where reality is not correlated (he will imbue mathematics with this capacity). He is pushing the question as to how ancestral statements can be considered potentially true in-themselves. What are the conditions that allow us to conceive of these statements as such and thus, given the questions they claim to answer? To resolve this dilemma Meillassoux will need to find a way to think primary qualities absolutely, that is, outside of any relation to the subject. He turns to Descartes to find a model that will allow him to achieve this aim.

Meillassoux is specifically interested in the Cartesian argument for the 'absolute existence of extended substance' and its link with the ontological proof in which the 'primary absolute' acts as guarantor for the absolute scope of mathematics, which is described as a 'derivative absolute' (*AF*, 29–30). If he can find a similar model, one unburdened by theological associations, he believes he should be able to carry out a robust defence of primary qualities. Descartes' proof for the existence of God (the primary absolute) runs as follows: (1) Given our idea of God as a being possessing all the perfections absolutely (2) then existence (since it is a perfection) is necessarily one of them; hence (3) God exists. Meillassoux notes that Descartes' proof allows one to move from an idea 'for us', that is, the very idea of God's existence, to its formal necessity as an ontological absolute. This seems an appealing option since he wishes to make a similar transition from what is 'for-us' to 'in-itself'. However, Meillassoux ultimately finds this model unsatisfactory since it relies heavily on the dogmatic assertion of a self-sufficient necessary being. His own project will aim to 'uncover an absolute necessity that does not reinstate any form of an absolutely necessary entity' on the basis that dogmatism is no longer a serious option for any contemporary form of philosophy (*AF*, 34).

Thus blocked from the dogmatic route to reality, Meillassoux also critiques other problematic approaches to the real. The first is the weak correlationism of Kant, which allows us to posit the existence of reality in-itself, but states that we cannot have any knowledge about it. The second approach is strong correlationism and it is characterised by two important decisions. The first is the one common to all forms of correlationism, which stresses 'the primacy of the correlate' (*AF*, 37). The second decision arises in opposition to weak correlationism and another option, namely speculative/subjective idealism (SI). SI is said to insist on the absolution of the correlate (*AF*, 37). There is no in-itself according to it and this means there is nothing but the subject-object dyad

(*AF*, 37).[3] Against SI, strong correlationism holds that the correlational forms can only be described and never absolutised (*AF*, 38–9). This means we cannot speak about what is outside our finite limitations. In relinquishing any grasp upon the in–itself we end up in a situation where discourses on the absolute are legitimate so long as they are irrational: 'philosophers seem to ask only one thing of these absolutes: that they be devoid of the slightest pretension to rationality' (*AF*, 45). The consequences of this are significant since we end up with fideism because strong correlationism allows for the slow emergence of scepticism concerning absolutes, which has the peculiar consequence of legitimising any belief about the nature of the absolute. This he calls the '*religionizing* of reason' (*AF*, 47).

We turn now to the central move in Meillassoux's ontology. This is the rendering of the facticity of the correlation into a form of knowledge (*AF*, 52). For Meillassoux facticity names the correlationist position that we can only uncover 'conditional' rather than 'absolute' necessity (*SR*, 428–9). We simply cannot say what constitutes the ultimate ground that could explain, as metaphysics once did, why things are the way they are. This means that we must we think according to those limits whether they are construed as epistemological or ontological. This is an important transition to register because it will involve Meillassoux re-rendering facticity not as an 'incapacity' but as a feature of the in–itself (*AF*, 53). The absence of reason will be taken as an actual feature of our reality. Or, put differently, he will turn the negative insight into a positive one. This corresponds to a shift from epistemological limitation to ontological knowledge. Meillassoux claims that facticity is then a 'real property' of the in–itself and has been hiding in plain sight (*AF*, 52). Unreason, this absence of metaphysical necessity, is said to warrant the designation of an 'absolute ontological property' (*AF*, 53).

How does Meillassoux convince us of this switch? What re-emerges is the problem of moving from the 'for-us' to the 'in-itself'. To make his point he depicts a dialogue that will bring together the various actors of *After Finitude* discussed so far. The dialogue concerns the nature of our 'future *post-mortem*' or death (*AF*, 55). At first we have two dogmatists: (1) a religious believer who holds that existence does not end with our death and that we continue to exist after it. (2) An atheist who holds that death is strictly the end. He then introduces (3) a strict correlationist,

---

3 One possibility that emerges from this is subjectivist metaphysics, which involves the hypostatization of some 'mental, sentient or vital term' (*AF*, 37). Meillassoux has called this a 'proliferation of subjectivations of the real' and has renamed it subjectalism (*IRR*, 3).

not explicitly identified as weak or strong, who holds that both are wrong since the best position on what happens after death is agnosticism. This is because knowledge is always of this world and neither believer nor atheist can claim to know what happens once we exit it. Both outcomes are possible, but that is as far our knowledge goes. Then into the dialogue (4) a subjective idealist enters and she argues that the two options are unthinkable since the only range we have is that of thinking. In response to both dogmatic positions and subjective idealism, the strict correlationist must maintain that all three positions are possible and she recuses herself from the debate.

Then finally a speculative philosopher enters, a stand-in for Meillassoux himself, and claims that the two dogmatists and the subjective idealist have misidentified the absolute. It is precisely 'the capacity-to-be-other as such', captured through the eyes of the strict correlationist, that the absolute indexes (*AF*, 56). This agnosticism means that when it comes to the in-itself anything is equally possible. We see that in some cases, for instance atheism, this includes the possibility of 'non-being' (*AF*, 57). Non-being is the ontological name for death and the commitment of strict correlationism to the facticity of the correlation means that the correlationist must recognise absolute possibilities, such as death, which are intrinsically non-correlational. The possibility of non-correlated realities is thereby assured from within strict correlationism. Meillassoux takes this admission of the capacity-to-be-other to be the 'faultline' leading out of the correlation (*AF*, 57).[4] For Meillassoux, we discover here a way to think realities subsisting beyond the correlation and not dependent on it. What subsists in-itself, irrespective of the correlation, is a *'time of a radical inhumanity'* and this is why he will place a strong emphasis on temporality when discussing the absolute (*MSC*, 12). In essence, he proposes that we turn the absence of metaphysical necessity, and the possibility for every entity to become otherwise, into an ontological principle that refers to an absolute time affecting all entities. In other words, the correlationist already takes for granted the existence of the contingency of the correlation; the point is to see that contingency as an index of reality as such.

Many have noted that a problem arises here. This hyper-chaotic time, ensuring the capacity-to-be-other of all entities, seems at odds with our

---

4 Strict correlationism cannot escape admitting this capacity due to a structural dilemma it faces. It wants to de-absolutise the correlation against subjective idealism because it is anti-absolutist, but to do this it would have to absolutise facticity in order to allow for non-correlated possibilities. However, it does not want to absolutise facticity because it is sceptical about non-correlated knowledge. This means it would have to de-absolutise facticity, which in turn absolutises the correlation as found in subjective idealism.

original desire to uncover a primary absolute that could justify mathematical discourse's warrant upon ancestral realities (*AF*, 64). To address this issue Meillassoux introduces 'determinate conditions' that entities are subject to from within this model (*AF*, 66). He begins with a demonstration that the thing-in-itself is non-contradictory. He provides an unusual argument to this effect: Suppose a contradictory entity existed. If it existed it would hold two states at once and thus be in contradiction with itself. It would both be and not be at the same time. If this were the case it would continue to *be* even in a state of *non-being* (*AF*, 69–70). However, non-contradiction is required for the transition between states stipulated by our commitment to the absolute scope of the capacity-to-be-other (*AF*, 71). There must be some determinative state to switch between and this requires non-contradictory entities. Regarding the existence of the in-itself his approach is straightforward: If one accepts the principle of unreason then one affirms the capacity-to-be-other of entities. This is 'unthinkable without the persistence of the two realms of existence and inexistence' and we can assert that there must *be* entities with the capacity to become other than they are lest this would not be possible (*AF*, 76).

This leads to a positive rendering of the terms we have encountered so far. We are said to be engaging in a '*logos* of contingency', which is to philosophise without accepting the principle of sufficient reason (*AF*, 77). The principle of unreason is renamed the principle of factiality in order to disassociate it from the potential negative connotation of irrationalism (*AF*, 79). This principle states that facticity is not a fact or factual. It is not contingent like entities or laws. In an affirmative manner, only contingency is necessary, thus the subtitle of the *After Finitude: The Necessity of Contingency*. The procedure whereby we discover the conditions of the absolute is called 'derivation', which produces 'figures' (*AF*, 79). Although we have secured some knowledge of the primary absolute, in particular the absolute scope of non-contradiction, we seem to remain within Kantian coordinates when it is the Cartesian ones we want to 'transition' toward (*AF*, 81). We must get from the absolute scope of logical principles to the absolute scope of mathematical statements (the secondary absolute). Despite this a subtle warning is given: 'we cannot present the complete resolution of the problem here' (*AF*, 81). What can be resolved is a quite specific problem that has traditionally been considered insoluble: Hume's problem of causal connection. It is the perfect dilemma since it motivated by the belief that there is an 'ineffable reason underlying all things' (*AF*, 82). To show why his ontology has broad appeal Meillassoux will aim to solve this case and he presents this as a first foray into factial speculation.

Meillassoux is aware of an obvious objection to the implications of a hyper-chaotic time, namely that there is in experience a manifest stability that is at odds with the claim that things could change for no reason at all. Hence, there must be constant physical or natural laws ensuring this stability. In short, 'if physical laws were actually contingent, *we would have already noticed*' (*AF*, 84). Taking Hume's example of billiard balls we know that 'given the same initial conditions, the same results invariably follow' (*AF*, 85). Hume's problem raises a simple dilemma: whilst we are certainly being reasonable to expect the same results to follow, it cannot be guaranteed as necessary *a priori*. Our only recourse in terms of gaining knowledge is our own experience, which is trapped in the present and only knows what happened in the past; we mistake our habits for physical necessity. The principle of non-contradiction can certainly tell us that 'a contradictory event is impossible', but as to whether any non-contradictory event will follow we have no assurance (*CLN*, 323). This is one of the most long-standing puzzles in modern philosophy and with typical confidence Meillassoux promises a novel solution to it.

There are, for Meillassoux, three possible responses to Hume's problem. The first is the metaphysical one. Here one demonstrates the existence of a necessarily perfect being who acts as a guarantor that our laws are the optimal ones for governing our universe. The second is the sceptical or Humean solution. Although we cannot demonstrate causal necessity *a priori* we can shift the problem toward the 'origin of our *belief* in their necessity' (*AF*, 88). This is the habituation we build up over time when confronted with the consistency of outcomes. The third potential response is the transcendental or Kantian solution.[5] It asks us to imagine what the consequences of the absence of causal necessity would be. For Kant, the consequence would be the impossibility of structured representation, objectivity, or even consciousness. The very 'fact of representation' refutes the contingency of laws (*CLN*, 325). Meillassoux believes all three positions adhere to the 'common assumption' that the truth of causal necessity cannot be called into question (*AF*, 90). This is precisely what he wishes to question.

He proposes a fourth speculative solution and from this perspective one argues not, as with Humean scepticism, that reason cannot demonstrate *a priori* the necessity of laws. Instead one claims that reason proves *a priori* the contingency of laws. What he does here is flip Hume's supposed deference to the principle of sufficient reason such that we embrace what reason tells us a *priori* about causal necessity – namely that it does not exist. This extends, in Meillassoux's ambitious critique, to the physical or natural laws themselves. If causal connection 'cannot be demonstrated' then we

---

5 Here Meillassoux has in mind the objective deduction of the categories in the 'Analytic of Concepts' from Kant's *Critique of Pure Reason*.

must abandon it and trust our rational instincts (*AF*, 91). However, we still have the dilemma as to why natural and physical laws are so consistently stable and why, despite what reason tells us, we do not encounter constant chaos. To destabilise this picture he zones in on what he calls the 'necessitarian inference' involved in our belief in causal necessity (*AF*, 94). This inference takes it that '*the stability of laws ... presupposes the necessity of those laws*' (*AF*, 94). It works as follows: (a) if laws could change for no reason they would do so frequently (b) but they do not and thus (c) they cannot and should be considered necessary. Accepting that (b) is incontestable he focuses on (a), which if undermined collapses the entire argument. He calls the force of the argument the 'frequentialist implication', which boils down to the belief that the contingency of the laws of nature would result in their frequent transformation (*AF*, 95).

There is a subtle move here in the suggestion that the argument for the stability of laws is based on a form of unacknowledged mathematical reasoning. Drawing on the work of Jean-René Vernes (1982), Meillassoux thinks that the frequentialist implication is enmeshed with probabilistic reasoning (*AF*, 95). To illustrate this point, he introduces the example of a gambler faced with a die that always lands on the same face, leading him to suspect that it is '*very probably* loaded' (*AF*, 96). In the classic scenario of the throw of the dice there are equally probable outcomes that we can calculate. In this scenario '*that which is equally thinkable* [a priori], *is equally possible*' (*AF*, 96). Once the dice are thrown and an outcome occurs we can assign probabilistic reasoning to chance reoccurrences. If, however, we started with this thesis of equiprobability and the same result kept occurring, we have reason to assume that we are not dealing with chance. We suspect a hidden cause is ensuring the outcome. If the dice landed on the same face not just for the duration of the game, but for our entire lives, then we are in the situation we find ourselves in with physical laws. This leads one to accept that there is some underlying reason why they always re-occur. It is perhaps impossible to ever know this reason, as Hume believes, but that *there is one* is not in doubt.

The problem is in treating the universe the same way we treat events within it, that is, using probabilistic reasoning. This would necessitate that we are in position to conceive of a complete set of all universes with alternative physical laws.[6] What Meillassoux has in mind here are possible worlds governed by different laws; each throw of the dice would represent a new possible world and its laws being put into effect (*IWB*, 448). In our example, the dice-universe always lands on ours leading us to make

---

6 Meillassoux notes that non-contradiction is still applicable here since otherwise they would not be conceivable alternatives (*CLN*, 329).

the frequentialist inference. It is improbable that our laws are contingent given the fact of the manifest stability of natural laws. Meillassoux will argue that the necessity we infer here should be considered a 'supplement' (*AF*, 98).[7] The argument for stability hinges on the conception of a dice-universe that would represent a 'Whole [*Tout*] of possible universes' from which our own universe can be considered one possibility (*CLN*, 330). But is such a Whole legitimate in this case? His answer is no. Events taking place within the universe can be calculated according to some defined total, but the totality being discussed in relation to physical laws is not one we actually encounter in experience nor is it possible that we could.[8]

Nor can the Whole be theoretically assured in a post-Cantorian age. Building on Badiou's use of Cantor he follows the now standard line that set theory disallows any consideration of a fixed totality.[9] To simplify, each attempt to construct the theoretical totality or the set required to undertake this calculation about possible worlds is immediately undercut by the impossibility of generating it. This is because, according to the lesson of Cantor, a larger set can always be constructed that includes *this* set resulting in the detotalisation of what we had taken to be the total. This operation can persist indefinitely. The Whole that would make this probabilistically based argument possible is not a dependable basis for the demonstration being made.[10] We are ignorant as to whether totalisation is possible and this is 'sufficient' to disqualify arguments made on its basis (*CLN*, 333). This is not a proof, but a suspension of the assumed legitimacy of the frequentialist implication that holds that if laws were contingent this would manifest often. We cannot say that frequent change is probable or stability improbable on the basis of such an inference.

Having undertaken his critique of causal necessity Meillassoux does not immediately provide his promised solution. He will later outline how this will be accomplished, but for now he turns to the earlier problem of ancestral reality. In doing so, he proceeds to introduce a more expansive sense to those statements that refer to a 'temporal discrepancy' between thinking and being such that both anterior *and* ulterior events are covered (*AF*, 112, italics removed). The term dia-chronicity is introduced to cover this wider sense (*AF*, 112). He turns his attention back to the event of modern science with Galileo and Copernicus as the figures responsible

---

7 Not to be confused with the '*pure supplements*' introduced by advents (*IRR*, 15).

8 See *PV*, 65 where recourse to experience is eliminated as a feasible option.

9 Meillassoux gives an account of the mathematics involved at various places. See *CLN*, 332–3; *AF*, 134 fn 11; and *PV*, 66–7. See also Gironi 2011: 42–3.

10 Meillassoux admits that other set-theoretical axiomatics may allow for the totality required, but the existence of this one axiomatic at least undermines it (*CLN*, 333).

for allowing such statements to gain traction. This event is linked to the 'mathematization of nature', the unleashing of formal languages, that renders the discourse on anterior and ulterior time meaningful without recourse to fabulation (*AF*, 112). This process of de-mystification is further accompanied by an awareness of the autonomy of the world, its indifference to us, and its subsistence regardless of our presence (*AF*, 115). We approach this non-correlated world in mathematical terms and on that basis hypothesise meaningfully about it. Thus Meillassoux will suggest that a more fitting name for the Kantian Copernican turn, which excised this Galilean-Copernican spirit from its remit, is the 'Ptolemaic counter-revolution' in philosophy (*AF*, 118).

While Kant is commended for excising dogmatic metaphysics from philosophy, he is condemned for missing the 'speculative import' of modern science (*AF*, 120, italics removed). In a way, Meillassoux is disappointed that as the natural sciences opened us up to the great outdoors, philosophy went another way and created nothing more than an insular field of limited possibilities. How then to revive the Galilean-Copernican spirit for philosophy? What speculative tasks remain ahead of us? *After Finitude* ends by outlining what this would require. In particular, Meillassoux believes we must discover a link between the capacity of mathematics as a formal language and the principle of factiality.[11] The motivation for this derivation arises firstly from the problem of ancestrality, which requires a derivation supporting the claim that 'what is mathematically conceivable is absolutely possible' and hence can subsist beyond correlated realities (*AF*, 126). Secondly, this derivation is needed to properly resolve the problem of causal connection and this would allow us provide ontological support for the intotalisation thesis in relation to manifest stability – since, as it stands, the intotalisation hypothesis remains merely one possible reading of set theory amongst others (*AF*, 127). Two absolutisations are required then: the ontic one concerning the possibility of ancestral realities and the ontological one concerning the 'non-Whole'. This is where *After Finitude* leaves off, and we can turn now to an entirely different facet of Meillassoux's thinking: his ethics.

Meillassoux's work is not simply focused on the nature of an abstract absolute, but includes an important ethical dimension. He is, following a long line of thinkers in the French and German tradition, not content with simply propounding a new ontological system, but wants also to reshape the way in which we regard our common possibilities of being

---

11 The first provisional attempt occurs in *IRR*, 18–38, but given that this occurs in the context of a conference paper we will need to await the first complete example of this demonstration.

in the world. Meillassoux develops his ethics according to a hope, one undergirded by rationalist considerations, in the emergence of future God that would redeem our fallen world. For Meillassoux, given the capacities of hyper-chaos, it is conceivable that the current stability of natural laws has been upended before – that is, the facts of the physical laws have themselves changed. Meillassoux argues there were previous Worlds – capitalised to distinguish them from the world of the non-Whole – prior to this one. They are (1) the World of inorganic matter; (2) the World of organic matter; and (3) the World of organic matter and thought. In this way, Meillassoux differentiates between the notion of World and 'world', since each World emerges *ex nihilo* from the 'world' of hyper-chaos. The essential point here is that once one is willing to accept Meillassoux's ontological vision that no non-contradictory possibility can be discounted, then we see the possibility of a new World to come, which has immense implications for ethics.

Meillassoux argues at various points that from one World to the next there is a qualitative leap that cannot be explained in terms of the physical laws of the previous one. Hence, each World is *sui generis* or self-causing: the World of thought could not have come out of the laws governing organic matter and organic matter, he avers, could not have been caused by simple matter. In this manner, speculative materialism 'affirms' the 'radical contingency of our world' (*IRR*, 11). The philosopher oriented toward contingency thereby has as her concern not 'being' (*l'être*), that is, what currently exists, but, as Meillassoux puts it, 'the perhaps' (*le peut-être*) (*TWB*, 11). What is possible, in the most pressing ethical sense, is for him not another World beyond *this one* in any vertical sense, as in vulgar forms of Platonism, but other Worlds to come. These Worlds would build on the current instantiation and merge with it immanently. The only restriction he places on these possible Worlds is that they bring more into reality than was there before. He believes that we can identify the most likely possibilities by identifying what is currently lacking in the current configuration, and it is these possibilities that are the province of the speculative philosopher.

The lack in question is expressed in the term divine inexistence. Meillassoux develops his ontological commitments toward an interest not in a God who *is* or who *is not*, but in a God who *may be* (or is currently in-existent). The appearance of this God would precisely be a fourth World beyond those mentioned already, one not certain to happen, but whose potential appearance gives us hope beyond the nihilism of the present. It would also be an addition to this World in that it would bring into being a more complete justice since this could solve what he calls the spectral dilemma. This refers to the haunting of our common existence by a mourning over all those lost in history, those whose deaths we cannot begin to put in rational order or make any sense of. There is no need to detail all those kinds of spectres Meillassoux describes – the dead child, the victims of heinous massacres of all sorts – since only the most affectless of us do not feel the existential weight of the horrors of this or that death, as well as all the Holocausts of history. To be human is to live under the shadow of this wide work of mourning. For Meillassoux essential mourning over these spectres is impossible in our current World. What words could console us concerning them?

This is Meillassoux's way of indirectly addressing the problem of whether we can accept a God who would allow such deaths to occur. In this way, Meillassoux follows, from a different direction, the view of Jacques Derrida, namely that our lives are always lived as a work of mourning. However, whereas Derrida saw this finitude as inexorable, Meillassoux argues that the nature of hyper-chaos ensures that it is possible that our condition could be otherwise. Who would choose to believe in a God who would allow such deaths? For the believer we have precisely the opposite problem than that faced by the nihilist. This is the dilemma that arises from the lack of a transcending principle at work in the world that would provide justice for the departed. Note well that the argument, as produced by Meillassoux, takes place at the ethical level. These are not dry proofs for a clockmaker God or a mere first principle that founds nature. This is not the God of the philosophers. Rather at its heart, the spectral dilemma concerns a personalist God, one who answers our prayers and who can provide mercy for the living and the dead alike. This God is not metaphysical, but ethical: a plea for any light with which to banish away our darkest fears. The answer Meillassoux provides for the atheist faced with the spectral dilemma is not in the form of various proofs for God's inexistence. We hear nothing of evolutionary theory or physicist accounts of the Big Bang that disprove the book of Genesis, or about the problematic logics of the cosmological proof, or all the well-worn paths of the non-believer. The atheist, rather, responds to the dilemma in precisely ethical terms:

You want to hope, [the theist says], for something for the dead ... You hope for justice in the next world: but in what would this consist? It would be a justice done under the auspices of a God who had himself allowed the worst acts to be committed ... You call just, and even good, such a God ... To live under the reign of such a perverse being, who corrupts the most noble words – love, justice – with his odious practices: isn't this a good definition of hell? ... To this hell you wish for them, I prefer, for them as for myself, nothingness, which will leave them in peace and conserve their dignity, rather than putting them at the mercy of the omnipotence of your pitiless Demiurge. (*DI*, 265)

Neither of these positions can be considered an ethical response to the dead, Meillassoux suggests: the atheist abhors the very idea of such a fearsome God, while the believer can only go on with the faith that life is something other than 'devastated by the despair of terrible deaths' (*DI*, 265). Countless books argue for and against the possibility of such a God, and the arguments are well-worn and historically repetitive. Few readers of Meillassoux's *After Finitude* would expect that his arguments regarding the divine inexistence would remain on such ethical grounds. While it's true that *After Finitude* provides an indirect proof against the existence of God, namely as a necessary being, here he goes further to say that even a necessary and impersonal God, as found in Aristotle, could not answer the spectral dilemma: both sides of the dilemma take on the existence of a personal God and this is correct, in so far as any other God would seem meaningless for our existence, save answering a metaphysical dilemma.

Meillassoux thus will map out a third position not often envisioned in the binary debates over God's existence or inexistence. His view is that both sides take for granted that were God to exist, then His existence would be necessary: 'to be atheist is not simply to maintain that God does not exist, but also that he could not exist; to be a believer is to have faith in the essential existence of God' (*SD*, 268). But God *doesn't* exist; this follows not only from the arguments of *After Finitude* but is required for any worthy God lest He remain responsible for the myriad horrors of this world. But that God *may* be also holds out hope for an existence that, as of now, confronts the lack of meaning for the deaths of history. Meillassoux goes further, saying that the problems of the worst regimes, such as the Soviet one, involve an inequality of the living and the dead, creating the latter in the name of those who will be alive in the future. Thus he argues that a God of justice will not just bring mercy to the living but to all those who have died. However, this requires the appearance of a World to come, since God 'cannot be posited except as contingent, in the sense that, if its thinkability supposes that nothing prohibits its advent, inversely, no destinal law can be supposed to guarantee its emergence' (*SD*, 271).

Meillassoux is not suggesting that under the current laws of nature we can hope for the rebirth of the dead. As we have seen, he does not adhere to the principle of sufficient reason whereby the laws of this universe are eternal. Rather, by radicalising Hume he has also overturned the latter's atheism. In this way, while nature does not provide for an all-powerful God, hyper-chaos provides for its hope beyond *this* World. Meillassoux's thinking is therefore never far removed from considerations of our mortal condition. His project is ultimately not about realism in any abstract sense, but is imbued, from his dissertation forward, with a touch of the absurdity of our current condition, one that gives us every reason, it seems, to find God unforgivable. Meillassoux gives us a veritable hauntology, a study of these spectres who, he says, 'refuse to pass over', who still belong to the world of the living, even as unending shadows that we can only meekly begin to countenance (*SD*, 262). He argues not only that this thinking of the possible God marks a future just world, but that it should have effects upon us in *this* one. Freed by an existential weight of utter hopelessness we can begin to act differently in this World.

In Kant's philosophy, the dignity of the human was founded in its ability to reason and on this basis give itself over to the moral law. For Meillassoux, the ultimate being is the one who can think the factiality of reality and thus have a rational hope for an immanent World to come (*IWB*, 462). This figure, of whom he suggests the human may just be one type, is notable for both its 'cognitive' and 'tragic' character: rational enough to understand the contingency of all, it also knows the ever-present possibility of its own death. As Meillassoux understands the fourth World, God will prevent the decay of our bodies, but given that God is not necessary, we cannot hold out the hope that He is eternal or everlasting. Thus even in Meillassoux's system, where justice and equality might one day win out, death is still a contingent possibility given the unpredictable power of hyper-chaos. While Meillassoux is interested in working out the fourth World's formal possibility, the point is to think how this 'dense possibility' effects our conduct in *this* World. This vision of a future is one that he thinks calls forth what he dubs the eschatological or 'vectorial' subject, 'one magnetically attracted by the emancipation of the World to come' (*IWB*, 463).

The vectorial subject, he argues, is produced through successive speculative stages: (1) first, a removal from despair by recognising the lack of limits for reason, since the latter can move speculatively to the absolute. This absolutisation of reason thus counters Kant's finite subject while deciphering a potential God. The vectorial subject provides both a hope for a future beyond this World and knows that this World may not arrive, but Meillassoux argues that this is anything but a political quietism. We know what a future World would be that could deliver us from injustice, and thus we work, here and now, to bring about the justice we can. (2) The second stage for the vectorial subject is nihilism, which Meillassoux understands as this subject's recognition of the coming World as horrifying. Meillassoux argues that the truly difficult moment is the realisation that the coming of the fourth World could mean an immortality from which there is no escape. This nihilism was first identified by Nietzsche in his famed 'Eternal Recurrence of the Same', which as Meillassoux rightly argues, is not a consideration of our finitude, but rather the possibility of our immortality. The 'greatest weight', the one that grounds Nietzsche's nihilism, is not death, but an everlasting (and tedious) life.

In such a scenario the vectorial subject faces an aporia beyond that which she faced in the spectral dilemma: either the coming World arrives and the vectorial subject sees the satisfaction of her greatest hopes, at which point she becomes meaningless, or it doesn't arrive and these hopes face no such satisfaction. If it's the former, then the vectorial subject, formed by a quest for justice, no longer has any meaning for going on; her purpose has been fulfilled and she loses her very reason for being. This also means that Meillassoux agrees with Marx that any true communism – equivalent to a future World of justice, as he sees it – is also the cessation of politics. This not to say, though, that a World freed of politics, that is, no longer with material inequities and misery, would be free of disquiet. It would still be a World with love and its betrayal, a World with the life of thought and horrific mediocrity, and all the other petty miseries life offers. The vectorial subject, then, looks forward to a World not of happiness, but a World of disquietude, one from which death cannot provide an escape. Our hope, then, is a peculiar one: to free human beings from material misery in order that they may experience the human dignity of disquietude and anxiety.

Having come to this, we conclude our brief *entrée* onto Meillassoux's thought, a form of thinking that is at once speculative and ethical, highly rationalist and deeply felt. In the dictionary that follows, our contributors have done a remarkable job of filling in the details of our broad sketch above. They don't always agree with Meillassoux, but their admiration for what is an increasingly audacious body of work means they are always fair. It is our hope to provide you the tools to follow him with all of his potential, whether in disquietude of the World to come or in disagreement with his major claims.

A

ABSOLUTE

Bart Zantvoort

The question of the absolute has historically been posed in two ways. Firstly: what is the ultimate ground or foundation for reality as a whole? This is framed in at least three ways: what is the first cause, the 'unconditioned', or the highest entity? Secondly: what are the absolute, non-relative properties of things? That is, what are the attributes of a given entity independent from the standpoint of an observer?

Meillassoux takes up this classical schema in an unusual way. Taking René **Descartes** as an example, he distinguishes between a 'primary absolute' and a 'derivative absolute' (*AF*, 30). For Descartes, the primary absolute is the existence of a perfect, all-powerful **God** (see **Cartesian in-itself**). The secondary absolute, which is the capacity of **mathematics** to describe the non-relative properties of things, can be derived from the primary absolute, because a perfect God would not deceive us in our use of mathematics. Meillassoux agrees with Descartes that we need to demonstrate the absolute reach of mathematics. But he thinks that after Immanuel **Kant**'s critique of dogmatism and his own destruction of the **principle of sufficient reason**, we can no longer invoke God or any other form of highest entity to do so. Instead, he proposes the principle of **factiality** as his own primary absolute.

This principle states that 'contingency alone is necessary' (*AF*, 80). According to Meillassoux, all beings are necessarily contingent, and we can know this absolutely. (It must be noted here that 'absolute' for Meillassoux seems to entail both that we can *know* 'absolutely' that contingency is necessary and that this principle is itself absolutely necessary). It is from this principle that the capacity of mathematics to describe absolute properties of things is supposed to be derived. Meillassoux uses 'absolute' to mean two very different things, however. In relation to the status of mathematics, as well as in the critique of **correlationism**, it means: that which is thinkable as existing independently of thought (*AF*, 57; 117). But in relation to the principle of factiality, it means: that which must be thought as absolutely necessary (*AF*, 62). Although Meillassoux rejects the traditional understanding of the absolute as an ultimate cause or necessary entity, he still maintains that the necessity of contingency can be demonstrated through a rational argument (*AF*, 60).

Initially, Meillassoux claims that mathematics is absolute only in the first sense: 'The absoluteness of that which is mathematizable means: the possibility of factial [that is, contingent] existence outside thought – not: the necessity of existence outside thought' (*AF*, 117). But he also claims that the absoluteness of mathematics (see **set theory**) has both an 'ontical' scope in so far as it pertains to 'entities that are possible or contingent, but whose existence can be thought as indifferent to thought', and an 'ontological' scope, since it 'states something about *the structure of the possible as such*' (*AF*, 127).

This ontological scope of mathematics would consist in a speculative resolution of David **Hume**'s problem. Hume argued that we cannot derive the necessity of the laws of nature from experience, and therefore we cannot know if they will continue to hold as they have in the past. Meillassoux, on the contrary, wants to prove the stability of the **laws of nature**. This proof would provide an absolute foundation for the derivative-absolute capacity of mathematical science: 'It is . . . necessary to establish the legitimacy of the assumption that the stability of natural laws, which is the condition for every science of nature, can be *absolutized*' (*AF*, 127).

The demonstration in *After Finitude* amounts only to a 'hypothetical resolution' of this problem (*AF*, 110; 127). Meillassoux argues that, although the laws of nature are contingent and could therefore change at any moment, this does not preclude the obvious fact of their stability. Probabilistic reasoning, which would lead us to expect these laws to change frequently if they are contingent, can only be applied to numerical totalities, whether these are finite or infinite. But, according to Meillassoux, the Cantorian transfinite, according to which the thinkable does not constitute a totality, gives us reason to think that the world as a whole might not be such a totality. Therefore, probabilistic reason does not necessarily apply to the world as a whole, and it is at least a plausible hypothesis that the laws of nature could be stable (*AF*, 107). But, as Meillassoux admits, this is only a hypothetical resolution of Hume's problem, because the version of set theory he uses is only one set of possible axioms among many (*AF*, 104). Therefore, we do not know *a priori* whether or not the world as a whole forms a totality or not. The absolute proof of the stability of the laws of nature would require him to derive the necessity of Cantor's theorem from the principle of factiality (*AF*, 110).

Contrary to many interpretations, therefore, Meillassoux is not trying to prove that the laws of nature could change at any moment. The ultimate ambitions in *After Finitude* are, in fact, to prove the following: (1) The *absolute necessity* of the principle of factiality; (2) The *absolute possibility* (*AF*, 117) of the world described by mathematics (the capacity of mathematics to accurately describe contingent entities, which exist independently from us); (3) The 'absolute and . . . unconditionally necessary scope' (*AF*, 127) of the Cantorian transfinite (see Georg **Cantor**), which will allow us to 'legitimize absolutely' the stability of natural laws.

Of these aims, only the first is accomplished in *After Finitude*. In 'Iteration, Reiteration, Repetition', Meillassoux takes up the project of proving the absolute status of mathematics again, but he has to conclude that he has not succeeded (*IRR*, 37). If, therefore, *After Finitude* serves as a critique of correlationism, demonstrating that the limits of knowledge have been too narrowly constructed, we are still awaiting Meillassoux's second critique in which he proves that thought, in the form of mathematics, can think the absolute.

ADVENT

Christina Smerick

The word Advent means a coming or an arrival. In the Christian tradition, advent is a liturgical time, before Christmas, when Christians anticipate the coming of the Christ child and reflect and repent upon the various ways in which they have failed to live toward the ethic articulated by Christ in Scripture. Advent is most strongly linked to the Incarnation of Christ – the entry of God into the world in bodily form. Advent is thus the revelation *of* God *in* Christ – an indication of the radical reconciliation between the divine and the human, the spiritual and the material. The advent of Christ in the world is a radical in-breaking of the divine not merely as a *deus ex machina* but as a human being, a material entity. Advent also implies a second Advent – the return of Christ to rule. Advent thus functions as a time to reflect both upon the past and the future, and draws attention to the notion that this present time is a time 'between' – between the Incarnation and the Return, a time of 'already and not yet'. Advent indicates both the yearning for deliverance and the hope for redemption.

Meillassoux's work utilises 'advent' to indicate the possible coming of a **fourth World of justice**, a radical, unforeseeable and yet anticipated novelty in which God may be possible. As such, it echoes the liturgical sense of anticipation and hope found in orthodox Christian traditions. However, the paradoxical nature of Advent in the Christian tradition, and its belief that God in Christ entered *this* already broken and 'known' world, does not seem to be implied or indicated in Meillassoux. Rather his argument is that it will literally be a new World to come, one that will bring the justice promised by the old messianisms which take God to be existing now, not in a possible future.

ANCESTRALITY

Rodrigo Nunes

The problem of ancestrality is Meillassoux's opening gambit in *After Finitude*, and thus, in a sense, also a major aspect of what his philosophy as a whole is recognised for. It sets the scene for everything that follows: the characterisation of **correlationism's** limits and its unholy alliance with **fideism**; the deduction of the principle of **factiality** and the attainment of an **absolute** in the form of **hyper-chaos**; the **derivation** of the 'determinate conditions' facticity imposes on all beings; and the defence of mathematised science's capacity to access a nature thought independently from humans (see **Cartesian in-itself**). It matters precisely as a *'philosophical* problem, one liable to make us revise decisions often considered as infrangible since Kant' (*AF*, 37). The extent of Meillassoux's attachment to it is nonetheless debatable since the book itself states the wish only 'to provide a rigorous formulation of it … in such a way that its resolution no longer seems utterly inconceivable to us' (*AF*, 37).

The argument starts by defining ancestral statements as those bearing on any reality prior to the emergence of the human species, or of life on earth in general, not by distance in time, which makes something merely *ancient*, but in terms of anteriority in time in relation to any sentient or sapient relation to the world. While ostensibly addressing **dia-chronicity**, the temporal lag that ancestral statements reveal between world and relation-to-world, the problem extends to scientific statements as a whole, to the extent that it concerns the capacity to think the world in itself, separately from its givenness to us. The problem, in a nutshell, is: how can we have knowledge of something that was given prior to there being any mind it could be given to?

If its resolution, which does not trouble scientists, seems inconceivable for philosophers, that is because of the dominance of correlationism. How can a correlationist, for whom being is co-extensive with being given to a human mind, interpret a statement that essentially concerns the givenness of something that was given before it could be given to any human mind? According to Meillassoux, what the correlationist does is distinguish between a superficial, realist sense ('x took place millennia before human life') and a more originary, correlational one ('x is given to us today as having take place…'). While the first indicates a chronological anteriority of being over the correlation ('x was given before givenness'), the second establishes a logical anteriority of the correlation over what is given ('x is given to us as given before givenness'). This means that the truth of the statement arises not from the dia-chronic anteriority of the past itself but from a present, universalisable experience, intersubjectively verified by the scientific community, being retrojected into the past to which it refers. That means it is *'a true statement*, in that it is objective, but *one whose referent cannot possibly have actually existed in the way this truth describes it'* (*AF*, 34). In this way, anything that occurs is only 'taking place for us'. Since she only accepts the statement's sense at the cost of denying its reference, the correlationist must turn it into nonsense; an ancestral statement, concludes Meillassoux, can only have sense if that is the literal, realist one.

One should ask, however, whether the argument does not presuppose rather than demonstrate the problem with correlationism that Meillassoux wishes to expose. That would mean that its upshot – that confrontation with ancestrality exposes 'every variety of correlationism … as an extreme idealism', incapable of taking science for its word and therefore 'dangerously close to contemporary creationists' (*AF*, 18) – relies on the assumption that any correlationism is an extreme idealism. This, in turn, would be disastrous, as it could not only deprive factial speculation of its strategic role, which is fighting the 'religionizing' of reason (*AF*, 47) that results from strong correlationism's ultimate coincidence with fideism (*AF*, 46–8), but, more importantly, of its whole point.

The place to test that hypothesis is the most important passage in *After Finitude*, where Meillassoux turns correlationism around by arguing that the 'very idea of the difference between the in-itself and the for-us' depends on 'what is perhaps human thought's most remarkable power – its capacity to access the possibility of its own non-being, and thus to *know* itself to be mortal', which in turn presupposes that contingency be thought as absolute (*AF*, 59): 'If I maintain that the possibility of my not-being only exists as a correlate of my act of thinking the possibility of my not-being, then *I can no longer conceive the possibility of my not-being*'

(*AF*, 57). This is the subjective idealist's position: in order to know myself to be mortal, I must be capable of thinking my death as not requiring my thought of it to be effective, and hence as something outside of the correlational circle (*AF*, 78).

Yet the question of my death requiring my thought of it to be actual only arises if I take my thought to constitute its objects in the sense of causing their ontic existence as something 'out there' in the world. And for whom, except an extreme subjective idealist, is a subjective act of thought the cause of something's existence? It is one thing to say that 'x only is for me if it is for me', a more subtle tautology than it seems, and another to say that 'x only is if it is for me', which is the position against which Meillassoux is arguing. If I subscribe to the former, I can draw a further distinction between two ways in which x can be for me: experience of my death is impossible, as the consciousness and sensory apparatus necessary to register it would be lacking. But I can think myself as mortal, for example, via the perfectly legitimate inductive reasoning that if I am similar to other living beings in most aspects, and living beings are, as far as I know, mortal, I must be similar to them in that respect, too. My own death can be an object of thought for me as an actual possibility whose occurrence is independent from my thought, even if it cannot be an object of experience. This is a much more modest alternative to either believing things do not exist unless I think them, or hyper-chaos.

That Meillassoux reduces the issue to a choice between the latter two becomes clear when he states that unless by thinking contingency as an absolute, like the speculative philosopher, '*it would never have occurred to you not to be a subjective (or speculative) idealist*' (*AF*, 59). It would seem that in forcing a choice between the speculative absolute and an extreme, solipsistic subjective idealism, Meillassoux makes his most important argument depend on an artificial restriction of our real philosophical alternatives. As a consequence, he builds his proof on the refutation of the weakest of all the positions he wishes to oppose and leaves unconsidered all sorts of possible non-extreme correlationisms for which the problem of ancestrality in all likelihood would not arise.

ANHYPOTHETICAL

Rodrigo Nunes

'He whose subject is being *qua* being must be able to state the most certain principles of all things', one that is 'non-hypothetical' and which 'every one must have who knows anything about being'; this is how

Aristotle (*Metaphysics* IV, 1005b9–1005b15) prefaces the **principle of non-contradiction**. Meillassoux picks up the gauntlet: a 'demonstrated first principle', the principle of **factiality** 'seems to reconnect with the most profound "illusion" of philosophy since its Platonic inception, that of an *anhypothetical* principle, that is, a founding principle of rational thought that is not irrationally posed (in a contingent way), but is instead itself founded in reason' (*DI2*, 54, his emphasis). In a very classical way, he is posing the problem of beginnings, though not so much where to begin his enquiry, but on what principle to found speculative philosophy – and rational thought as a whole. If philosophy 'is the field of necessary discursivity', its point of departure must consist in 'identifying that which, amidst the facticity of being, is itself not factual' (*DI2*, 43–4).

If the speculative defence of the rights of thought over the absolute is not going to be a relapse into **metaphysics**, its first principle must not be metaphysical. While metaphysics is characterised by affirming the existence of necessary beings, speculative reasoning cannot allow itself the complacency of running up a chain of sufficient reason in order to arrive at a being that is necessary or *causa sui*. What it does, instead, is to establish a necessity 'that is not the necessity of a being, since no being is necessary, but of the contingency of beings – a contingency that is not itself a being' (*DI2*, 53). At the same time, this first principle must break with 'hypothetical rationality' (*DI2*, 54) – the idea that beginnings can only be posed in the form 'if ... then...', rather than demonstrated. It must be a '*first demonstration*', i.e., 'demonstrated without being deduced from another statement'; only then can it be '*the anhypothetical principle demanded since Plato as the first principle of philosophy*' (*DI2*, 54, his emphasis).

For Meillassoux, the principle of factiality does more than fit the description of 'a fundamental proposition that [cannot] be deduced from any other, but which [can] be proved' indirectly, 'by demonstrating that anyone who contests it can do so only by presupposing it to be true, thereby refuting him or herself' (*AF*, 60–1); it is in fact a stronger candidate for first principle than Aristotle's. All that can be shown of the latter is that it is impossible to *think* a contradiction, allowing the strong correlationist to claim that, while unthinkable, it might be possible in absolute terms. In turn, factiality concerns absolute contingency not only for-us, but in-itself, so that to think the possibility of the contingency of contingency is merely to posit a higher contingency, thus presupposing what one seeks to deny. It is thus both anhypothetical and absolute.

One should note Meillassoux's statement concerning the 'faultless' 'consensus' in 'contemporary thought' around 'hypothetical reason' – the idea that 'the beginning of reason can only be *posed* – as axiom, postulate, thesis, hypothesis etc.' (*DI2*, 53–4, his emphasis). One could easily expect this to apply to philosophy, given the ascendancy of correlationism; the fact that Meillassoux extends it to 'the hypothetico-deductive reason deployed by logic and mathematics' and 'the inductive reason deployed by experimental sciences' (*DI2*, 53–4), however, complicates the picture painted at the start of *After Finitude*. If the sciences understand themselves as hypothetical, what purchase can the argument of **ancestrality** retain? Is there a correlationism of the sciences themselves? What would that mean for the concept of **fideism**?

ARCHE-FOSSIL

Rodrigo Nunes

Arche-fossils – 'materials indicating the existence of an ancestral reality or event; one that is anterior to terrestrial life' (*AF*, 10) – are what ancestral statements are about. They are that which the problem of **ancestrality** is meant to show **correlationism** as incapable of thinking. Two examples of arche-fossil are 'an isotope whose rate of radioactive decay we know, or the luminous emission of a star that informs us as to the date of its formation' (*AF*, 10). Since **speculative materialism** deals only with the necessary conditions 'that belong ... to a contingency delivered of all constraints other than that (or those) of its own eternity', it does not concern itself with existing things, which are by necessity contingent (*IRR*, 12). Thus, as Meillassoux clarifies, the arche-fossil was employed in *After Finitude* 'only so as to problematize the contemporary self-evidence of correlationism', by way of arguing that the problem of ancestrality appears insoluble for as long as one stays within the correlational circle (*IRR*, 12).

It is the fact that the arche-fossil indexes a lacuna of manifestation rather than in manifestation – not a spatio-temporally distant event or being, but specifically one that is prior to any correlation – that allows Meillassoux to expose correlationism's embarrassment, which comes in the face of contemporary science's apparent capacity to think nature independently from any phenomenological experience of it, or even '*a world wherein spatio-temporal givenness itself came into being within a time and a space which preceded every variety of givenness*' (*AF*, 22). Yet Ray **Brassier** makes the perspicuous point that, to the extent that his defence of the absolute rights of objective reality pivots around establishing a rift between ancestral time and spatio-temporal distance, it harbours a concession to correlationism, for 'surely it is not just ancestral phenomena which challenge the latter, but simply the reality described by the modern natural sciences *tout court*' (Brassier 2007: 59). To insist that only the ancestrality presented by the arche-fossil transcends correlational constitution, therefore, is to create an exception where there is none: science tells us that we are surrounded by mind-independent processes all the time, and the fact that these are 'contemporaneous with the existence of consciousness, while the accretion of the earth preceded it, is quite irrelevant' (Brassier 2007: 60).

Meillassoux's choice of isotope dating as an example is perhaps an even greater trouble for his argument. Not, *pace* Hallward, because measuring is a human, convention-based practice – the point about the reality of what is measured still stands – but because this being an area in which precision is paramount, and thus highly dependent on advanced technology, it displays rectification much more habitually than, say, the formalisation of certain physical relations into mathematical functions (see the back and forth between Hallward 2011 and Brown 2011). As such, it brings into sharper focus the difficult spot in which Meillassoux's defence of mathematised science places him in regard to the revisability of scientific claims (see Johnston 2011). Estimates of the age of the universe have varied a fair amount throughout the last century, during which the Hubble constant, the first relatively accurate measurement of the rate of expansion of the universe, was recalculated several times. It was only with the discovery of microwave cosmic background radiation in the 1960s that a way was found to determine the Hubble constant without the need to refer to galaxy distances, thus increasing accuracy. Throughout the last decade, the exact measure changed literally every two years, as the data from the Wilkinson Microwave Anisotropy Probe measurements were released, providing ever greater precision – so that the actual figure has been revised even after the publication of *After Finitude*.

A correlationist rejoinder to Meillassoux could therefore be that the universe coming into existence is something that effectively took place 13.75 billion years ago, at least according to today's best science; but the event of this becoming an object of our knowledge – thus being true for us – only took place as recently as 2010, when scientific consensus stabilised around this measurement.

ARCHI-FACT

An alternative name for the facticity of the correlation. See, for example, *MSC*, 17–18.

ATHEISM/THEISM

Paul O'Mahoney

Atheism is a profession of non-belief in the existence of any **God**, which is opposed by both theism and deism. Theism is the belief in the existence of at least one God, who evinces a concern for the world. This world can thus be influenced by God and in many belief systems it is also the creation of the God. As such, theism is a belief with a specific content, where the nature of the deity is accessible to human beings, sometimes through reason, though for others this access can only come through revelation. With this theism is distinguished from deism. Deism is the assumption that, although God or gods do exist and may have created the world, they do not intervene in this world. Deism thus rejects all accounts of religious revelation or the miraculous interaction of a deity with creation. All revealed religions therefore count as theistic. The modern origin of theism is commonly dated to the 1660s, attributed to Ralph Cudworth, who used it in his *The True Intellectual System of the Universe*, first published in 1678. Cudworth was concerned to refute atheism, along with all moral and political philosophy derived from or conducive to atheistic principles.

Two things can immediately be noted about Meillassoux's position. First, he offers a stronger conception of atheism. Second, though deism counts as a religious belief, Meillassoux's use of the term 'the religious' in all cases clearly implies theistic beliefs (see **irreligion**). Atheism and the religious are considered opposites. Each denies to the other the power to refute its position; this is one feature of contemporary **fideism**, where even atheism is reduced to a mere belief and can therefore essentially be equated with religion. It is Meillassoux's stronger and stricter interpretation of atheism that allows him to propose a third option to these alternatives, which apparently exhaust all possibilities. Rather than the beliefs that there is or is not a God, for Meillassoux:

The two theses are in truth stronger than these factual statements: for their sense lies in the supposedly *necessary* character of either the inexistence or the existence of God. To be atheist is not simply to maintain that God does not exist, but also that he could not exist; to be a believer is to have faith in the essential existence of God. (*SD*, 268)

Both positions are then seen to be tied to or derived from a belief in necessity and, ultimately, belief in the **principle of sufficient reason**. By virtue of his denial of any necessity save for that of **contingency**, and his consequent assertion of the 'omnipotence of Chaos', Meillassoux can posit God as an eternal possibility. This would be the personal God who brings with Him the promise of justice and the **resurrection** of the dead as a real possibility:

It is a question of maintaining that *God is possible* – not in a subjective and synchronous sense (in the sense that I maintain that it is possible that God currently exists), but in an objective future sense (where I maintain that God could really come about in the future). At stake is the unknotting of the theo-religious link between God and necessity (God must or must not exist) and its reattachment to the virtual (God could exist). (*SD*, 269)

In Meillassoux's definition, God must henceforth be thought of as '*the contingent, but eternally possible, effect of a Chaos unsubordinated to any law*' (*SD*, 274). This permissible (and for Meillassoux rationally defensible) hope is the ground of his discussion of **divine inexistence** and is Meillassoux's primary contribution to theological or religious debates.

B

BADIOU, ALAIN

Christopher Norris

Alain Badiou was Meillassoux's teacher and mentor at a formative stage in the latter's intellectual development and has continued to encourage and actively promote the younger man's work. Badiou's influence is everywhere evident in Meillassoux's thought, although it doesn't always take the more overt forms of explicit agreement or closely convergent thinking. Certainly there is a lot of common ground between them, both as a matter of shared philosophical commitments and the range of topics to which their work has been addressed. The intellectual kinship comes out most clearly in the opening section of *After Finitude* with its now famous attack on **correlationism** – that is to say, on the epistemology of Immanuel **Kant** along with all the proliferating woes in its wake – and its dramatic, not to say imperious, statement of the adversary case for an outlook of intransigent or hard-line objectivist **realism**. It is also apparent in Meillassoux's high regard for **mathematics**, the physical sciences, and art (especially poetry) as among philosophy's prime 'conditions' or essential means of critical orientation. Both of them tend to philosophise through a combination of passionate critical engagement with various thinkers of the past, although Badiou's range is much wider in this respect, and speculative ventures well beyond the limits of orthodox history of ideas or philosophical commentary. Despite that, they are both axiomatic thinkers in the sense usually associated with mathematics, logic and the formal sciences, that is, starting out from certain assumed, though not necessarily self-evident, premises and then proceeding to derive their consequences by a deductive (or quasi-deductive) sequence of argument.

Beyond that, more specifically, there are numerous shared points of reference, for instance, the set theory of Georg **Cantor** and the poetry of Stéphane **Mallarmé**, that may safely be said to exemplify Badiou's 'influence' on Meillassoux's developing project, although often their modes of engagement with these topics have been markedly divergent. Indeed it is the differences between them that I shall focus on here since the commonalities are less to the point in this context. One such difference concerns their respective deployments of set theory as a means to articulate ontological issues and to argue for a realism (in Meillassoux's case, a speculative realism). Badiou takes developments in this area since Cantor to have established a number of cardinal truths not only in mathematics but also, by more than loose analogy, in politics and art. That claim is advanced on the strength of a detailed working-through of the formal arguments (proof-procedures) involved and a likewise rigorous working-out of what they signify or demonstrably entail when transposed to those other contexts. Thus it is a question of showing, via methods like Cantor's technique of diagonalisation and results like the power-set axiom, how any given political situation or current stage of development in the arts is always, by the strictest necessity, exceeded, surpassed, or potentially thrown into crisis by that which finds no place in the dominant 'count-as-one'. Among such excluded and socio-politically disenfranchised minorities are the *sans-papiers* or undocumented migrant (mainly North African) workers in France whose unrecognised collectivity forms the equivalent of that absolute excess that comes into play once the power-set axiom is applied, as by Cantor, to the multiple 'sizes' or orders of infinity.

Badiou is a realist about mathematics in so far as he takes it as axiomatic (1) that 'set theory is ontology', and (2) that any genuine 'event', whether in mathematics, politics, or the arts, is ineluctably marked by that unpredictable occurrence that disrupts, invalidates and potentially transforms some existing ontological scheme. It is the moment, typically evaded or repressed by many philosophers from Plato down, when 'consistent multiplicity' gives way to the outbreak of an 'inconsistent multiplicity' which, again potentially, heralds the advent of some radical change or advance. At the same time this realism is qualified by Badiou's emphasis on the subject as 'militant of truth', that is, the subject who comes into existence solely as a result of taking up that specific challenge and thereafter investing their best efforts in its carrying-through. Meillassoux is also a realist, as witness – most strikingly – those now famous pages in *After Finitude* where he deploys the **arche-fossil**, that is, the immemorial relic of a time before the advent of any sentient life-forms, as a supposed knock-down argument against all **correlationism**, whether of a Kantian (epistemological) or latter-day (post-linguistic-turn) persuasion. However his realism differs from Badiou's in finding no such procedurally specified role for the human subject, perhaps because it might seem to soften or compromise his hard objectivist stance, and also, as fairly leaps off the page toward the end of *After Finitude*, in the kinds of consequences he draws from set-theoretical reflection on the multiple orders of infinity. It is here that Meillassoux advances his extraordinary reading of David **Hume** where he steals a spectacular march on the latter's much-debated outlook of epistemological scepticism with regard to causal explanations and our grounds (or lack of them) for supposing the uniformity of nature. This Meillassoux rejects in favour of a nominally realist outlook according to which it is reality that changes, for all that we can possibly know, along with those putative **laws of nature** that, once acquainted with Cantor's discovery, we must conceive as subject to radical mutation from moment to moment across the infinities of possible worlds that might pop into and out of existence.

I shall not here go into the problems with this speculative venture from the viewpoint of a realist outlook compatible with the sorts of causal-explanatory reasoning basic to the physical sciences. My point is that it stands in striking contrast to Badiou's insistence that if we are capable of making discoveries or achieving advances in mathematics, the physical sciences, politics, or art then this entails a number of precepts decidedly at odds with Meillassoux's version of Hume. These are, firstly, that in any given situation, there are uncounted multiples that objectively exceed whatever is known, recognised, or grasped concerning that situation and, secondly, that for this reason truth exceeds knowledge, that is, it must be thought of as objective, recognition-transcendent, or 'epistemically unconstrained'. Moreover, thirdly, if indeed 'mathematics is ontology' then certain kinds of formal reasoning (from Cantor's diagonal procedure to the concept/method/technique of 'forcing' elaborated by Paul Cohen) are capable eventually of delivering truths that go beyond a presently existing state of knowledge but that are none the less latent or (so-far unknowably) contained within it. Scientific revolutions thus occur not as the result of some obscure Kuhnian process of rationally under-motivated paradigm-change but by the working-through among 'faithful' or 'militant' subjects of a truth-procedure whose outcome is, of course, not epistemically guaranteed in advance but whose validity is all the same a matter of objective warrant. It is, to say the least, unclear how any such procedure could possibly work if one subscribes to Meillassoux's itself obscurely motivated doctrine of infinitised ontological relativity.

Another difference between the two thinkers has to do with Meillassoux's emergent interest in developing (perhaps more aptly, 'trying out') a speculative theology based on the same line of argument. This involves the idea that even if, in our presently existing reality, there is nothing that answers to the name or description 'God' nevertheless there might – indeed must – be infinitely numerous worlds amongst the infinitely many infinities thereof in which no laws of nature or anything else would debar such a being from existence. However playful or doctrinally disengaged, the kind of thinking here displayed is again maximally remote from Badiou's militant atheism and his clear determination that speculative interests, despite their undeniable centrality to his work, should not do anything that takes away from the force of its political and intellectual commitments. The same applies to Badiou's readings of literature, especially Stéphane Mallarmé's poetry, which must be seen as very much an integral part of his overall project since, for better or worse, their approach is predominantly thematic, rather than formal, and aims to discover in literary texts an analogue or allegory of his own mathematical, ontological, political and, of course, art-related interests. When Meillassoux reads Mallarmé, on the other hand, he does so in pursuit of an arcane numerological thesis that may perhaps be textually warranted or true to Mallarmé's intent but which leaves a distinct impression that the poem functions mainly as a pretext for Meillassoux's conceptual acrobatics.

Despite these divergences of intellectual temperament and orientation it is worth repeating that Meillassoux owes a great deal to his early mentor and would surely not have written a book like *After Finitude* (at any rate the first, more convincing part) had it not been for Badiou's example. To some extent the aforementioned problems may derive from precisely that affiliation since, as other commentators have noted, they are problems that also affect Badiou's work, though in a different form. Thus it is often hard to grasp how Badiou's highly abstract mathematical ontology can be thought to hook up in any convincing way with the various sectors of reality, whether scientific or political, where they are supposed to have critical traction. Of course this is a version of the issue that has long exercised philosophers of mathematics, namely, in the plaintive words of physicist Eugene Wigner, the 'unreasonable effectiveness of mathematics in the physical sciences'. However that issue is rendered especially acute with thinkers like Badiou and Meillassoux since they each, in different ways, raise abstraction or speculation to a high point of philosophic principle even while (again in different ways) making large claims concerning its real-world applicability or purchase.

In Meillassoux's case it is further exacerbated by his seeming lack of acquaintance with the large body of recent Anglophone work in realist, especially causal-realist, epistemology and philosophy of science that has appeared in the wake of old-style logical empiricism. A knowledge of this work might have helped not only to buttress his own position but also to strengthen its scientific credentials, provide it with more substantive metaphysical content, and perhaps prevent or damp down that chronic oscillation between ultra-realism and a strain of ultra-speculative thought that, if taken with less than a large pinch of salt, would undermine that whole project. Indeed one suspects that some of the current excitement around speculative realism has to do with its coming as such a dramatic turn-around after so many movements of 'Continental' (especially French) thought with a strongly anti-realist, constructivist or 'correlationist' bias.

BRASSIER, RAY

Pete Wolfendale

Ray Brassier is a Scottish philosopher largely responsible for popularising Meillassoux's work in the Anglophone world. He published one of the first critical engagements with Meillassoux's work in English and was the translator of the first English edition of *After Finitude*. He was also one of the principal organisers and one of the four speakers at the infamous 'Speculative Realism' conference at Goldsmiths' College in 2007, though he has since distanced himself from that term. He has consistently criticised what he sees as the avoidance of epistemological problems in Anglophone Continental philosophy, as well as the ignorance of and sometimes hostility toward the natural sciences often associated with it. There is a profound affinity between Brassier's criticisms and Meillassoux's critique of **correlationism**, in so far as they both insist on the necessity of taking the results of natural science literally, but there is equally an affinity between their positive positions, in so far as they are both committed to the revival of **rationalism** in contemporary philosophy. Nevertheless, Brassier has a number of important disagreements with Meillassoux, some of which have grown more serious as his position has developed and changed in recent years. We will begin by presenting an outline of Brassier's thought in his book *Nihil Unbound*, and the criticisms of Meillassoux found therein, before addressing how these have developed since its publication.

Nihil Unbound connects a number of different themes, structured around the core contention that **nihilism** is 'not an existential quandary but a speculative opportunity' (Brassier 2007: xi). He takes it that nihilism is the logical conclusion of the progressive disenchantment of nature by science begun in the Enlightenment, through which conceptual thought comes to be seen as something manifest in causal processes amenable to naturalistic explanation and normative value comes to be seen as something projected upon nature by these same processes. This more or less passive consequence of the work of reason is to be neither opposed nor ameliorated, but rather to be embraced. However, this differs from Nietzsche's own active nihilism in so far as it does not aim to overcome the will to truth, because this constitutes the normative core of reason that drives disenchantment. This point is crucial to Brassier's thought, in so far as it functions as a fundamental constraint upon what he characterises, following Wilfrid Sellars and Paul and Patricia Churchland, as the project of replacing the manifest image of man in the world with the scientific image. The aim of *Nihil Unbound* is to steer a path between a self-destructive naturalism that violates this constraint and a soporific correlationism that preserves rationality at the expense of neutering scientific naturalism.

Although it is possible to see Meillassoux's work as already navigating this difficult path, Brassier provides two important criticisms that recommend against following him, both of which turn on Meillassoux's responses to objections to his opening argument that correlationism is incompatible with the scientifically ratified truth of the **arche-fossil**. On the one hand, he maintains that Meillassoux's claim that the arche-fossil is not merely a lacuna in the given, but rather a lacuna of givenness itself, depends upon an asymmetry between time and space that can only be motivated by appealing to a logic of time that supersedes the scientific account of time in precisely the way that correlationism does. He thus demands that the non-correlation of thought and being be conceived in non-temporal terms. On the other hand, he maintains that Meillassoux's claim that any transcendental structure of thought must be empirically instantiated in an existent thinker invalidates his own appeal to the **intellectual intuition** of absolute contingency. He thus demands that thought's ability to think its non-correlation with being must not be premised upon an access to being that is secured through an ontological privilege.

Brassier meets the first demand by appropriating Francois **Laruelle**'s general account of philosophy as founded upon a decision that divides the real (being) into an *a priori* component which constitutes thought and an *a posteriori* component that constitutes its object, before uniting the two in the form of a pre-established harmony that is sufficient to encompass its own intelligibility, and deflating it into an account of correlationism more specifically. He thereby transforms Laruelle's non-philosophical suspension of philosophical decision into a philosophical 'scision' of the correlation between thought and being premised upon the necessity of thought's empirical instantiation. The bare fact that the real determines thought *in-the-last-instance* is taken to foreclose its intelligibility to thought, in so far as the distinction between them is operative only from the side of thought itself. This 'unilateral duality' of thought and the real forms the original basis of Brassier's transcendental realism.

Brassier meets the second demand by appropriating Alain **Badiou**'s rationalist account of thought, in so far as its mathematical abstraction enables it to preserve the normative core of reason while making possible a subtractive ontology that obviates the need for an access to being that reflexively secures its own ontological status. However, he transforms Badiou's subtractive approach to being on the basis of the mathematical thought of the empty set – the void – by re-founding it upon the limit-case of scientific comprehension – being-nothing – the real as evacuated of all positive content, or as what is common to all stages of the indefinite process through which science attempts to grasp nature. Brassier re-articulates this conceptual limit as a metaphysical terminus – extinction – the ultimate annihilation of all matter, which he then uses to reformulate the Freudian death drive as a relation that every material entity bares to this terminus. This irrevocably unbinds the interests of reason from the interests of living, liberating the will to truth from the will to survive, while simultaneously incarnating the indifference of being to thought that grounds the 'non-dialectical negativity' of unilateral duality. Whereas *After Finitude* posits the necessary possibility that everything can become otherwise (and thereby the necessity that there is something rather than nothing) as thought's point of contact with the absolute, *Nihil Unbound* posits the inevitability that everything will become nothing as thought's subtractive purchase upon the real.

Brassier has departed from the position put forth in *Nihil Unbound* in at least three substantial ways since its publication. The first of these is his rejection of Meillassoux's sympathetic characterisation of the circle of correlationism as an argument from pragmatic contradiction in favour of David Stove's characterisation of it as an instance of the fallacy of equivocation, called 'the Gem' (Brassier 2011: 56–64). The realisation that correlationism is premised upon an equivocation between concepts and objects motivates a transcendental response to correlationism more direct than the Laruellian scision attempted in *Nihil Unbound*, in so far as the latter also ignores the conceptual content of thought in order to treat it as an object among others. The second departure is his abandonment of Badiou's account of thought as ultimately too abstract to be naturalistically tractable. The realisation that Badiou and Meillassoux's focus upon mathematics as the paradigm of rationality leaves them unable to account for the specificity of empirical science motivates a more concrete analysis of the empirical instantiation of thought in causal systems that can be related to their objects through perceptual interactions. The final departure consists in distinguishing the project of nihilism from the metaphysics of extinction, in so far as the latter depends upon precisely the sort of pseudo-scientific appeal to temporality that plagues the argument from the arche-fossil.

Taken together, these departures announce two fundamental shifts: a shift away from the Cartesian rationalism of Meillassoux and Badiou toward the rationalism inherent in the **German Idealism** of Immanuel **Kant** and G.W.F. **Hegel**, and a shift away from the combination of transcendental minimalism and brute realism of Laruelle's non-philosophy to the resurrected Kantianism and thoroughgoing naturalism of Sellars. These shifts have not modified the core of Brassier's project, which remains that of preserving and harnessing the intellectual force of nihilism. However, this is no longer simply constrained by the need to protect the normative force of reason from its own progressive disenchantment of nature, but is motivated by the need to articulate the relationship between the normative and the natural as such, or between what Sellars calls the 'space of reasons' and the 'space of causes'. This involves combining the general critique of epistemic and categorial givenness provided by Sellars with the more specific critique of phenomenal selfhood provided by Thomas Metzinger as the basis of a functionalist account of rational agency capable of bridging the gap between the transcendental structure of conceptual norms and their empirical instantiation in the behaviour of causal systems (see, for example, Brassier 2011). This rigorously anti-phenomenological approach puts Brassier's current work in even greater conflict with Meillassoux's, in so far as the latter's account of the genesis of thought from life *ex nihilo*, and the independence of sensible secondary qualities from mathematisable primary qualities that it facilitates, ultimately preserve much of the phenomenological account of experience traditionally favoured by correlationism.

$$\boxed{C}$$

CANTOR, GEORG

Paul Livingston

Georg Cantor was the creator of **set theory** and the modern theory of the mathematical infinite. His discovery of a rigorous, mathematical way to treat actually existing infinite sets revolutionised the foundations of mathematics as well as philosophical thinking about infinity, with implications that continue to be actively explored today. Prior to Cantor, philosophers had argued that the infinite can exist only potentially and never actually (for example, Aristotle), that the concept of an actually existing infinite quantity is contradictory or paradoxical in itself (for example, Locke and Galileo), or that the actual infinite must be identified with the absolute or the divine, and hence cannot be understood by a finite intellect (for example, Aquinas) (Moore 2001: 17–44, 75–83). Against each of these interpretations, Cantor showed that it is mathematically possible and useful to discuss an open hierarchy of infinite sets – the so-called 'transfinite hierarchy' – and that their ordering and relationships could be rigorously modelled and understood.

Around 1874, working on the problem of finding general trigonometric representations for functions, Cantor discovered that infinite sets of differing sizes could be distinguished and that the set of natural numbers or positive whole numbers (1, 2, 3...) is smaller than the set of all real numbers (numbers with indefinitely long decimal parts). This led Cantor to posit the bases of what would become set theory, and in 1883 he defined a set (*Menge*) as 'any many [*Viele*] which can be thought of as one, that is, every totality of definite elements which can be united to a whole through a law', commenting also that 'by this I believe I have defined something related to the Platonic *eidos* or *idea*' (quoted in Hallett 1986: 33). His definition of sets allowed him to introduce the concepts of 'set cardinality', that is, the 'size' of sets considered in terms of the possibility of putting them into one to one correspondence with one another, and the 'power set', which is the set of all subsets, the arbitrary re-groupings of the elements of a given set.

These ideas led him to be able to prove what has become known as 'Cantor's Theorem': any set, whether finite or infinite, has a power set that is strictly larger than itself (in the sense of one-to-one correspondence). In proving the theorem, Cantor invented the powerful and general technique of 'diagonalisation', which later found application in many developments of set theory and proof theory, including (in a proof-theoretic version) as one of the central steps in proving Kurt Gödel's incompleteness theorems. Cantor was also able to formulate what became known as the 'continuum hypothesis', a hypothesis about the relative size of the set of natural numbers and the set of real numbers, or of the set of points on a continuous line. In particular, on one formulation, the continuum hypothesis holds that there is no set of any transfinite 'size' or cardinality between that of the natural numbers and that of the real numbers. Cantor worked unsuccessfully to prove or to refute the continuum hypothesis for much of the rest of his life, and the problem of the truth or falsity of the hypothesis sustained set-theoretical research for many decades. It was finally proved by Gödel (in 1939) and Paul Cohen (in 1963), respectively, that the continuum hypothesis can neither be refuted nor proven from standard set-theoretical axioms.

In the first decades of the twentieth century, Cantor's ideas were quickly applied by philosophers and logicians such as Bertrand Russell, Gottlob Frege and Ernst Zermelo to axiomatise set theory and put all of mathematics on a firm set-theoretical foundation by showing how numbers and other mathematical objects could be defined in terms of sets. However, from the beginning, the development of set theory was beset by a series of interrelated paradoxes, some of which may have already been known to Cantor. The most famous of these is Russell's paradox, which states that the set of all sets is not an element of itself (that is, the set is not an element of itself if it is, and it is an element of itself if it is not). After Russell pointed out the paradox, set theoreticians have resorted to various devices to ensure that contradictory sets such as the Russell set cannot arise or be formed. Most generally, these devices appeal to varieties of the intuition that a set that would be 'too big', that is, roughly as big as the set of all sets, if that were to exist, cannot be formed. Despite (or because of) this resolution by fiat of the paradoxes in the standard axiomatisation, their impact has continued to be felt in logical, mathematical and especially metaphysical thought.

Although Cantor provided, for the first time in history, the rigorous basis for a mathematical treatment of the infinite, his own views about the infinite were shaped by theological and religious ideas. In particular, Cantor distinguished between the mathematical infinite, which he treated with his theory of the transfinite hierarchy, and the absolute or 'unincreasable' infinite, which he identified with God. Perhaps anticipating or reflecting the set-theoretical paradoxes, Cantor termed the 'too-large' infinities that cannot exist without contradiction 'inconsistent multiplicities'. For example, according to Cantor, the totality of all that can be thought is such an 'inconsistent' or 'absolute' infinite, and so cannot be conceived without contradiction.

In *Being and Event*, applying his programmatic identification of ontology with mathematics in terms of what is called Zermelo-Fraenkel set theory, Alain **Badiou** argues that the set-theoretical paradoxes of the 'too-large' infinities demonstrate in a rigorous fashion the non-existence of a 'one-all', that is, as is shown by the axioms under the impetus of the paradoxes, there is no universe or consistent totality of all that exists (Badiou 2007: 23–30). Although being in itself, for Badiou, can only be thought as 'pure inconsistent multiplicity', every presentable whole results from the operation of a 'counting as one', which produces it as a limited and consistent unity.

In *After Finitude*, Meillassoux follows Badiou in appealing to Cantor's set theory to establish metaphysical conclusions about infinity and totality. Meillassoux maintains that Cantor's set theory shows that the 'totalization of the thinkable ... can *no longer* be guaranteed *a priori*' (*AF*, 103). This result, according to Meillassoux, has implications for the structure of modality. In particular, the axioms of post-Cantorian set theory provide 'the resources for thinking that the possible is untotalizable' (*AF*, 105). That is, given the fact of the non-existence of the one-all, there is no single, total set of possible worlds or scenarios. This, in turn, allows the disqualification of the 'necessitarian inference', which deduces the necessity of physical laws from their apparent stability by reference to a supposed totality of possibilities accessible to *a priori* reasoning, and thus helps to support Meillassoux's own thesis of an overarching 'absolute' and 'necessary' contingency (*AF*, 105–6).

There are at least two significant problems with Meillassoux's attempt to apply Cantorian conclusions to support the thesis of 'absolute contingency' (Livingston 2012 104–6). First, it is not clear that Cantorian set theory has any direct application to the theory of possible worlds, or even if so, what that application demonstrates. Probability is well-defined even over sets of transfinite cardinality, so the appeal to the transfinite hierarchy itself cannot block what Meillassoux calls the 'necessitarian inference', and even if Cantor is taken to have demonstrated the non-existence of the set of all sets, it is not clear how considerations about probability are to be linked to this (non-existent) 'total' set. Second, it is not clear that Cantor's theorem or the set-theoretical paradoxes have to be interpreted as showing the non-existence of a set of all sets at all. Alternatively, it is possible and cogent to consider them to demonstrate simply the necessary inconsistency of this totality, and indeed to indicate the kinds of structural inconsistencies and paradoxes that must arise with the existence of totalities of certain kinds. But since the structure of inconsistent totalities is not simply unthinkable (and indeed can be modelled with what is called 'dialetheiac' logics, certain 'non-well-founded' set theories, and formalisations of critical, dialectical and deconstructive thought about contradiction), it is not clear that either Badiou or Meillassoux is justified in interpreting Cantorian set theory as excluding this possibility.

CARTESIAN IN-ITSELF

Sebastian Purcell

Rehabilitating the idea of the Cartesian in-itself after the Kantian Critical project (see Immanuel **Kant**) as a means for critiquing contemporary forms of **correlationism**, such as phenomenology and the linguistic turn in mid-century Anglo-American philosophy, is the basic metaphysical objective of Meillassoux's **speculative materialism**.

The Cartesian in-itself is best understood in relation to the distinction between **primary and secondary qualities**, terms which were first coined by John Locke, but which are clearly present in René **Descartes'** thought. For the latter thinker secondary qualities are those which exist both in relation to my own conscious perception and the object itself. For example, if you were to place your hand over a candle flame, the heat you would feel is something registered in your own consciousness. The flame itself does not feel the heat. Yet, your own feelings of heat are not hallucinations because they are prompted by proximity to the flame. This means that while secondary qualities exist in relation to you, they do not exist solely in your mind, but also bear some relation to the object. Primary qualities, by contrast, are those properties of the object that would exist even if you were not around to perceive them, and which are thus understood to be inseparable from the object. For Descartes these properties are those that pertain to spatial extension, and so are subject to geometric proof. They include width, length, movement, depth, size and figure.

Meillassoux generalises Descartes' account of primary qualities and makes it compatible with advances in contemporary mathematics. The Cartesian in-itself satisfies the following two conditions: it is all the aspects of the object that can be formulated in mathematical terms, and it is those aspects that can be meaningfully conceived as properties of the object itself (*AF*, 3). By 'mathematical formulation' and 'meaningfully conceived' Meillassoux intends those aspects that are subject to proof by means of modern mathematics' most basic abstract algebra, namely **set theory** in its standard Zermelo-Fraenkel formulation, and standard non-formal methods of mathematical proof (see Georg **Cantor**).

Support for the Cartesian in–itself is today often thought untenable because of what might be called the correlationist critique. It runs thus: even if you think of an object in mathematical terms, then it is you who are thinking it. What you are thinking is thus an object for you, and this means that it is a secondary rather than primary quality. The sort of objectivity that the Cartesian in–itself maintains, then, is supposed to constitute a form of objectivity on its own, but it turns out to be a self-contradictory notion. Instead, the post-Kantian sense of objectivity is more generally accepted, which maintains that something is objective if its representation in my mind is universalisable, not independent.

Meillassoux agrees with this critique of the Cartesian in–itself, and responds in two ways. First, he develops the ancestral argument to show that the post-Kantian position, correlationism, is itself deeply troubled. Second, he demonstrates how, from within the correlationist framework, it is nevertheless possible to make one's way to the outside, by adopting a strong correlationism and seeing what it must take as **absolute**, namely the fact of the contingent relationship of thought and world itself.

CAUSATION

See Hume, David.

CHILD (*INFANS*), THE

Leon Niemoczynski

According to Meillassoux's ontology described in his theorisation of the **fourth World of justice**, the Child can be interpreted to be the birth of an infant that is the **symbol** of the rebirth of humanity, or it can be interpreted as The Child of Man, a mediating Christ-like figure who brings divinity itself under the universal conditions of contingency (*DI*, 334). Although Meillassoux's descriptions of the literal birth of the *infans* are vague, according to *L'Inexistence divine* the birth of the child marks a key moment in the messianic **eschatology** (or **eschaology** as coined in 'Immanence of the World Beyond') indicating a knitting together of Greek reason and Judeo-Christian faith with hope in the contingent conditions of **hyper-chaos** that enable future change (*IWB*, 463).

Meillassoux states that the child represents 'the God to come' present in humanity's 'womb' (*DI*, 335). This is to say that humanity can be pregnant with hope for a future to come, to see the birth of a new World, just as in the past conditions have given birth to Worlds of life, matter and thought. Thus, the *infans* represents a 'spirit of expectation' making each human a 'forerunner of God' (*DI*, 232). According to Meillassoux, however, there will always be some ambiguity regarding the birth of the child during, before, or after the advent of the fourth World of justice. This is due to the indifferent power of the surcontingent that covers the predictability of any symbolic birth that is to happen. Regardless of the unpredictability of this symbolic gesture made by the birth of the child, Meillassoux ventures that it is a requirement in the **advent** of the incarnation of universal justice.

The child, or *infans* in Latin, suggests for Meillassoux 'the unborn child' or one 'who does not speak' (*DI*, 225). This symbolisation assures the impossibility of any specific religious vision for the advent of the fourth World. 'The child is the one who teaches us that its power is not the manifestation of a superior power of providence, but of contingency alone' (*DI*, 225). The child teaches others that power is not to be had in an authoritative transcendent manner in its own right, but is solely an 'immanent end' (*DI*, 225). The child also teaches humanity 'the impossibility of despising ourselves with respect to what makes us human ... thus [the child] cannot be loved as Lord but ... as one who knows itself to be equal'. It is part of the divine gesture that has made itself 'human among humans' (*DI*, 225).

In short, the child represents the supreme abandonment of power during the time in which a Christ-like messianic figure, a 'mediator', assumes the power of rebirth, inaugurates a process of bodily **resurrection** so that justice can be brought about for the dead, and relinquishes power once justice is accomplished for which the advent was this event's founding condition. Thus the child is a human mediator between humanity's current World and universal justice.

CONTINGENCY

Nathan Brown

The centrality of this concept to Meillassoux's enterprise is signalled by the subtitle of *After Finitude: An Essay on the Necessity of Contingency*. The primary claim of Meillassoux's philosophy is that only contingency can and must be thought as absolutely necessary. 'The absolute', he argues, 'is the absolute impossibility of a necessary being' (*AF*, 60). Thus, his effort is to think contingency in a manner that is speculative rather than either empirical or metaphysical. Contingency is thought as an **absolute**, as a property of the in-itself rather than of observable reality. Yet grasping this absolute does not require the metaphysical assertion than an absolute entity exists; on the contrary, it is precisely the impossibility of the existence of such an entity that delivers the veritable concept of contingency. It is through the concept of absolute contingency that Meillassoux thus opens an alternative passage between empiricist scepticism and dogmatic **rationalism** to that cleared by Immanuel **Kant**'s transcendental philosophy.

Several distinctions are required to isolate the specific concept of contingency that we find in Meillassoux's work. Contingency must be distinguished from both facticity and chance. Empirical contingency must be then distinguished from absolute contingency. Empirical contingency is distinct from facticity in so far as the former is 'predicated of everything that can be or not be, occur or not occur, within the world without contravening the invariants of language and representation through which the world is given to us' (*AF*, 40). Empirical contingency is that which, within the framework of these invariants, is not necessarily the case. Facticity, on the other hand, pertains to the modality of these invariants themselves: these are factical in so far as we cannot establish their necessity or contingency. That is, these invariants of language and representation through which the world is given to us constitute a **fact** rather than an absolute since we cannot seem to establish whether or not they are necessarily the case.

The concept of absolute contingency is to be distinguished from empirical contingency, however, in so far as the former results from converting the deficit of knowledge implicit in the concept of facticity into a positive item of knowledge concerning the modality of the real. 'Facticity can be legitimately identified with contingency', Meillassoux writes, 'in so far as the former must not be thought of as comprising a possibility of ignorance, but rather as comprising a positive knowledge of everything's capacity-to-be-other or capacity-not-to-be' (*AF*, 62). The burden of the central chapter of *After Finitude* is to demonstrate, by way of **anhypothetical** demonstration (*AF*, 60–2), that facticity can only be thought as an absolute: one can only remain rationally consistent by thinking those factical constants apparently governing the world as necessarily unnecessary, and therefore necessarily subject to the possibility of alteration without reason (without any higher law or constant governing this alteration). While empirical contingency (or 'precariousness') designates the perishability of determinate entities, a 'possibility of not-being which must eventually be realized', absolute contingency (or contingency proper) 'designates a *pure possibility*; one which may never be realized' (*AF*, 62). What is absolutely contingent is a real possibility that may come to pass for no reason whatsoever, but that also may not come to pass, since nothing necessitates it.

Absolute contingency is therefore unbound from the necessary **finitude** that governs empirical contingency.

Meillassoux's concept of contingency is further sharpened by its distinction from chance and **virtuality**. The paradigm of chance is a throw of the dice abiding by laws of probability: the outcome of the throw is not determined, but its indeterminacy is limited by the physical and mathematical invariance of the context in which it is thrown. Absolute contingency, on the other hand, breaks with any predetermined set of cases or context of physical laws that might frame the preconditions of an event; it is thus 'capable of affecting the very conditions that allow chance events to occur and exist' (*AF*, 101). The most technical formulation of this distinction is offered in 'Potentiality and Virtuality': '*Chance* is every actualisation of a potentiality for which there is no univocal instance of determination on the basis of the initial given conditions. Therefore I will call *contingency* the property of an indexed set of cases (not of a case belonging to an indexed set) of not itself being a case of a set of sets of cases; and *virtuality* the property of every set of cases of emerging within a becoming which is not dominated by any pre-constituted totality of possibles' (*PV*, 72). Contingency is thus a property of virtuality: it is the condition of all possibilities that occur outside a pre-constituted totality of possibles.

In both 'Potentiality and Virtuality' and Chapter 4 of *After Finitude*, Meillassoux elaborates 'a mathematical way of rigorously distinguishing contingency from chance' (*AF*, 104) through the application of Georg **Cantor**'s theory of the transfinite to the sort of probabilitistic reasoning that has been applied to David **Hume**'s problem of induction. It should be noted that, in doing so, Meillassoux does not ground his concept of absolute contingency upon an ontological interpretation of Hume's problem of induction. Rather, his argument concerning the implications of transfinite mathematics is only intended to counter a possible objection to his anhypothetical proof of the principle of **factiality** in Chapter 3. In a word, Meillassoux's mathematically grounded distinction between chance and contingency aims to displace any recourse to the 'improbability' of absolutely contingent events on the basis of past experience or any probabilistic reasoning requiring a closed set of cases.

COPERNICAN REVOLUTION

Fabio Gironi

The expression Copernican Revolution refers to the sixteenth-century definitive rehabilitation of the heliocentric model of the solar system, generally attributed to the influential work of Polish astronomer Nicolaus Copernicus. Meillassoux singles it out as a momentous scientific *and* philosophical conceptual shift, decisively overthrowing anthropocentrism and establishing the epistemic priority of the natural sciences. He moreover employs the term, and its polemical subversion **Ptolemaic counter-revolution**, to construct a critique of the philosophical project of Immanuel **Kant** and the post-Kantian tradition, guilty, in Meillassoux's reading, of a reactive subversion of Copernicus' insight.

In the *Preface* to the second edition of his *Critique of Pure Reason*, Kant proposed, by way of clarification of his own transcendental method, an analogy between it and a number of revolutions in the mathematical and physical sciences, all singular instances of a general type: a *Revolution der Denkart*, a radical shift in our methods or ways of thinking wherein the rational agent was seen to constitute or 'put something in' the object of inquiry. Most famously, Kant refers to Copernicus' conceptual shift in astronomy which, as Kant's transcendental idealism does, postulates that a certain kind of *activity* is to be attributed to the cognising subject, who therefore contributes to the phenomenon under examination. As Copernicus, against common-sense intuitions, attempted to explain the *apparent* movement of the celestial bodies by having the Earth-bound observer move across outer space, so Kant, against contemporary epistemological theories, conceived *appearances* to depend upon an *a priori* discursive movement across our internal conceptual space.

Meillassoux, like numerous commentators before him, criticises Kant's analogy as misconceived. Unlike Copernicus, who demoted the Earth-bound observer from a privileged to a subordinated position, Kant's philosophical turn amounts to an *anthropocentric* shift, where the peculiar modes of cognition of rational agents are given the priority as *unique* and uncircumventable modes of access to independent reality. Preserving the astronomical analogy, Meillassoux argues that Kant's revolution, then, is best described as a Ptolemaic counter-revolution, considering how the subject is immovably reinscribed at the centre of the epistemological process. Meillassoux accuses Kant of a reactionary betrayal of the Copernican conceptual turn, subordinating the factual discoveries of science (which only a *naive* realist would take literally) and their '*speculative import*' (*AF*, 120) to the subject-centred conditions of possibility of any knowledge whatsoever, and thus laying the foundations of that correlationist 'transparent cage' which for centuries to follow curtailed the ambition to attain knowledge of objectively existent non-human reality.

For Meillassoux the Copernican turn, correctly interpreted as untamed by transcendentalist caveats, indexes the irrevocable unmooring of humans from cosmic centrality, both spatial and conceptual. The modern science spawned by the encounter between the Copernican demotion of the human and the Galilean mathematisation of nature is uniquely able to deliver a 'non correlational mode of knowing' (*AF*, 119) of the glacial reality indifferent and anterior to human thought, a fiercely non-correlated '*great outdoors*' (*AF*, 7), stripped of subject-dependent qualities and reduced to its mathematically describable primary properties.

CORRELATIONISM

Levi R. Bryant

Meillassoux's concept of correlation is arguably among his most significant and controversial contributions to philosophy. In *After Finitude*, he defines correlation as 'the idea according to which we only ever have access to the correlation between thinking and being, and never to either term considered apart from the other' (*AF*, 5). Although Meillassoux does not himself specify this, correlationism presumably comes in a variety of different forms, and is therefore not restricted to theories focused on the relation between mind and being. Thus the relation between transcendental ego or lived body and the world in phenomenology would be one variant of correlationism, while the relation between language and being in Wittgenstein, Derrida and Lacan, or between power and knowledge in Foucault, would be other variants. In each case we encounter the claim that being cannot be thought apart from a subject, language or power.

Meillassoux argues that correlationism has been the central notion of philosophy ever since Immanuel **Kant**, whose core epistemological hypothesis is twofold. On the one hand, Kant argues that objects conform to mind, rather than mind to objects. Kant claimed that in traditional forms of epistemology the mind was conceived as a mirror that reflects being as it is in-itself, independent of us. He argues that mind does not merely reflect reality, but rather *actively structures* reality. Consequently, on the other hand, he argues that we can never know reality as it is in itself apart from us, but only as it appears to us. If the mind takes an active role in structuring reality (for us) we are unable to know what it is in-itself because we cannot determine what, in appearances, is a product of our own minds and what is a feature of things as they are in themselves. This is because we cannot adopt a third-person perspective that would allow us to compare things as they appear to us and things as they are in themselves. Consequently, knowledge is restricted to appearances and we must remain agnostic as to what being might be like in itself.

The claim that modern philosophy is inspired by Kantian correlationism is not the claim that most modern philosophers embrace the specific details of Kant's philosophy. Clearly Wittgenstein, for example, does not adopt Kant's account of transcendental categories, pure *a priori* intuitions, or the transcendental ego when he speaks of language games. Rather, the correlationist gesture consists solely in the claim that we can only think the relation between being and thinking and that therefore our knowledge is restricted to appearances.

Correlationism is not merely the thesis that we must relate to something in order to know it. Obviously we had to discover dinosaur fossils to know anything of the past existence of dinosaurs. For Meillassoux, it is not relation *per se* that makes a position correlationist, but rather the assertion of a very specific, unsurpassable relation. As Meillassoux remarks:

Correlationism rests on an argument as simple as it is powerful, and which can be formulated in the following way: No X without givenness of X, and no theory about X without a positing of X. If you speak about something, you speak about something that is given to you, and posited by you. Consequently, the sentence: 'X is', means: 'X is the correlate of thinking' in a Cartesian sense. That is: X is the correlate of an affection, or a perception, or a conception, or of any subjective act. To be is to be a correlate, a term of a correlation . . . *That is why it is impossible to conceive an absolute X, i.e., an X which would be essentially separate from a subject. We can't know what the reality of the object in itself is because we can't distinguish between properties which are supposed to belong to the object and properties belonging to the subjective access to the object.* (*SR*, 409, my emphasis)

Correlationism is thus not the thesis that we must relate to something in order to know it, but rather that what we know of anything is true only *for us*. In this regard, correlationism is a form of scepticism for it asserts that whether or not things-in-themselves are this way is something we can never know because we can only ever know things as they appear to us, not as they are in themselves. For example, for the correlationist there is no answer to the question of whether carbon atoms exist apart from us and whether they decay at such and such a rate because we only ever know appearances. This is Meillassoux's support for scientific realism. For the correlationist we are never able to get out of the correlation between thought and being to determine whether or not carbon itself has these properties or whether it is thought that bestows these properties, which is sometimes the view of scientific functionalism. Meillassoux calls this unsurpassable relation the correlationist circle.

One of Meillassoux's central projects lies in finding a way to break out of the correlationist circle. He seeks to determine whether it is possible to think the absolute or being as it is in-itself apart from mind, and what characteristics the absolute might possess. Meillassoux's discussion of **ancestrality** or statements about time prior to the existence of human beings is not an argument against correlationism *per se*, but is designed to present readily familiar and widely accepted claims about cosmic time prior to the existence of life and humans that ought not be permissible within a correlationist framework. If correlationism is true, what entitles us to make claims about the nature of the universe billions of years prior to the emergence of life or mind? Meillassoux presents his account of how we might break out of the correlationist circle in his discussion of the principle of **factiality** in *After Finitude*.

CORRELATIONISM: WEAK AND STRONG

Michael Austin

Correlationism is the often unstated view that being only exists for subjects, that there is a direct correlate between subjective mind and the world of objects, or perhaps more accurately, that thinking beings have no access to the world except by way of cognition, so that any claim to think or discuss things-in-themselves is taken as either imaginative whimsy or pure absurdity. Like tea though, correlationism can be taken either weak or strong. While correlationism broadly understood maintains that we have access only to the correlate of Thought and Being, it is the possibility of anything existing outside of the correlate that ultimately allows for the distinction between weak and strong correlationism. Meillassoux suggests several historical figures as a way of understanding the distinction between these positions, with the former represented by Immanuel **Kant** and Edmund Husserl and the latter by Ludwig Wittgenstein and Martin **Heidegger**.

Weak correlationism accepts the move of Critical philosophy, claiming that we must take account of how and what we know prior to any talk of **metaphysics**. Where various weak correlationists differ is in what this 'taking account of' means. For instance, Husserl will maintain that in order to understand the world, we must grasp it as purely through experience as possible, through phenomenological description. Through eidetic reduction, we can capture things in their most abstract, as features or qualities shared across types, grasping the *eidos* of things. Beyond this experience, we can know nothing, but like Kant, Husserlian phenomenology will not presume to be equipped to *dismiss* the possibility of things-in-themselves. Kant's agnostic position concerning the in-itself is more than simply stating that things in the world could be other than what they are (e.g. this or that thing need not exist *necessarily*), but tells us that it is impossible to claim that things must necessarily appear as they do. In other words, by saying that while we cannot *know* things other than through rational cognition, that is, that it is impossible to know any object except through the categories of rationality, it remains possible to think or imagine that things *could in-themselves be otherwise*, that things may not be wholly reducible to their mere appearances. What we have access to, says the weak correlationist, is merely the correlate of thought and being, that small space where the two converge, while what lies outside of this convergence remains thinkable but ultimately unknowable. Things-in-themselves remain forever unknowable to rationality. The noumenal remains very much an open question for the weak correlationist, as we can neither affirm nor dismiss anything about things outside of their givenness to human experience.

The strong correlationist argument picks up from its weak cousin, namely with the question, 'why claim there are things-in-themselves at all?' Simply stating that the idea of things-in-themselves is thinkable and therefore non-contradictory is not enough, as I can think all sorts of non-contradictory things which most likely do not exist, from unicorns to self-transforming machine elves. In fact, Terrence McKenna's tryptamine-induced elf hallucinations make just as much sense as the mysterious things-in-themselves, argues the strong correlationist, neither of which exist necessarily by virtue of not being self-contradicting. The strong correlationist will insist that we must therefore abolish the very idea of things-in-themselves as incoherent speculation. We know of no reality, no being, outside of our own thought and to propose that there even exists such a thing is entirely groundless and presumes knowledge attained outside of thought to begin with, which is impossible. There is no agnosticism for the strong correlationist, as there is an absolute confluence between thought and being, with neither existing without the other and the possibility of there being one without the other entirely absurd. What can be said to exist is what we can know (being-for-thought), with the limit to our thinking being identical to the limits of existents. There is no objective knowledge, as all knowledge is knowledge of the givenness of things, that is to say, we know things only in so far as they are *for-us*. For the strong correlationist, there can be no being outside of thought, as the very possibility of such a thing existing is not only incoherent, but illogical. That is to say, while the weak correlationist accepts the possibility of a world outside of the correlation of Being and Thought, the strong correlationist *absolutises the correlation itself* since our knowledge extends only to the bare givenness of the world. This means that it is impossible to think the fact that there is a world at all, as our rational discourse extends only as far as the givenness of such a world, that is, our relation to it.

CREATION *EX NIHILO*

Peter Gratton

This is a traditional theological/philosophical term meaning creation from out of nothing. It is most commonly associated with monotheistic religions wherein a creator **God** brings forth the universe from nothing. The concept acts as a bulwark against the problem of the infinite regress of causes. Meillassoux dissociates the term *ex nihilo* from its theological context and argues that if one drops one's belief in causal necessity then the idea of events emerging from nothing becomes perfectly conceivable. His case for **hyper-chaos**, and the novelty it can produce, means he is committed to a the idea of a universe that is not constrained by a predetermined set of possibilities and can produce events from out of nowhere or nothing, that is *ex nihilo*.

DEATH

Daniel Sacilotto

For Meillassoux, death or the mortality of the living is first a corollary of his theses concerning the **necessity of contingency** of being in general. In this sense, death designates the possibility of thought's non-being or, put differently, the impossibility of its necessity, since the world goes on without it. Thought in these terms, the possibility of death corresponds with the materialist attempt to think that which does not depend on thought for its being. Death is thus named 'the pure other of ourselves' (*IRR*, 19). The possible absence of thought would then be an ontological consequence of the argument for **factiality**. For if every entity is necessarily contingent, it follows that the same applies for thought, or the agents of thought.

However, thought's contingent being seems to operate also as a premise that supports the argument for factiality, rather than as a consequence of the latter. It informs a pivotal point in the dialectic proposed by

Meillassoux between the idealist, who absolutises the correlation, and the speculative materialist, who absolutises the facticity defended by the correlationist. **Idealism** resists the claim that we couldn't even think thought's non-being, and thus denies that death is impossible. This renders thought itself absolutely necessary. Meanwhile, the correlationist insists on the epistemic restraint that is the facticity of thought. According to the correlationist, we simply do not know whether thought is necessary or not. And it is this possibility that **speculative materialism** argues cannot be taken to be merely for-us, lest we grant the idealist the impossibility of thinking our non-being (*AF*, 57).

Nevertheless, we should note that all Meillassoux has shown is that in order for us not to be idealists we must be able to determine that the possibility of thought's non-being is **absolute** rather than relative or for-us. But his argument does not give reasons to decide between idealism and speculative materialism, or explain why we ought to reject the absoluteness of the correlation, beyond the declared avowal of materialism. In order to go beyond correlationist ignorance, something else is needed. To do this, Meillassoux lends credence to the correlationist's insistence on facticity by now appealing to our knowledge of our own contingency and mortality. We know ourselves to be mortal, he claims. In response to the alleged epistemic modesty of the correlationist, Meillassoux is then able to claim: 'The very idea of the difference between the in–itself and the for-us would never have arisen within you, had you not experienced what is perhaps human thought's most remarkable power – its capacity to access the possibility of its own non-being, and thus to know itself to be mortal' (*AF*, 59).

Meillassoux provides no further support for how this knowledge is gauged, but it clearly conditions the purported derivation of the necessary contingency of all beings, and not only our own. Thus although the contingency of our thought would apparently follow from the principle of factiality, the latter actually turns out to presuppose knowledge of the former.

Looking past this difficulty, it is important to realise that just because it is necessary that we can die, given the contingency of all beings, it doesn't follow that we will or must die. Once the principle of factiality is granted, the prospect of death nevertheless leaves open the possibility of its non-occurrence. This is crucial for Meillassoux, in so far as the advent of the **fourth World of justice**, which is the object of hope in his ethical programme, requires the possibility of the dead not only being resurrected, but joining the living in eternal life and equality. The possibility of death, tethered to the contingency of being and thought, should thus not be taken to entail its inevitability, or its incompatibility with the prospect of eternal life.

Finally, in a more metaphorical register, mathematics is described as complicit with death by virtue of the radical indifference of its formal ideography to the meanings of natural language, and to the proximate ends of human life. In so far as it allows the thought of that which exceeds the horizon of our experience and existence, mathematics grants access to 'the Kingdom of death', which is to say, it can think the **Cartesian in-itself** or the absolute, that which is not a mere correlate of thought (*IRR*, 19).

DELEUZE, GILLES

Jeffrey Bell

Gilles Deleuze (1925–1995) is probably Meillassoux's most important interlocutor, the philosopher who is both closest to his own concerns and yet the one with whom he most strongly disagrees. On the one hand, both Deleuze and Meillassoux place great emphasis on **contingency**, and each draws from the work of David **Hume** in important respects in order to make the case for contingency. The central thesis and subtitle of Meillassoux's *After Finitude* is that the only thing that is necessary is the **necessity of contingency**. Deleuze and Guattari, similarly, will call out in *What is Philosophy?* against what they label the cult of necessity and will reaffirm Nietzsche's own advocacy of the roll of the dice, the chance and contingency inseparable from all things. In *What is Philosophy?* they will also give philosophy the task of creating concepts, a task that entails affirming and embracing a fundamental chaos. Similarly for Meillassoux, chaos, or what he calls **hyper-chaos**, is fundamental, and the nature and role of this chaos is one of the principal themes of his own philosophy.

Despite these similarities, there are three points that Meillassoux singles out where the differences could not be starker. First, whereas Meillassoux's project sets out to critique what he calls **correlationism**, Deleuze, by Meillassoux's lights, actually affirms a strong version of correlationism in that the correlation itself becomes the **absolute** in Deleuze's system. With the traditional understanding of correlationism, the real is always and only real as correlated to a subject that has access to it. One can entertain the thought of a world without correlation, but then again this would be a thought and we are once again within the circle of correlationism (hence the problem of **ancestrality**). Deleuze, Meillassoux argues, does not even entertain the possibility of a world without correlation, but absolutises it. He offers a 'vitalist hypostatization' (*AF*, 64), to use Meillassoux's term, of this correlation by arguing that all reality is simply a correlate of a life.

The second point of difference concerns the philosophy of becoming. According to Meillassoux, one only truly overcomes the 'cult of necessity' and truly affirms contingency when one abandons any attempt to establish a philosophy of becoming. The reason for this, Meillassoux claims, is that absolutising becoming involves affirming contradictory entities – an entity that simultaneously is and is not – and yet it is just such entities that are not contingent for they always include all their possibilities; they cannot not be since they already presuppose their not being! Deleuze's philosophy of becoming is thus incompatible, Meillassoux concludes, with the effort to overcome the cult of necessity.

The third and final point of disagreement concerns the **principle of sufficient reason** (PSR). Simply put, while Meillassoux rejects the PSR, Deleuze endorses it. Meillassoux's reason for rejecting the PSR is quite straightforward: it is a consequence of the necessity of contingency in that there is no reason for anything being or not being the way it is. Deleuze, by contrast, is inevitably drawn, Meillassoux believes, to a version of the PSR by virtue of his own version of strong correlationism. It is thus only by overcoming correlationism and the related philosophy of becoming, therefore, that one can truly support the two points upon which Meillassoux and Deleuze agree.

Deleuze and Meillassoux are thus so close yet so far away philosophically, and thus it is no surprise that Meillassoux devotes a fair amount of energy to contrasting his own position with Deleuze's, beginning with the strong correlationist label he attaches to Deleuze's project. In his longest treatment of Deleuze, the essay 'Subtraction and Contraction', Meillassoux offers an illuminating and creative take on Deleuze's thought. Meillassoux's treatment of Deleuze here is very fair and nuanced, but, as with his teacher Alain **Badiou**, there is a tendency to read Deleuze as a dualist, a virtual-actual dualist in this case. These dualist readings are problematic. For one, the virtual is not, Deleuze makes clear, a separable reality determinately distinct from the actual. If this were the correct reading, then the strong correlation between Life – taken here as the virtual writ large – and the determinate actualities would indeed be how to read Deleuze. For the sake of brevity, it should be noted that Gilbert Simondon's work was profoundly influential upon Deleuze's, and an important part of Simondon's philosophical work was to understand the process of individuation from metastable states. A metastable state is not a determinate state but is rather the dynamic condition for the possibility of differentiating between determinately distinct states. There is a tendency in Meillassoux's reading of Deleuze, as there was in Badiou's, to assume a world of two fundamentally distinct and already individuated states – the virtual and the actual – when in fact it was precisely the effort to understand the emergence of individuated states that best characterises Deleuze's entire project. Perhaps the conclusion to draw is that Meillassoux has in Deleuze a worthy interlocutor.

DERIVATION

This is Meillassoux's technical term for the procedure of uncovering the conditions of **hyper-chaos**. A condition revealed through derivation is known as a **figure**.

DESCARTES, RENÉ

Devin Zane Shaw

Descartes (1596–1650) is often considered, especially in the Continental tradition, as the founding figure of modern philosophy for rejecting the authority and Aristotelianism of the Scholastics and grounding philosophy on the *cogito* or thinking subject. The legacy of his work remains a point of contention in contemporary French philosophy. On the one hand, for the post-Heideggerian tradition, including Jacques Derrida and Jean-Luc Nancy, Descartes' distinction between thinking substance (*cogito*) and extended substance makes possible the technicity that reduces nature or being to the calculable world of standing reserve. On the other hand, a number of philosophers influenced by existentialism or Jacques Lacan, such as Alain **Badiou**, Jacques Rancière and Slavoj Žižek, lay claim to the Cartesian subject to reformulate a radical concept of political subjectivity and praxis.

Unlike for his predecessors, for Meillassoux the *cogito* is of secondary conceptual importance; in *After Finitude* he focuses on Descartes' distinction between the primary qualities of the in-itself that can be formulated in mathematical terms and secondary qualities that are subjective and sensible (see **Cartesian in-itself**). By desubjectivising nature through **mathematics**, Meillassoux argues, Descartes' thought provides a model for speculation that escapes from the correlationist circle. To set out his speculative position, Meillassoux examines Descartes' metaphysical argument to justify 'the absolute existence of extended substance', that is, extended substance in-itself and not 'for-us'. This argument has four steps: (1) An absolutely perfect being must necessarily exist; (2) Deception is an imperfection; (3) I have an idea of bodies extended in space; therefore (4) bodies must exist independently of the *cogito*, since God is not a deceiver given that deception is an imperfection.

Meillassoux argues that Descartes' metaphysical claims to the speculative problem of the absolute are ultimately untenable. **Metaphysics**, on his account, is that type of thinking that holds that the **absolute** is a necessary entity or being, such as God, that can be explained through the **principle of sufficient reason**. While all metaphysics is speculative, that is, concerning the absolute, Meillassoux will stake out a position that he claims is speculative without being metaphysical or correlative, since first, it does without attempting to demonstrate a necessary being, and second, it does without relying on the principle of sufficient reason, as the principle of sufficient reason ultimately fails, since it requires an infinite regress of reasons for a being's necessity. Rejecting speculative thought, as **correlationism** does, leads to the undesirable consequence of the return of the religious; it 'legitimates all those discourses [such as **fideism** and mysticism] that claim to access an absolute, the only proviso being that nothing in these discourses resembles a rational justification of their validity' (*AF*, 44–5). These discourses can talk about the absolute but there is no possibility of rationally adjudicating between them – thus they prioritise belief over reason as a means for accessing the absolute.

Though he argues that Descartes' metaphysical claims about the absolute in-itself seem to be 'irrevocably obsolete', Meillassoux claims that the speculative solution to demonstrating the intelligibility of the absolute follows the same procedure. Descartes' argument establishes the existence of a primary absolute from which it derives a 'derivative absolute', the absoluteness of mathematics (*AF*, 30). For Descartes, the primary absolute is the perfect being that guarantees the existence of extended bodies that can be described in themselves in mathematical terms. To avoid falling into dogmatic metaphysics, Meillassoux proposes, 'we must uncover an absolute necessity that does not reinstate any form of absolutely necessary entity' (*AF*, 34). He argues that speculative philosophy must demonstrate the necessary ontological structure of the absolute rather than a necessary entity. Claiming, as he does, that the speculative thesis holds the 'absolute necessity of the contingency of everything' allows him to bypass the use of the principle of sufficient reason, for the necessity of contingency means that anything could become otherwise without reason. (However, that the absolute has the ontological structure of contingency or pure possibility is necessary). Rather than Descartes' necessary God, Meillassoux holds that absolute contingency is the 'primary absolute' from which it is possible to derive the absolutisation of mathematics. To complete the Cartesian structure of his speculative argument, Meillassoux continues by attempting to demonstrate that the 'derivative absolute' is the absolutisation of the Zermelo-Fraenkel axiomatisation of **set theory**, which elaborates a specific condition of contingency, namely that absolute contingency is transfinite and non-totalisable.

Despite constructing his speculative argument by analogy to Descartes, there is a significant difference concerning how they absolutise mathematics. The difference arises due to the dual meaning of the term 'derive'. In the case of Descartes, to claim that the absolutisation of mathematics is derived from God, the 'primary absolute', means that the existence of extended substance is dependent upon God. For Meillassoux, 'derivation' is a 'demonstration which establishes that a statement is a condition of facticity' (*AF*, 127). Thus his absolutisation of Zermelo-Fraenkel set theory elaborates conditions of the ontological structure of absolute contingency as pure possibility. Nevertheless, statements about the ontological structure of the absolute, such as 'only those theories that ratify the non-All harbour an ontological scope' (*AF*, 127), are a different type of claim from ontical statements, such as that 'the origin of the universe was 13.5 billion years ago' (*AF*, 9). It remains to be seen how the ontical absolutisation of mathematics relates to the ontological absolutisation.

DIA-CHRONICITY

Paul J. Ennis

Toward the final stages of *After Finitude* Meillassoux discusses the idea of dia-chronicity as the 'temporal discrepancy' that exists between thinking and being in terms of both anteriority and ulteriority (*AF*, 112, italics removed). The dia-chronic statement is one that refers to non-correlated events whether we mean by this ancestral statements, as in the opening chapter of *After Finitude*, or futural events such as the extinction of our species.

DIALETHEISM

Raphaël Millière

Aristotle, in Book Γ of the *Metaphysics*, famously states that 'the same attribute cannot at the same time belong and not belong to the same subject in the same respect', and he adds that this idea, known as the **principle of non-contradiction** (PNC), 'is the most certain of all principles' (1005b19–24). In *After Finitude*, Meillassoux draws the outline of an argument to prove this principle. He writes that such a proof would 'point out that paraconsistent logics were not developed in order to account for actual contradictory facts, but only in order to prevent computers, such as expert medical systems, from deducing anything whatsoever from contradictory data ... because of the principle of *ex falso quodlibet*' (*AF*, 78–9). Therefore, he says, paraconsistent logic only deals with *contradictory statements*, and not *worldly contradictions*; thus it doesn't threaten the idea that there are no true *ontological contradictions*, even if we can, for pragmatic purposes, speak of true *logical contradictions*.

Meillassoux seems fully aware that paraconsistent logic, in which some (but not all) contradictions are true, is nothing but a *formal system*: it has no bearing, in itself, on reality, and neither can it be used as a metaphysical thesis to undermine the ontological PNC as found in Aristotle. However, this shouldn't come as a surprise: arguably, formal systems can never be used to 'solve' metaphysical issues, and this has nothing to do with the alleged utilitarian aim of paraconsistent logic as a way to deal with inconsistencies in (medical) databases.

Nonetheless, this doesn't mean that a genuine metaphysical thesis denying the ontological PNC is not defensible; in fact, it has been minutely advocated as 'dialetheism', most notably by Richard Routley and Graham Priest, who coined the term. Dialetheism argues that there are some sentences such that both they and their negations are true – in other words, there are genuinely true contradictions. Paraconsistent logic *does* support dialetheism by showing that its main thesis is logically intelligible, but the latter is nevertheless independent of the former: indeed, while paraconsistent logicians provide ways of thinking that some contradictions are true in some *possible* worlds, most of them do not really believe that *our* world is one of them. Thus dialetheism is a much more radical view, but Priest has shown at length that it may actually be used to solve classical paradoxes about time, change and motion (Priest 1987). Moreover, one cannot rule out dialetheism as easily as Meillassoux thinks; David Lewis, for instance, acknowledged that his opposition to dialetheism was, in the end, entirely dogmatic: 'I am affirming the very thesis that Routley and Priest have called into question and – contrary to the rules of debate – I decline to defend it. Further, I concede that it is indefensible against their challenge' (Lewis 1998: 101).

Interestingly, Priest (1987) also tackled in detail some issues related to the 'limits of thought', which are arguably also Meillassoux's main subject in *After Finitude*; he has given thought-provoking applications of dialetheism to such issues, including Berkeley's so-called 'master argument' (*one cannot conceive of an unconceived object*), one of the very first attempts to show how naive realism falls into a 'pragmatic contradiction' as Meillassoux puts it. According to Priest, this 'pragmatic contradiction' is a true one, typical of the limits of thought; therefore, a correlationist philosopher is not entitled to conclude that realism is false, but only that reality (including the very fact of the correlation) is contradictory.

DIVINE INEXISTENCE

Leon Niemoczynski

The Divine Inexistence: An Essay on the Virtual God is the title of Meillassoux's 1997 doctoral thesis. As he remarked in *After Finitude*, 'the divine inexistence' is to be the subject and title of a much larger, forthcoming work, as *After Finitude* covered only the first 150 pages of the whole of 'The Divine Inexistence'. In addition to the dissertation, there are two noteworthy pieces that Meillassoux has published that cover important topics found in *The Divine Inexistence*. Those pieces are the essay 'Spectral Dilemma' and a lengthy book chapter called 'The Immanence of the World Beyond'.

In all of these texts Meillassoux argues against **atheism/theism** (for each accept and work within the terms of theistic thought), questions 'a/theism' or any '**God** after God' a/theological perspective and its anti-realist **fideism**, and opposes orthodox onto-theological religion and its corresponding longing for satisfying transcendence (defined as 'exteriority in general') (*DI*, 8). A more admissible alternative, claims Meillassoux, is a third option that he calls in different places 'divinology', simply 'philosophy', or '**irreligion**'. For Meillassoux, knowledge of God's existence is not constrained by the limits of human reason and thus relegated to be an object of faith found within some unknowable noumenal realm (see Immanuel **Kant**). Rather, 'divinology' does not reject God at all. It places an 'immanent form of hope' in God's current inexistence and the potential for this 'virtual God' to appear in the future. Meillassoux's claim is that philosophy can believe in God precisely because God does not currently exist.

In *After Finitude*, Meillassoux concludes that only contingency is itself necessary. This is important regarding the divine inexistence because Meillassoux does not accept God in terms of **onto-theology**, as a necessary being or *causa sui*. Because metaphysics deals with necessity and necessity has been rejected through the principle of **factiality**, we cannot admit God (a necessary being) into metaphysical theology *de facto*. After the 'death of God' we have no grounds to admit God back into our ontology if necessity demands that re-appearance by way of faith. Later, Meillassoux equals his rejection of necessity with the insufficiency of reason. If everything has the property of being absolutely contingent, it does not have to be that way in virtue of its creation, we cannot provide a sufficient reason as to why something should be some way rather than another way. Using a principle of 'insufficient reason', then, Meillassoux states that there is no reason why anything, including God's existence, is necessary, which means there can be no **ontological proofs** for the existence of God.

Another important aspect of divine inexistence is Meillassoux's argument that while he cannot accept the principle of sufficient reason, he nevertheless does accept the law of non-contradiction. If an entity were somehow both itself and not itself, that is, self-contradictory, it could not change, since of course, since it's already all that it could be. Thus, it would a necessary being, since it does not change, yet would defy the necessity of contingency Meillassoux already derives in the first sections of *After Finitude*. This means that anything can appear, without reason, save for the contradictory.

When we apply this reasoning to God, we find that God as a necessary being cannot exist. But given the nature of **hyper-chaos** and the fact that anything can appear without reason, save for contradictory beings, Meillassoux is able to state, 'if there is no law for becoming, then becoming is capable even of God' (*DI*, 6). Thus, God 'inexists', or, does not exist now but, in accordance with the principle of factiality, may exist at some point in the future. God is thus **virtual**, though neither possible nor necessary. Rather, God's possible existence is necessary. Given his critique of the principle of sufficient reason, which states every effect must have a cause, Meillassoux states that there can be **creation *ex nihilo***, that is, effects that arise from no previous cause. He thinks this has occurred in the three worlds of matter, life and thought. But it is the **fourth World of justice** that relates to divine inexistence, since for Meillassoux this justice requires a divine being capable of the **resurrection** of the dead. Therefore, this divine being's appearance, among others, is ethically most important.

DOGMATISM

Robert S. Gall

Meillassoux's references to dogmatism need to be understood within the context of Immanuel **Kant**'s definitions and analyses of dogmatism in his Critical philosophy. In *The Critique of Pure Reason*, Kant defines dogmatism as:

the presumption that it is possible to make progress with pure knowledge, according to principles, from concepts alone . . . and that it is possible to do this without
having first investigated in what way and by what right reason has come into possession of these concepts. Dogmatism is thus the dogmatic procedure of reason,
without previous criticism of its own powers. (32 [B xxv], his emphasis)

With Kant, then, dogmatism became synonymous with **rationalism** and
its attempt to give an absolute description of the world – uncontaminated
by experience – based upon reason alone. What is 'dogmatic' about such
an attempt is 1) the unquestioned belief that reason is capable of acquiring
and extending knowledge without appeal to experience, and 2) the unquestioned belief in the concepts used by reason to extend our knowledge. Kant
rejected both dogmatism (rationalism) and scepticism (**empiricism**) in
formulating his Critical philosophy that has served, by Meillassoux's own
account, as a blueprint for philosophy since the nineteenth century.

Since Meillassoux aims to revive the Cartesian thesis that we can know
the properties of an object as they are in the object itself in mathematical
terms (see **Cartesian in-itself**), he recognises that he is obliged to deal
with the charge that he is proposing a return to a pre-critical, dogmatic
metaphysics. He deals with this by trying to redefine our understanding of
dogmatism and its relation to metaphysics and the absolute. Generalising
from the example of René **Descartes**, Meillassoux argues that what
defines dogmatism is the claim that there is some necessary being. In
Descartes' philosophy, an absolute, necessary being (**God**) is deployed
to found a world absolutely outside us, based upon the **ontological
argument** and tied to the **principle of sufficient reason**. However, as
Kant has shown us, all claims of a necessary being fail because nothing
can be shown to be necessary by definition. No thing exists just because
of what it is. Rejecting dogmatic **metaphysics** then 'means to reject all
real necessity, and *a fortiori* to reject the principle of sufficient reason, as
well as the ontological argument' (*AF*, 33). That nonetheless leaves open
the possibility of knowing a different kind of absolute (a non-necessary
absolute) in mathematical/geometrical terms. It is this possibility that
Meillassoux pursues in *After Finitude*. In this way, Meillassoux attempts
to remain an heir of Kant without giving up the notion of an absolute that
is known through (mathematical) reason. However, one of Kant's conditions for dogmatic philosophy is that there is no criticism of the powers
of reason within that philosophy. Meillassoux does not appear to question
the powers of reason; he does not question the ability of logic to ground
itself and seems to take it as given that reason is its own justification. To
his Kantian or post-Kantian critics, then, Meillassoux's philosophy would
still qualify as dogmatism.

E

EMPIRICISM

Adrian Johnston

Before addressing Meillassoux's positioning *vis-à-vis* empiricism proper as an epistemological orientation in philosophy, I should say a few words about his relations with things empirical, specifically as per the empirical sciences resting upon *a posteriori* observation and experimentation. To begin with, Meillassoux, following French philosopher and historian of science Alexandre Koyré, singles out Galileo Galilei of 1623's 'The Assayer' as the one-and-only father of modern science. On this contentious account of the birth of scientific modernity, the Galilean distinction between primary and secondary properties of observed objects – the former are mathematisable/formalisable and, therefore, supposedly indicative of the mind-independent real features of natural beings in and of themselves, whereas the latter are non-quantifiable qualities perhaps limited to being phenomena peculiar to the observing mind – is the sole locus of origin for the modern sciences. In other words, Koyré and Meillassoux, like a number of other French thinkers from the mid-twentieth century to the present, such as Louis Althusser, Jacques Lacan and Alain **Badiou**, among others, believe that the essence of scientificity strictly speaking consists in mathematical or mathematical-style formalisation.

The reaffirmation of this Koyréan thesis apropos scientific modernity already signals Meillassoux's favouring of a French neo-rationalist epistemology, with Koyré's narrative completely sidelining and ignoring the 1620 *New Organon* of British empiricist Francis Bacon. (I will return to the topic of British empiricism shortly.) Bacon's canonical text lays the foundations of the empirical and experimental approach that has come to be known as 'the scientific method'. Against Koyré, Meillassoux, et al., Bacon, not to mention Galileo as an observer and experimenter, instead of as a pure mathematician, cannot defensibly be denied the title of (co-) founding figure of modern science. In fact, it would not be unfair to say that Meillassoux's version of the distinction between **primary and secondary qualities** – he opens *After Finitude* with a declaration that he intends to revivify and redeploy this early-modern distinction long ago having fallen out of general philosophical fashion – is Cartesian, rather than Galilean, or, for that matter, Lockean, with John Locke, another British empiricist, also adopting this distinction for his own purposes.

Meillassoux seeks to elaborate a rationalist ontology that is both **realist** and materialist, one in which knowing subjects truly can know and not simply think material objects *qua* asubjective things-in-themselves. As per the subtitle of Jean-René Vernes' *Critique of Aleatory Reason* (1982), a book influencing the author of *After Finitude*, Meillassoux too plays 'Descartes *contra* Kant' (more precisely, *contra* the critical, empiricism-inspired dimensions of Immanuel **Kant**'s transcendental idealism). Although Meillassoux's ontology and philosophical *modus operandi* owes much more to rationalism than empiricism, he partly motivates his system-building endeavours through recourse to the latter as well as to the empirical sciences of nature.

Meillassoux's **arche-fossil** argumentative device is extrapolated from those natural sciences studying entities and events presumably predating the genesis of sentient and/or sapient life. On a realist interpretation, these experimental, *a posteriori* sciences refer to beings enjoying actual existence utterly independent of whatever statuses they might possibly have as objects-*qua*-correlates of any consciousness whatsoever. Through recourse to such disciplines as cosmology and geology – Meillassoux emphasises that most practising scientists are spontaneous robust realists about their targets of investigation – he aims to manoeuvre Kantian and post-Kantian anti-realists (that is, idealist and phenomenological 'correlationists') into confronting a stark binary alternative between either (1) absolutising as eternal and ubiquitous the subjectivity of the correlationist version of the subject-object co-relationship or (2) conceding the sentient and sapient subject and its co-relationships to be non-absolute, namely, to have arisen contingently in space and time as factical geneses surfacing out of asubjective real being *an sich*. Just as the V.I. Lenin of *Materialism and Empirio-Criticism* (1908) contends, following Friedrich Engels, that all alternatives to militant realist materialism boil down in the end to the solipsistic subjective idealism of George Berkeley, Meillassoux wields his arche-fossil so as to force various types of correlationists to choose between an anti-realism resting on an absolutised subject (an understandably unpalatable option too implausibly extreme and anti-scientific for most of them) or a realism at least implicit in acknowledging the factical spatio-temporal emergence of thereby de-absolutised subjects.

Apropos empiricism per se as a philosophical orientation, Meillassoux leans heavily on David **Hume** in particular. More precisely, he proposes an ontological construal of Hume's problem of induction, a gesture akin to G.W.F. **Hegel**'s speculative move of ontologising Kant's critical-epistemological 'Transcendental Dialectic'. Although Locke and Hume, unlike other British empiricists such as Bacon, Hobbes and Berkeley, exhibit a reluctance to indulge in ontology foreshadowing Kant's same wariness, Meillassoux insists upon reading Hume's problem as more than merely epistemological. In fact, Meillassoux goes so far as to claim – this assertion is absolutely central to Meillassouxian ontology – that the problem of induction is already its own solution. In other words, the impossibility of any purported law of nature being deemed via induction to be a necessary connection *qua* forever-unbreakable rule is a matter of ontological insight rather than epistemological ignorance. The combination of a realist rendition of the inductive-yet-mathematised empirical sciences of nature with a related rendition of Hume's problem of induction leads Meillassoux to advance an ontology (un-)grounded on the core idea of **hyper-chaos**, namely, the concept of the omnipotent power of a lawless contingency unconstrained by sufficient reasons as the sole necessity operative across the temporal expanse of existence. As hyper-chaotic, the being and beings of Meillassoux's ontology can, at any time, possibly undergo an unimaginably large number of radical transformations deviating from past and present observed patterns of behaviour. With his system under-construction being based on the foundation of a hyper-chaotic ontology, Meillassoux faces the daunting challenge of defusing the many profound difficulties this Hume-indebted vision generates.

ESCHAOLOGY

Meillassoux's name for an **eschatology** based on **hyper-chaos** as introduced in *IWB*, 463.

ESCHATOLOGY

Christina Smerick

The word eschatology means, in its literal sense, the study of what is last as a final resolution or completion. Eschatology therefore focuses upon the final condition of a being, be that a human being (personal eschatology) or the entire world (cosmic eschatology). Theistic religions tend to understand time as linear and therefore hold to an expectation of a conclusion to time, an end in which everything is destroyed and something new is brought into being, or an end in which everything is redeemed and made new. Theistic religions, particularly Islam and Christianity, sometimes refer to this as the Day of Judgement.

Eschatology has not only a temporal sense as indicated above but a teleological sense as well. The 'end' is not merely the completion or ending of a linear temporality but is also a fulfilment of a particular purpose, a completion of a task or a goal. Despite all appearances, those who adhere to an eschatological worldview have faith that there is a process or goal in and for this world that will be achieved by God. Rather than resignation in the face of suffering and evil, eschatology holds fast to the belief that all will be redeemed, resurrected, made new, or made clear at the end of history. Thus, eschatology could be best summarised experientially as audacious hope, or, more negatively, as 'insane expectation' (a phrase used by David Hart). Christian eschatology is focused upon here because it resonates most strongly with Meillassoux's own eschatological writings.

In twentieth-century Christian theology, eschatology once again came to the fore. Early twentieth-century theologians refocused their attention upon the 'insane expectations' claimed in Christian doctrine. On the popular front, eschatology assumed a central position in fundamentalist movements in America, which themselves were a response to the historical-critical method of Biblical scholarship popular among academics at the turn of the century. Fundamentalist eschatology relies upon a particular interpretation of apocalyptic Biblical literature ('apocalypse' meaning an uncovering or revelation) such as the Book of Daniel and the Book of Revelation.

There are varying forms of fundamentalist eschatology. Dispensationalism is the belief that God is revealed to humanity at various times, in various 'dispensations'. Dispensationalism is one version of 'premillennialism', which holds that the end of this age will inaugurate a time of peace under the leadership of Christ. Dispensationalism holds that the last dispensation of God will happen at the 'millennium', the end of this present age and the start of a 1,000-year reign under Christ's leadership. Premillennialist eschatology holds that the Day of Judgement will follow this reign. Amillennialism, held by scholars more than laypeople, argues that Christ's reign has already begun and that it began at his **death, resurrection**, and the coming of the Holy Spirit (at Pentecost). Postmillennialism holds that this present age is progressive, that Christ will come to reign once the entire world is converted to belief in Him.

While these differences at first may seem to the internal debates of fanatics, they are not theoretical. They reflect not only what each group hopes for but also how they view the current conditions of humanity. If one holds that Christ will come to reign before all are saved, one's understanding of the meaning and purpose of this age shades toward the negative. What is happening now is essentially hopeless and purposeless, because the only hope is Christ's coming when all will be made right. Our own actions have no purpose. A postmillennialist, however, will believe that our actions contribute to the coming kingdom, and therefore are of critical importance.

Putting Meillassoux's work into context with the above is no small feat, especially as he certainly would not identify himself with any of the aforementioned movements. However, his work focusing upon **divine inexistence** and the **creation** *ex nihilo* of worlds aligns strangely but significantly with eschatological concerns expressed in twentieth- and twenty-first-century Christianity. Most resonant is his argument that reality is a **hyper-chaos** that creates *ex nihilo* worlds, and that a **fourth World of justice** is at least logically possible, a world through which God comes into existence. Therefore, he holds forth an audacious hope that human beings may become immortal and God may come to reign in this fourth possible world. While Meillassoux does not hold to a present God, an existent God, and is thus far removed from anything like an orthodox Christian or theistic position, he nevertheless hopes for a future God, or rather for a world to emerge, *ex nihilo*, in which God does exist. This God would not be produced from a previous world (of matter, life or thought), but it is possible in that anything is possible. This possibility, of a world of Justice, of God, should not remain at the level of theory, however, but should inform and shape our behaviour in this world without God. Meillassoux writes: 'We must revive the extreme hope of eschatology in order to act – and right away – in view of an unconditional equality for all people, whose ultimate realisation no longer depends on us but on an omnipotent God who guarantees the "soundness of our folly"' (*IWB*, 454). His work expresses a personal eschatology in that he suggests that the lives of the dead need completion or fulfilment. His work expresses a cosmic eschatology in that there could be a world-to-come in which every life is fulfilled and death is no more. God is not to blame for the current injustices of the world, for God does not (yet) exist. But God could exist, in the future, and this is what would make the sufferings of this world meaningful and at the same time annihilated – for this coming world of justice can only work, for Meillassoux, if death itself dies and the dead are bodily resurrected – all of them.

Placing Meillassoux's philosophical eschatology alongside traditional theistic eschatologies is obviously problematic. However, the problems or questions that emerge from a careful reading of any eschatology are the same, and are ethical in their scope. Meillassoux argues that the extreme hope of eschatology should shape our behaviour in this world, but that the creation of this world of justice is not dependent upon any action or happening in *this* world. In this sense, he echoes both the premillennial and postmillennial ethical viewpoints, even as they contradict one another. While Meillassoux is no dispensationalist, in that he does not hold to any intervention or appearance of God in the worlds we are currently aware of, he does hold forth the hope for a future dispensation, one that would be the first coming of God.

ETERNAL RECURRENCE

Daw-Nay Evans

Nietzsche calls the 'eternal recurrence' the 'greatest weight' and the 'highest formula of affirmation that is at all attainable' (Nietzsche 1974: 341; 1954: 1). He introduces the concept in *The Gay Science* and *Thus Spoke Zarathustra*. Some view it as a philosophical embarrassment, while others see it as the cornerstone of Nietzsche's thought. For those who view the eternal recurrence as crucial to appreciate Nietzsche's thinking, two different interpretations have emerged. The first contends that the eternal recurrence is a cosmological theory about the nature of time. The second contends that the eternal recurrence is a thought experiment that should be construed as an ethical command akin to Kant's categorical imperative. Despite these internecine battles, there is little doubt that the eternal recurrence is Nietzsche's answer to the problem of nihilism that is the Platonic-Christian worldview. The latter is static and linear, whereas the world in which things eternally recur (or are said to recur) is fluid and cyclical.

The presentation of the eternal recurrence as a true doctrine first appears in §109 of *The Gay Science*. This version does not contradict the more popular, hypothetical version presented in §341 of that same text. As a cosmological theory, the eternal recurrence is non-teleological. There is no overarching purpose or aim to time as such. Indeed, the narrative of progress so prominent in many religious and philosophical traditions is absent in the eternal recurrence. Without a beginning or an end, this cyclical theory of time stands in stark contrast to its competitors. As a consequence, the same things that occurred in the past will infinitely repeat themselves in the same manner in the future. On this reading, at least two questions arise. First, given the truth of recurrence, how is it significant for my life? When one becomes aware of the truth of recurrence, it should have transformative power such that you change your behaviour in the same way you changed it countless times before. In other words, the moment you become aware of the reality of recurrence is *the* moment you decide to live in a manner different than you did in the past. Even though this is a life you have lived numerous times before, you have yet to live *this* particular life in its entirety. Thus, you have no idea what your future entails until you experience it for yourself. Second, what actually recurs? Some have argued that to save Nietzsche from the fallacy of 'misplaced concreteness' we should think of that which eternally recurs as a reconfiguration of energy as opposed to the repetition of events, ideas and persons in their concrete sameness. If we move from a classical atomistic theory of time to a more dynamic energy theory, then what repeats is not literally the same things of the past but the energy of which those things are composed. For these reasons, the eternal recurrence is fatalistic but fatalistic in a way that leaves room for personal growth and change.

As a thought experiment, the eternal recurrence is a test to determine if we would choose to affirm our life as it has been lived on the assumption that time eternally recurs. For those who view the eternal recurrence as more myth than reality, the psychological disposition it should motivate does not require it to be literally true. There are two ways in which Nietzsche's eternal recurrence is analogous to Kant's categorical imperative. First, both Nietzsche and Kant view their theories as tests. Just as Kant's categorical imperative is a test to determine if our actions have moral worth, the eternal recurrence is a test to determine if our lives are worthy of affirmation. Second, both Nietzsche and Kant view their theories as having descriptive force. Kant's categorical imperative follows from understanding ourselves as rational agents, while Nietzsche's eternal recurrence, even as a thought experiment, follows from taking a fatalistic worldview seriously. Kant and Nietzsche are different in terms of the scope and magnitude of their views. Kant's ethics is meant to be universally applicable to all rational agents. Nietzsche's 'ethics', so to speak, apply to a select few.

Amor fati means accepting things as they are and not wanting them to be different. For Nietzsche, only those strong enough to stare into the abyss of a meaningless universe will accept the truth of eternal recurrence or, alternatively, affirm the idea of eternal recurrence. The challenge is to view one's life as a totality whose tragedies and triumphs are woven into a beautiful tapestry to be repeated again and again.

ESSENTIAL SPECTRE

The unmournable dead whose horrific deaths motivate the **spectral dilemma**.

F

FACT

Robert Jackson

In Meillassoux's system facts play a crucial part in answering the question as to why there is something rather than nothing, and more specifically why anything at all did not necessarily have to be. To see why this might be so, Meillassoux distinguishes, and then shortly after rejects, two models of the principle of unreason: a Kantian weak model and an enforced strong model, both of which follow from the two models of **correlationism**. The weak Kantian interpretation of **factiality** suggests that if something is (as a fact) then it must be contingent without then entailing that this something must exist. Maybe nothing exists. The strong interpretation, emphatically endorsed by Meillassoux, demands that not only is something contingent, but also that there must be contingent things. The weak principle claims that if a fact exists, it must be contingent, but the strong principle claims facts do not support whether or not factual things exist.

Now, endorsing the weak principle means endorsing facticity as a fact, because if nothing existed, there would not be any factual basis for it. This leads to an unacceptable regress that is self-refuted by the absolute nature of the strong interpretation, which evacuates all necessity from those facts and identifies absolute possibility. For if there was a weak arena of factual things, there will always be the assumption of a 'second-order' realm of factual things upon which it can change (*AF*, 74). Supporting that would require a third order and so on. Therefore, it is not a fact that things exist; rather it is an absolute necessity that contingent factual things exist. In order for contingency alone to be necessary, something must exist. This is a direct consequence of the principle of factiality because the absolute facticity of everything that exists cannot be thought as a fact. Meillassoux refers to this as the 'non-iterability of facticity', that facticity and facts cannot be applied to themselves (*AF*, 79).

FACTIALITY

Robert Jackson

The principle of factiality (*principe de factualité*) denotes the final stage of absolutising the facticity of the correlate. It is the necessity or non-facticity of facticity. It is also referred to as the principle of unreason. The typical definition of facticity as Meillassoux uses it is found in the work of Martin **Heidegger**. There one understands facticity as the brute, contingent fact of one's existence, which can only be described in terms of its **finitude**, and not deduced as something that had to be the case or necessary. Meillassoux is mostly concerned with the facticity of the correlate's contingent existence: that it could be otherwise. Moreover he is especially concerned with its facticity as an anti-absolutist gesture that only narrows contingent possibilities for the correlate, that is, there can be no absolute if facticity is only 'mine' or 'for me'.

Thus his pivotal argument in Chapter 3 of *After Finitude* is to establish and expose the contradictory nature of the strong correlationist position, and convert its facticity into an **absolute** for **speculative materialism**, whilst crucially distinguishing it from absolute idealism. The speculative materialist thesis is endorsed over idealism, and is favourable, in so far as the latter cannot pass through the 'meshes of facticity' (*AF*, 51). Idealist absolutism maintains that the correlation of being and thought itself is absolute and necessary. Whilst idealism can only absolutise the necessity of the correlationist circle, entailing that the in-itself is necessarily constituted by subjectivist traits, factiality only seeks to absolutise the 'absolute other' facticity of the correlate, entailing that the absolute other of contingency can be deduced in itself. I can deduce an absolute possibility that something can happen outside of thought and that a 'being-other' of the correlate's constitutive thought is absolutely possible.

To put it another way, if the facticity of strong correlationism was believed to be rooted in its finitude, that is, the failure to think the in-itself, Meillassoux modifies its function as a feature of the in-itself absolutely. It is because of strong correlationism's implicit admission of the absoluteness of contingency that the unthinkable can occur, and being an absolute, this entails that nothing, not even the correlationist position, is necessary. The facticity of the correlate presupposes an absolute within it. Therefore, not only is the correlate absolutely contingent, but rational thought can go one further, and know that reality is, in itself, absolutely contingent. The principle of factiality thus evacuates necessity from absolutely everything that exists and paradoxically only contingency alone is absolutely necessary.

In separating speculative materialism from idealism, Meillassoux believes he has introduced an entirely new absolute which simultaneously defeats the sceptical finitude of the facticity, and transforms its blind spot into an absolute knowledge of the things themselves. His strategy therefore hinges on the ability of the speculative materialist to convince the correlationist that his position conceals absolute contingency, namely that there is no reason why the correlationist must exist indefinitely. Thus the speculative materialist defeats the idealist (who absolutises the correlation), the dogmatic metaphysician and naive realist (who thinks that there must be a hidden reason for facticity in reality itself) and the correlationist (who can only de-absolutise facticity, by postulating it for us and not in-itself). If the strong correlationist remains sceptical of this and seeks to de-absolutise factiality, he can only do so on the basis of re-introducing it: by affirming the absolute possibility of everything and therefore implicitly presupposing the absolute.

FERVOUR

The manner of being belonging to the **vectorial subject** oriented toward bringing the **fourth World of justice** into being.

FICHTE, JOHANN GOTTLIEB

Devin Zane Shaw

Johann Gottlieb Fichte (1762–1814) is best-known for his *The Science of Knowledge* (1794), in which he set out his doctrine of a system of transcendental idealism grounded in the activity of the absolute I. Rather than evaluating Fichte's philosophy as ultimately idealist or realist, which has been the subject of recent debate, Meillassoux claims that *The Science of Knowledge* is 'the *chef-d'oeuvre*' (or masterpiece) of **correlationism** (*SR*, 409). In it Fichte attempts to show that all versions of **realism** fall victim to a pragmatic contradiction: after positing the absolute I, he proceeds to show that any attempt to think the thing-in-itself leads to a contradiction, that is, it must make recourse to the act of thinking of the in-itself. Meillassoux argues that **speculative materialism** must demonstrate that the correlationist's reliance on facticity, in Fichte's terms, 'freedom', entails a pragmatic contradiction in so far as it implicitly absolutises facticity.

Fichte's work follows Immanuel **Kant**'s suggestion in the *Critique of Practical Reason* (1781) that it should be possible to derive both theoretical and practical reason from a common principle, which Fichte posits as the absolute I. In addition to the absolute I, in Part I of *The Science of Knowledge* he proposes two other principles, that of opposition and of ground. The three principles have, on his account, ontological, ethical, epistemological and methodological implications (we will here consider only the ontological and epistemological implications). Fichte posits the absolute I as an infinite and unconditioned activity in both form and content that functions as a regulative ideal, while he also attempts to deduce from this activity the categories put forward by Kant in *Critique of Pure Reason* (1781). For example, from the first three principles, the principles of identity, opposition and ground, Fichte argues we can deduce the categories of reality, negation and limitation as moments of the self's activity.

The crucial moment of correlation occurs when Fichte posits the principle of opposition, which opposes the not-self to the self. (Technically speaking, he writes that the proposition '~A is not equal to A' has its transcendental basis in the not-self, just as the proposition of identity 'A=A' has its transcendental basis in the activity of the absolute I.) While formally the not-self is unconditioned, its content is conditioned by the first principle of the system, the self's activity. While his account suggests that the self and not-self are unconditionally opposed, Fichte argues that this opposition is overcome by the first synthesis in the system, the principle of ground, which demonstrates that the self and not-self interact through mutual limitation. It is possible to demonstrate that Fichte is a correlationist because he holds that the not-self must be grounded in the self's activity before any form of objectivity is possible: 'in order to set up something as an *object*, I have to know this already; hence it must lie initially in myself, the presenter, in advance of any possible experience' (Fichte 1982: 109).

FIDEISM

Paul O'Mahoney

Fideism refers to the belief that human reason cannot attain certainty in metaphysical, religious or moral matters, and that consequently beliefs formed in these areas must in large measure be a matter of faith. Historically, there have been prominent fideist strains in Catholicism, but the Church today proscribes the doctrine, holding faith to be rationally informed rather than wholly independent of reason. This is worth recording because Meillassoux sees the influence of this historical, religious phenomenon in contemporary fideism. His claim is that contemporary fideism is the outcome of a sceptico-fideist tradition inaugurated by Montaigne, who is called its 'founding father'. The classical document of Montaigne's fideism is his 'Apology for Raymond Sebond'. There, Montaigne explicitly acknowledges his debt to and admiration for classical scepticism, and defends adherence to traditional, historically transmitted religion or morality on the grounds that unaided reason cannot establish final certainty about such things. This tradition is considerably radicalised by the sceptical arguments of David **Hume**.

Hume's critique undermines human reason, denying it the potential to attain certainty in 'matters of fact'; most famously, he denied the evident necessity of causal relations. It is Immanuel **Kant**'s response to Hume, however, which is the stronger spur to fideism. In salvaging necessity by making causality one of the categories of human reason, and restricting reason's province to phenomena, rendering inaccessible the noumena or the unknowable 'things-in-themselves', Kant instituted what Meillassoux calls **correlationism**. His **Copernican Revolution** is thus the anteced-ent of twentieth-century anti-realist traditions (see **Ptolemaic counter-revolution**). Contemporary fideism is for Meillassoux 'essential' or 'fundamental'. It is a consequence of a shift from Kant's position, where the thing-in-itself is unknowable but thinkable, to one where it is even deemed unthinkable. Any **absolute** is therefore categorically closed off to thought or reason. This is strong correlationism, where Kant's was weak, and Meillassoux makes strong correlationism a synonym for fideism. The thinkers he implicates most strongly in the rise of fideism are Wittgenstein and Martin **Heidegger**, two of the figures most com-monly associated with what Richard Rorty called the linguistic turn in twentieth-century philosophy. They are implicated in what is called by Meillassoux 'communitarian or intersubjective solipsism', where inter-subjective agreement is posited as the only possible or available standard for what counts as true.

With the sceptical critique of metaphysics leading to the undermining of human reason, and the denial of its ability to achieve absolute knowl-edge, the consequence is that belief in the power or superiority of reason to faith becomes itself a matter of faith since it can't be proved: fideism becomes fundamental.

FIGURE 73

FIGURE

Fintan Neylan

A core concern of Meillassoux is discerning what properties we may establish about the **absolute**. Because Meillassoux conceives the absolute in the terms of its classical meaning, that is, as mind-independence, the properties we may derive must be thinkable by us, but not relative to us. Such non-relative properties are determined by establishing what he calls figures and he argues that **speculative materialism** can derive a number of them. Traditionally the goal of deducing absolute properties was achieved through positing necessary metaphysical entities, but ever since Immanuel **Kant** this route has been barred. Although agreeing with Kant's critique of **metaphysics**, Meillassoux points out that his Critical philosophy went too far in its disqualification of all knowable mind-independence. For what Kant missed is that there is a *non-metaphysical* mind-independence which **speculation** can access when it grasps the absolute.

In grasping absolute **contingency**, speculation may discover certain features of it: while it is not subject to any higher rule of restraint, there are instances in which chaos limits itself. Not arbitrary binds, these constraints are conditions which even **hyper-chaos** must not breach. It is within the capacity of speculation to establish certain statements about hyper-chaos as instances of such auto-limitation, and hence as conditions for its existence. These conditions of hyper-chaos are known as figures. Because such conditions would be invariant across any possible world which hyper-chaos can muster, the properties of the absolute which those statements express may be considered absolute, mind-independent properties. As these conditions, figures give a non-metaphysical account of mind-independence because they are properties which must hold regardless of any situation hyper-chaos manifests.

After Finitude identifies three such figures to be demonstrated: that the absolute is non-contradictory, that the absolute exists, and finally that mathematics' discourse has both absolute scope and that it requires possibility to be untotalisable. While the initial two figures are derived as an immediate consequence of hyper-chaos, this last condition about mathematics is an example of how figures are to guide the project of speculative materialism in future works. The speculative method is defined as the procedure whereby figures are discerned in order to overcome difficulties encountered by factial ontology. Thus mathematics' ability to discuss mind-independent entities and the structure of possibility is identified as a condition in order to resolve the question of how the mathematical sciences are possible – the central concern of *After Finitude*.

If we grant the last of these will be proven, through figures speculative materialism establishes the outlines of its mind-independent ontology. For it thus states these three properties (non-contradiction, existence, and the capacity of mind-independence and possibility to be expressed in mathematics) are properties of the absolute, holding regardless of the existence of any other entity.

FINITUDE

Daniel Sacilotto

In its broadest sense, finitude designates an entire configuration of philosophical thought, roughly corresponding with the emergence in modernity of what Meillassoux names **correlationism**, and which becomes radicalised and reiterated throughout the twentieth century in various forms. In its germinal weak or Kantian form, the thesis of finitude designates fundamentally an epistemic limitation in the possibilities open to the transcendental subject. This constraint has at least two salient characteristics. First, it exemplifies what Immanuel **Kant** designates as the facticity of thinking, and which marks the foreclosure of thought given the conditions of the categories of understanding. Thus, although we can have *a priori* knowledge about the twelve categories that structure the understanding, and consequentially the way in which things must appear to us in judgement, we are in principle barred from knowing why we have twelve categories and why things appear in the way they do. These conditions are merely given and accessible to us, but we are foreclosed access to the reasons for why these conditions obtain thus. Similarly, on the side of intuition or perception understood in the widest sense, the subject is constrained by the receptivity of the senses, which for Kant anchors the faculties to the external world as well as one's own gaze upon the life of one's mind. In contrast, 'infinitude' is conceived in terms of the absence of such constraints. Thus the 'mind of God' is said to be infinite in its power in so far as it is subject to no reasons which it does not know (it is not 'factical'), and in so far as his thought produces the thing thought (it is not constrained by the senses onto an external world).

Finitude has a second, properly ontological dimension, correlated to what Meillassoux calls the contingency of being or the entity, that is, the possible non-being of that which is. This is precisely the aspect that becomes exploited later by the 'strong correlationists', for whom facticity, not just in terms of our epistemic limitations, must be recognised, more radically, in its ontological scope. Canonically, Martin **Heidegger** conceives of Dasein's existence as properly individuated through the (non)-event of death, where the temporal phenomenological horizon that constitutes its being-in-the-world is definitively closed. It is thus the event of death or the finite contingency of Dasein's being that marks that experience as its own. For Meillassoux, to go 'after finitude' requires that we overcome both the epistemic and ontological constraints described in correlationist philosophy. In a first moment, Meillassoux's argument for the principle of **factiality** seeks to establish the possibility of a knowledge of the **absolute**, precisely by recognising facticity as an ontological absolute rather than a mere epistemic constraint (*AF*, 59). Ontologising sceptical doubts raised by David **Hume** and others, Meillassoux thus takes thought's inability to find reasons for its own being as evincing the fact that there just *are* no reasons for things to be. This is precisely the thesis of factiality, according to which what we can know absolutely is that things are necessarily contingent, giving knowledge of an ontological principle that extends beyond that which is relative to the subject. And since the argument for factiality is meant to prove the necessity of the contingency of every being and law, it follows that the subject must likewise be contingent, that is, it must be mortal.

However, the overcoming of finitude has another radical, ontological dimension. In the course of showing that the laws of nature are themselves contingent, Meillassoux seeks to show that the necessary contingency of every being and law in principle leaves open the possibility that the mortality of human life may itself be subject to change (see **death**). But doesn't the apparent stability of laws, and thus our phenomenological experience of death, attest to their probable occurrence, if not their necessity? Mortgaging his argument to Alain **Badiou**'s use of Georg **Cantor**'s Theorem (see **set theory**), Meillassoux claims that there is no 'infinity of all infinities', that one cannot 'totalise' the field of possibilities open to being and so calculate 'probabilistically' that the frequency or apparent stability of a law or event is a reason for its necessity, or the likelihood of its recurrence. In other words, it defeats what Meillassoux calls the 'frequentialist implication' (*AF*, 103). Although it is not clear how this set-theoretical operation should yield insight into what is possible or not in the world, it is clear Meillassoux takes this result to open the possibility of an eventual transformation of the human beyond its present mortality. Thus, in the final stage envisaged in his account of **divine inexistence**, the **advent** of the fourth ontological order, the **fourth World of justice**, calls for going after finitude for humanity in another sense, namely by God's banishing death and thus providing a world of immortality.

FORMALISM

Paul J. Ennis

The second part of Meillassoux's lecture, 'Essay on the Derivation of Galileanism', has the aim of providing a 'factial derivation that would legitimate *the absolutizing capacity of modern science* – that is to say, Galilean science' (*IRR*, 18). The **derivation** required will be in the form of the capacity to 'think a meaningless sign' as the 'minimal condition' of any formal language whether we mean this in logical or mathematical terms (*IRR*, 18). The derivation will function by establishing that there is a bond between the **meaningless sign**, sometimes called the empty sign, and absolute contingency.

Meillassoux provides us with a new distinction in this lecture. The properties constitutive of the primary absolute are now named primo-absolutising properties (*IRR*, 18). For instance, facticity (in his sense) and non-contradiction are primo-absolutising properties that apply to all entities. This is the absolute considered in the ontological register. Deutero-absolutising properties are those related to the derivate or secondary absolute and they are absolute separation and persistence (*IRR*, 19). This is the ontic register. The ability to generate deutero-absolutising statements is his focus in this essay, but it is approached with the first type in mind. To grasp the latter Meillassoux wishes to find a criterion of formal languages and, in particular, to identify one belonging to **mathematics** that would help explain its relationship to absolute contingency (*IRR*, 20).

Meillassoux tells us we will be discussing logico-mathematics in the modern sense of formalism, that is, post-Hilbert. What is the general feature of all mathematical formalism? Meillassoux looks at the example of **set theory** in its standard Zermelo-Fraenkel (ZF) axiomatic form (*IRR*, 20). He characterises it as a first-order logic with a foundational role for mathematics and claims that it differs from the sense of axiomatic we find in Euclid. He portrays the Euclidean approach as one that begins with definitions, then establishes postulates, and then states its axioms. The definitions precede the axioms and this, for Meillassoux, distinguishes Hilbert's formal axiomatic from Euclid's. In modern formalism *'one does not begin with any initial definition'* (*IRR*, 21). We have undefined terms subject to specific relations. For instance, in set theory we have 'base-signs' as meaningless signs (for example, β) naming undefined sets (the terms in this context) (*IRR*, 21). The set is simply this meaningless sign with no reference to anything outside itself. Since set theory is foundational it follows that the meaningless sign is the 'initial object' of mathematics (*IRR*, 21). Relations are considered in terms of 'operator-signs' that perform operations on the base-signs, designated by meaning-less signs, for example ∈ as the sign of membership or V for disjunction (*IRR*, 21). Through the manipulation of base-signs by operator-signs we begin to see how the relations between terms are built up. Formally, then, we have only relations between signs and never the informal intrusion of definition or meaning.

Meillassoux claims that the ZF axiomatic can produce sets such as the empty set, which allows one to construct the succession of ordinals, and thus to provide a foundation for numeration. The relevant point we can extract from his treatment of axiomatic set theory is that it becomes pos-sible to differentiate between the uses of meaningless signs in informal or formal languages. In informal languages we can have meaningless signs, decontextualised letters, or randomly constructed words, but the tendency is to avoid them since the aim of natural language is commu-nication. In formal languages, however, syntactically, the meaningless sign plays an 'essential, structural role' in that we depend on them being undefined (*IRR*, 23). Formal meaning is, then, 'the rule-governed use of meaningless (or non-signifying) syntactical units' and for this reason constitutes the register '*capable of producing deutero-absolutizing truths*' (*IRR*, 23).

FOURTH WORLD OF JUSTICE

Fintan Neylan

In the face of the existence of pain and suffering, one might imagine that the rational, non-religious response consists in shrugging one's shoulders and accepting that this is just how the universe of **immanence** is, namely, a random one full of despair and void of hope (see **finitude**). Even with his acceptance of a scientific worldview, Meillassoux takes issue with such despair being regarded as the only rational response. While acknowledging that the transcendental option of hope usually provided by religions must be ruled out, he is adamant that this does not strip an immanent ontology of hope altogether. For despite the actually existing despair we find at present, through the principle of **factiality** one can rationally envision a just world emerging within the current universe.

Factial ontology considers not just the extremities of what is possible as real, but the import of such non-contradictory possibilities on what currently exists (see **principle of non-contradiction**). To the existence of a world rife with misery, the factial response is that there may emerge a **World** free of injustice, seated within the already existing world. Humans, as beings capable of reason, can rationally conceive of hope through this possible World of justice, and are not required to consign such notions about a better world to a latent mystical impulse. Through the factial, justice becomes a possible World that can serve as an object of rational hope in a universe of suffering. It allows the concept of hope to have coherence in the current world of pain and not seem like an irrationality. Ontologically, justice is to appear after the already emerged Worlds of matter, life and thought. As with the previous three, the World of justice is to emerge through **creation** *ex nihilo*.

For Meillassoux, such an emergence of a World must in some way be an *ex nihilo* novelty. In each of the previous emergences, we see an addition of an element that could not have existed beforehand: the addition of life to a dead universe of matter and the addition of thought to an unthinking universe of life. This last World is crucial, for the capacity to know absolute **contingency** emerges only in thought. This capacity that is afforded to rational beings forms a core piece of Meillassoux's project, for a World is defined as that which currently constitutes this capacity and *ex nihilo* occurrences as novelties which would further define this capacity. While it is contingent like everything else, this knowing relationship between a contingent being and contingency is marked out as that which cannot be 'surpassed'. With the World of thought comes a bar on the emergence of additional elements, for to thought there can be nothing added which would enable a 'superior' manner in which the absolute may be grasped.

The appearance of humans in the World of thought is by no means an accident, because humans are named as the realisation of this capacity. Having nothing to do with a particular biological make-up, for Meillassoux the human is a being that can grasp its contingent existence in relation to the absolute truth of contingency, the realisation of this unsurpassable relationship. The human is accorded a special place in factial ontology, for *ex nihilo* novelties are specified by the fact that they define it. The emergence of the next World, which Meillassoux argues will be the World of justice, is complicated by the unsurpassability of the human: as a World it must involve some form of *ex nihilo* novelty that further defines the human, but this novelty is barred from being an addition which would exceed the World of thought. This complication leads Meillassoux to suggest that the World of justice would entail the immortality of humans as its *ex nihilo* novelty.

Entailed in being human is the awareness of a universal equality between all rational beings, despite the actual existence of deep inequalities, for example, pain, suffering and unjust death in our current universe. Hope is both this awareness and an orientation toward the realisation of such a radical equality, that is, a World of justice.

Meillassoux sets great store by the fact that we can be orientated to a World that is not yet actual, that we have an idea of justice, a universal regardless of the fact it does not exist. Because we always hope for justice, he argues that we are already defined by it. He bolsters this claim by the fact that, while anything conceivable is possible in the factial, there is only one possible novelty which would further define the human. In lieu of not being able to surpass the human, this further defining novelty would have to be a different style of emergence: instead of an exceeding, the novelty would consist in redefining what the human actually is, that is, a rebirth of the human in just form. This recommencement of the human would be a recompense for our undergoing in the current World events that violate the strict equality of which we are all aware. In order to actualise justice, the emergent novelty would be the rebirth of humans as immortal, free from pain, suffering and early unjust death.

Meillassoux thus inverts the Christian apocalyptic vision in his conception of the coming of a World of justice: it is not an event in which humanity is judged and reproached, but one of redress and rectification for the horrors and injustices humans have endured over countless millennia. The World of justice is one where the equality of all rational beings is finally respected. But the coming of this World is to be of benefit not only to future generations, but for the dead too: what is hoped for is the rectification of all injustices past, present and future, which includes early death. The deceased are to be raised from the grave in order that the past injustices done to them can be redressed through the bestowal of immortality.

Thus the World of justice is the only possible World which can further define the human, one in which immortality would emerge. As a real possibility, justice defines the human by being an object of hope. It is important to stress that Meillassoux's considerations of justice are a detailing not of one extravagant notion among others but of the only possibility that adheres to the limits set down by the emergence of the human. For though its actualisation would be an ontological remaking of the human as just, it would not be a surpassing. As such, it will be the fourth World to appear *ex nihilo*, coming after matter, life and thought.

$$\boxed{\text{G}}$$

GERMAN IDEALISM

Sean J. McGrath

German Idealism began in the last decade of the eighteenth century with a variety of responses to unresolved questions generated by Immanuel Kant's Critical project. It lasted until the 1840s, with Schelling's Berlin lectures, alternatively considered the completion of German Idealism (as depicted by Walter Schulz) or the first act in its overcoming (as depicted by Horst Fuhrmans). One could root the movement in the rejection on logical, metaphysical and ethical grounds of Immanuel Kant's claim that the objects of human cognition are appearances and not things-in-themselves. Where Kant seemed to maintain the **realism** of objects, at least as a possibility, it was not clear how this was consistent with his epistemology. If a subject only ever knows phenomena, and if phenomena are by definition objects *for* a subject, the conditions of the possibility of which lie entirely in the *a priori* structure of transcendental subjectivity (space, time, the categories of the understanding and the ideas of reason), what sense could there be to Kant's claim that the *matter* of cognition (by distinction from its form, which is *a priori*), that is, sense data, is *a posteriori* and mind-independent?

Fichte first demolished the notion of things-in-themselves on the ground that a mind-independent object is a contradiction in terms. This led to the argument, common to Fichte, the early Schelling and Hegel, that in order for mind to think a limit, it must already be beyond that limit, on its other side, as it were. It follows that a reason that sets limits for itself, that is, reason that has achieved transcendental knowledge, is in fact limitless or **absolute**. The thesis that mind or spirit posits its own other in order to overcome it and in that act comes to know itself or realise a richer mode of operation, which Fichte first formulated and Hegel perfected, is the basic presupposition of German Idealism. In its inclusion of intuitive or non-discursive modes of experience as well as its thematisation of the unconscious, German Idealism was closely bound up with Romanticism. Nevertheless it would be a mistake to describe German Idealism as the philosophy of Romanticism since it was not primarily a literary or artistic endeavour and stood some critical distance from Romantic art, politics and literature. In histories of philosophy, German Idealism is generally considered the next step after Descartes, Spinoza and Leibniz on the rationalist side, and Locke, Berkeley and Hume on the empiricist side. As such it is read as a systematic attempt to heal the split between **rationalism** and **empiricism**, subjectivity and sensibility. However, the German idealists created such novel philosophical structures and were possessed of such seemingly inexhaustible genius that it is a misreading to reduce them to a response to any previous or contemporaneous intellectual movement.

The German idealist rejection of a real limit to reason precipitated a resuscitation of **metaphysics** and inaugurated the most fertile period for speculative philosophy since the heyday of Greek philosophy. Fichte, Schelling and Hegel are notable for their systematic treatments of every dimension of philosophy, from logic to political philosophy. The immediate reaction to German Idealism, especially in the work of Kierkegaard, Marx and Nietzsche, should be included in any assessment of its historical influence since these authors are inconceivable without that against which they revolted. The inconclusive relation of the parts of Kant's Critical project to one another inspired an intense search for a general system of philosophy, where system meant, as Karl Leonhard Rheinhold was the first to point out, that all of its parts could be derived from a single principle. This first principle could only be *the absolute*, the unconditioned which precedes all conditioned concepts or beings, all that which is limited by opposites. This assumption made the German idealists sympathetic to Spinoza and his effort to found philosophy in the concept of the infinite or substance. However, the German idealists criticised Spinoza's insufficiently nuanced account of subjectivity; for Schelling and Hegel, the absolute must be considered both subject and substance if it is truly absolute. The failure of German Idealism to achieve an absolute system, already announced in the lectures of the late Schelling, was the departure point for the non-foundationalism of Kierkegaard, Marx and Nietzsche.

The rise of German Idealism was closely connected to the pantheism controversy, in which Moses Mendelssohn sought to defend the Spinozism of Gotthold Ephraim Lessing. At issue here was the question of whether Spinoza's identification of **God** and nature amounted to atheism, and more broadly, whether a deductive rationalist philosophy was compatible with a theistic and morally oriented worldview. Friedrich Heinrich Jacobi argued that it was not: any attempt to rationally deduce truth was fatally flawed since God, the truth itself, entirely transcended reason. Jacobi allied Spinozism with Kant's transcendental idealism and declared that both produce only a pseudo-religiosity, which he called 'nihilism', because it amounts to finite reason's denial of anything other than itself and humanity's worship of its own image. For Jacobi genuine religion and morality is grounded in the immediate non-conceptual certainty in revelation which the tradition calls faith, not reason. All three of the German idealists rejected this argument, albeit in different ways, and insisted that the basic beliefs of Western religion were fully compatible with *a priori* reasoning. In Schelling's late lectures a concession was made to Jacobi: *a priori* reasoning, however necessary, Schelling argued in Berlin in the 1840s, is merely negative; the real is excluded from it. Our knowledge of the real is always *a posteriori* and as such a disruption of the ideal. The paragon of such an interruption is biblical revelation. However, the late Schelling held that *a posteriori* revelation can become the foundation for a new mode of philosophy, which he called 'positive philosophy', when its truths are appropriated by reason. Such an appropriation becomes the ground for a genuine philosophy of history and metaphysical empiricism.

This represented a radical change of perspective for Schelling, who had started as a supporter of Fichte's idealism. Fichte argued that reason's other, which he called the not-I, is generated unconsciously or 'posited' by reason itself, so that in the activity of overcoming its otherness, either by reducing the object to conceptual knowledge, that is, science, or by mastering wild nature so as to make it habitable by rational beings, that is, ethics, reason can come to know itself for what it truly is, not an object but a pure subject that subsists only in its proper activity. The early Schelling pursued this thesis in his first major works but then supplemented it, to Fichte's dismay, with a philosophy of nature, arguing that the unconscious self-positing subject can also be approached through a systematic study of nature in itself. Nature understood as endlessly productive ground (which Schelling called, after Spinoza, *natura naturans*), by distinction from its objects produced (*natura naturata*), is nothing other than a pure activity that generates limits (finite entities) for the sake of overcoming them. Nature annuls the finite by sacrificing the individual to the universal, in organic life, the single organism to the species through reproduction. Thus the absolute subject and absolute nature coincide in the early Schelling; they are to be considered as 'indifferent' to one another. Hence alongside a transcendental philosophy of the subject, such as Fichte's, Schelling advocated a transcendental philosophy of the object, such as was being developed in various ways by romantic scientists under the banner *Naturphilosophie*.

Along with the poet Hölderlin, Hegel had been Schelling's classmate in Tübingen from 1790–93. His first work mediated the dispute between Fichte and Schelling by describing Fichte's work as 'subjective' idealism by distinction from Schelling's 'objective' idealism. Fichte's absolute subject is a denial of the identity of the *I* and the *not-I*, Hegel argued. Schelling established the identity of the subject and object by means of his notion of the objectivity of the subject, on the one hand, the subject as a product of nature, and the subjectivity of the object, on the other, nature as absolute 'non-thinged' productivity. The truth of the matter could only be found in a position that was neither subjective nor objective but maintained the unity of the subject-object or the absolute. Schelling's philosophy prepared the way for such an absolute idealism. Schelling found Hegel's early position entirely congenial to his identity-philosophy, which was the next stage of his thinking (after transcendental philosophy and nature-philosophy). To his surprise, when Hegel published his *Phenomenology of Spirit* in 1807, Schelling discovered that Hegel rejected the premise of his identity-philosophy entirely.

Hegel attacked Schelling's early notion of the absolute, the ineffable origin of thought and action that could only be known through intuition, as obscurantist, and called for a reinstatement of public and discursive reason. According to the mature Hegel, Schelling's conception of the identity of subject and object elided the distinctions that determine the different forms of consciousness, distinctions which are crucial for the concrete universalisation of reason or spirit (*Geist*). This point has led non-metaphysical interpreters of Hegel to argue that Hegel's is not a philosophy of the absolute at all but rather a much more modest philosophy of the conditions of intelligibility (John Burbidge, Robert Pippin). In any case, sublimation (*Aufhebung*) is the key to Hegel's logic and the basis of his approach to metaphysics and ethics. Reason's essential activity consists in the negation of that which initially resists it (alternatively sensation, particularity, nature, art and revelation), which leads to the discovery that all apparent immediacy is in fact nothing but inchoate or concealed mediation. The 'notion' is not an ineffable absolute or a transcendent God but the concretely experienced truth that reason has no other: the otherness that it encounters in nature and in itself is nothing other than itself in an alienated form. Freedom consists in the activity of finding oneself in one's other. In this regard, Hegel's system is a qualified return to Fichte, with the caveat that the notion need not begin in subjectivity and is not the apotheosis of the subject: the truth of reason can be discovered anywhere and is no more subjective than it is objective.

A summary of German Idealism would not be complete without a word on aesthetics. The anonymously written *Oldest Program for a System of German Idealism*, variously attributed to Hölderlin, Schelling or Hegel, posits that the absolute idea is beauty that is only adequately expressed in art and mythology. This premise was basic for the early part of Schelling's career. In various ways, the early Schelling argued that art is higher than discursive philosophy for it alone gives concrete expression to that which reflection must always hold apart: the ideal and the real, the subject and the object, freedom and necessity. Hegel rejected this subordination of philosophy to art and maintained, to the contrary, that art, like its ally, religion, is mere picture-thinking, a concrete expression of the absolute idea or 'notion' in an inferior and sensuous form, which is necessary at a certain stage in the history of spirit but which needs to be cancelled and preserved (*aufgehoben*, sublimated) by philosophy. This is the presupposition for Hegel's infamous claim that art comes to an end in the nineteenth century: its function had been taken over by idealist philosophy.

When Hegel died in 1831, he was without doubt the most influential thinker of his generation, with a following among both conservatives (right Hegelians who took the point of the system to be the triumph of reason) and radicals (left Hegelians who emphasised the necessity of war and revolution in the dialectic of history). In 1841, Frederick William IV, King of Prussia, called Schelling to be Hegel's successor in Berlin and paid him the largest salary ever granted a university professor in Germany up to that time, in the hope that Schelling would purge German intellectual life of Hegelianism. Schelling had not published in decades. It was, however, widely known that he had been working on both a critique of Hegel and an alternative to Hegel's system (especially in the *Ages of the World* drafts and in the lectures delivered at Erlangen and Munich). On the opening day, the Berlin lecture hall was filled to capacity with the younger generation, who were weary of idealism and hungry for change, among them Kierkegaard, Engels and Bakunin. Most of the auditors left disappointed. While the late Schelling hardly displaced Hegel in the history of philosophy, his positive philosophy has recently been recognised by many scholars as the inception of late nineteenth-century **materialism**, Marxism and existentialism. Schelling's positive philosophy begins from the assumption that reason is insufficient to the real; reason is only fully rational when it is 'ecstatic', outside itself and receiving the truth of that which it did not itself generate. In this final act, German Idealism came full circle and returned to the point of its inception, the notion of self-mediated reason, only to emphatically deny its sufficiency.

GOD

Anthony Paul Smith

The arrival of *After Finitude* was greeted by many as a corrective to the so-called 'theological turn' in French philosophy. This 'theological turn' referred to the renewal of interest in questions of religion by major thinkers like Jacques Derrida and Emmanuel Levinas. Meillassoux's *After Finitude* was thought to represent a move away from questions related to God, whether they be philosophical or theological in character, as Meillassoux took explicit aim at a kind of **fideism** he located as existing under the postmodern condition of scepticism concerning the possibility of knowledge of the **absolute**. This scepticism disempowered philosophy to respond to religious claims to truth.

While Meillassoux's antipathy toward the nefarious elements of religion is explicit in *After Finitude*, especially in his remarks on the anti-scientific character of religious creationism, it soon became clear that his project was not atheist in any straightforward sense. It was with some surprise that readers discovered his unpublished doctoral thesis bore the title *L'Inexistence divine* (*Divine Inexistence*). Readers were then met with ideas arising out of that thesis in the publication of his essay 'Spectral Dilemma' in English translation in 2008 and the less well-known but expanded version of the essay, which was published in English as 'The Immanence of the World Beyond' in 2010. In these essays readers saw the emergence of a certain naming of God arising out of the outline of the system presented in *After Finitude* and the ethical importance of this conception of God for Meillassoux's project became clearer.

Meillassoux's argument that the only necessity is contingency has as a consequence that the laws of nature are also grounded upon **hyper-chaos**. This leads to a theory of virtualities that may emerge from this **hyper-chaos** and Meillassoux claims that among these virtualities we may also count God. In short, for Meillassoux, God does not exist, but may emerge and so exist in the future. This has led some philosophers to criticise him for seemingly sneaking religion back into philosophy. Most notable amongst these critics is Adrian Johnston, who mockingly compares this theory to one which would see the possible emergence of a 'Flying Spaghetti Monster'. Johnston's criticism confuses Meillassoux's conception of God, a conception which he calls 'irreligious', with the current standard theistic conception of God propagated by religious leaders.

While Meillassoux's irreligious conception of God emerges out of his theory of hyper-chaos, it is developed primarily in relation to an ethical problem he names the **spectral dilemma**. This dilemma arises in relation to horrific deaths that remain unmourned or for which mourning does not bring any satisfaction when confronted with the horror of these deaths. These horrific deaths may be the death of a child, the murder of a people, or the sacrifice of one generation for the sake of another future generation. Meillassoux claims the standard atheist and religious responses are different forms of despair in the face of these spectres. The first has to give up hope of absolute justice and the second posits that justice is to be carried out by a being which has allowed the worst injustices to exist. What

Meillassoux responds to with his vision of a God that 'may be' (or may come to exist) is not the hope in an all-powerful being to worship. Rather God is a name for the human hope in an absolute egalitarian justice which he claims is found in all revolutionary and messianic projects.

While Meillassoux argues for the possibility of a God who may arise in the future to bring justice, he has not yet gone on to develop a theory of the character of that God. The name of God is something of a placeholder, though at points in these essays his conception of God may appear to be positing simply the standard theistic account of a God who is all-powerful, all-knowing, eternal, and so on. However, his refutation of the religious response to suffering includes a rejection of the eternity of God (as it contravenes the principle that only contingency is necessary), leading the way to a claim that this irreligious conception of God will require a new science of the divine to replace theology. Meillassoux calls this new science 'divinology', for which his past works appear to provide only a prolegomena. The future work promises to combine his speculative philosophy with a strong emphasis on a theory of absolute justice in the face of human suffering.

GRANT, IAIN HAMILTON

Peter Gratton

One of the four original participants in the 2007 **speculative realism** conference, Iain Hamilton Grant's work is focused on renewing a particular form of Platonism to get past the problems of **correlationism** in Immanuel **Kant**. He is principally known within speculative realist circles for *Philosophies of Nature after Schelling* (2006). His task in this work is to think a philosophy of nature that is not mechanistic, where nature is more 'subject' than object. Greatly influenced by F.W.J. Schelling's reading of Plato, Grant contends that nature cannot be the mere correlate of human thought, but is in fact the productive power of all that is. To articulate this nature, following Schelling, we must have a 'speculative physics' that would give us a natural history of its processes, which also remain stubbornly irreducible to what can be thought. This history would focus on processes that deeply 'unthings' or 'de-objectifies' all that is. In this way, Grant is critical of Graham Harman's **object oriented ontology**, since the latter would focus only on what are the ephemeral effects of an underlying physics. In other words, his principal argument against Harman is that the productivity of nature is prior to any particular objects. The mark of being, then, is power, which upends all substantial forms of being.

For Schelling, what was the 'prius' or absolute prior to substances or things was not a ground or ultimate substance, as in **onto-theology**, where one substance (e.g., God) subtends all others, but rather a dynamism that we can never think, since thought itself is a product of that power and dynamism and thus could only provide a schema that cannot do justice to this prius. The ultimate 'ground', then, is a certain becoming that is less a ground than the shifting sands of reality. But Grant is also critical of those who would make this 'ungrounding' power a form of vitalism, which he rejects on the basis that it exports the qualities of the living (and in particular the human) onto being itself. Finally, Grant is not allergic, like the other speculative realists, to the label of idealism. His argument is that the infinite idea, the unconditioned, is precisely that which is prior to and productive of all things, and which, as Plato notes, cannot be given to the senses. Reading the Plato of the *Timaeus*, among other writings, Grant finds that this infinite ungrounding power cannot be given over to one idea or another on the flip side of materiality, since that would make the idea finite and conditioned. Thus, through rich readings of the tradition, Grant finds room to critique correlationism and substance philosophies, but not a powerful idealism that would critique all forms of Kantianisms remaining in the twenty-first century.

HARMAN, GRAHAM

Peter Gratton

Harman was one of the original four speakers at the 2007 **speculative realism** conference and is perhaps the most inveterate populariser of the movement through his books and weblog (http://doctorzamalek2. wordpress.com). One of four self-identified as following **object oriented ontology**, along with Timothy Morton, Ian Bogost and Levi Bryant, Harman has argued that philosophers have either 'overmined' or 'undermined' objects. To undermine them means to take objects as mere epiphenomena of some deeper effect, as in the powerful nature of which Iain Hamilton **Grant** speaks, empiricism, atomisms, and all manner of process philosophies, as well as materialisms, whether Marxist or the more traditional varieties. To 'overmine' objects means to treat objects only in so far as they relate to one another, as in the actants of Bruno Latour's mature philosophy, or the 'correlationism' that also comes under sharp critique from the other speculative realists. From his earliest work to his most recent, Harman has argued that objects in themselves are prior to any of their relations at the sensual level. As such, objects in themselves are indubitably real, but cannot be made the correlates of thought, since we can only ever access the sensual level of the object. While an import exponent of Meillassoux in several important works, including *Quentin Meillassoux: Philosophy in the Making* (2011), Harman is critical of his work for still being too correlationist, since Meillassoux uses the correlationist circle as the starting point for his pivot to the real. And inasmuch as Meillassoux is given to discussions of the chaotic in-itself and set theoretical insights into the absolute, he both under- and overmines the objects that Harman has put at the centre of his work.

HEGEL, G.W.F.

Bart Zantvoort

By identifying himself as a speculative philosopher of the **absolute**, Meillassoux unmistakeably and, without doubt, knowingly places himself in relation to Hegel. Like Hegel, Meillassoux aims to boldly sweep away the theoretical clutter of scepticism and the critical project of Immanuel **Kant** and claim that thought can think the absolute. But, although Hegel is mentioned in many places in *After Finitude*, these references are rather disjointed, and without exception critical. Despite his dismissal of Hegel as a 'subjectalist' (*IRR*, 8), their projects are much more similar than they might at first appear. Most of Meillassoux's criticisms of Hegel are not new. He claims, firstly, that Hegel is a thinker of absolute identity. Because Hegel thinks that all finite entities are contradictory he is forced to conclude that the true is a self-identical whole, in which all differences are contained (*AF*, 70). Meillassoux makes the inverse argument that, because a necessary entity is impossible and a contradictory entity would be necessary, contradiction is impossible. Secondly, Hegel subordinates contingency to necessity. For Hegel, according to Meillassoux, the absolute constitutes a 'rational totality', in which contingency is a necessary but secondary moment (*AF*, 80). And finally, Hegel is a metaphysician, because he postulates a necessary entity, mind or spirit (*Geist*), as absolute.

More interesting, however, is the role Hegel plays in the core argument of *After Finitude*, the argument for the principle of **factiality**. This principle entails that all determinate things are contingent and could be otherwise than they are (*AF*, 79). According to Meillassoux, the correlationist argues, in Kantian fashion, that the laws of nature and logic – what Meillassoux calls the 'structural invariants of our experience' – might appear to be necessary for us, but we cannot know if in reality ('in themselves') they are actually different from the way they appear to us. But, Meillassoux argues, this leaves the correlationist fixed on the horns of a dilemma (*AF*, 59). Either the correlationist admits that the structural invariants of our experience could *really* be otherwise, and that therefore everything, including the laws of nature and logic, is contingent. Or else, he has to admit that these laws could *not* really be otherwise, which means that they are absolutely necessary. But this is precisely the idealist position, which Meillassoux ascribes to Hegel, and which the correlationist seeks to avoid. According to Meillassoux, Hegel's idealism consists in 'absolutizing the correlation' of thinking and being (*AF*, 37). While Kant thinks that the categories that structure our experience are merely a fact for us – we cannot know whether or not they truthfully represent the world as it is in itself – and can therefore only be described, Hegel thinks that these categories can be deduced, and therefore are proven to be necessary (*AF*, 38).

Although Meillassoux does not distinguish clearly between the subjective idealist and the speculative or absolute idealist (*AF*, 59), it is Hegel's position as described above which is crucial in establishing the principle of facticity. Meillassoux forces the correlationist to choose between **speculative materialism** and (Hegelian) idealism. Since he rejects the latter on the basis of the arguments already given, speculative materialism must be correct.

While Meillassoux clearly distances himself from Hegel, even as he takes over his terminology, their positions are similar in a number of ways. Firstly, although it is true that Hegel thinks the categories of the *Logic* (such as being and nothing, identity and difference) are necessary and can be deduced, isn't Meillassoux doing something similar when he tries to derive non-trivial knowledge – his 'figures' – from the principle of factiality (*AF*, 80)? He demonstrates, firstly, the impossibility of a contradictory entity, and secondly, the necessary existence of a contingent entity. But he goes much further than this. The project he outlines in *After Finitude*, even if he does not manage to execute it there, is to prove two major points: firstly, the absolute reach of mathematics, that is, it's capacity to describe the world as it is in itself (see **Cartesian in-itself**), and secondly, the 'absolute and . . . unconditionally necessary scope' of the Cantorian transfinite (*AF*, 127) (see **set theory**; Georg **Cantor**). The latter would allow him to derive the stability of the laws of nature absolutely from the principle of factiality (*AF*, 127). But if this stability can be derived, does this not mean that it is necessary? What is the difference, then, between the Hegelian 'deduction' and Meillassoux's 'derivation'?

Secondly, one of the core elements of Meillassoux's argument is the rejection of the **principle of sufficient reason**. Although Hegel is undoubtedly a philosopher of reason (*Vernunft*), he does not subscribe to the principle of sufficient reason (*Grund*). As he shows in the section on 'Ground' in the *Science of Logic*, every 'coming into existence' of an entity depends on a moment of irreducible contingency, a 'groundless ground' that retroactively integrates the conditions for this entity into a causal chain. Although the existence of a thing or the occurrence of an event depends on a set of conditions, these conditions do not make the event necessary. The only reason for something to happen is, ultimately, just the fact that it happened, or what Meillassoux calls facticity. But after the event has happened or the thing has come into existence, its conditions become a necessary part of its causal explanation. In this way, Hegel allows for contingency while also explaining the obvious existence of causes in empirical reality, something which one can say Meillassoux fails to do.

Finally, it could be argued that both Meillassoux and Hegel abolish the difference between the world as it appears to us and the world as it is in itself in order to show that thought can think the absolute. Meillassoux's argument is the following: the correlationist claims that we can only know things as they appear to us, not as they are in themselves. But in order to make this distinction, while at the same time escaping idealism, the correlationist has to admit that the laws of logic and nature could really be otherwise than they are. For Meillassoux, this shows that there is no unknowable in-itself that serves as a reason or ground for the world we experience. The facticity of the given is all there is: 'there is nothing beneath or beyond the manifest gratuitousness of the given – nothing but the limitless and lawless power of its destruction, emergence or persistence' (*AF*, 63).

This, however, is also Hegel's approach, to show that there is no mysterious 'essential' world lying behind the given, but that what appears to us is the world in itself. The separation between thought and reality is, according to Hegel, a necessary illusion, born of the frustrations we experience in exercising our limited capacity for knowledge and action. Hegel thinks that we can overcome scepticism by showing its origin in the development of consciousness, and that philosophy can achieve self-transparency of method, which allows it to think the world as it is in itself while at the same time retroactively justifying and securing its own procedure. Through a very different line of reasoning, the points of convergence and divergence of which remain to be explored, Hegel and Meillassoux thus work toward the same aim, which, in typically Hegelian fashion, Meillassoux invokes in the last words of *After Finitude*: the reconciliation of thought and absolute (*AF*, 128).

HEIDEGGER, MARTIN

Marie-Eve Morin

For Meillassoux, the German philosopher Martin Heidegger is one of the chief representatives of strong **correlationism**. In *Being and Time*, Heidegger seeks to raise anew the question of the meaning of Being. He looks for the horizon in terms of which Being itself can be understood. Heidegger sees it as necessary to put ontology, the study of beings *qua* beings, on a secure footing. Heidegger first turns to an analytic of Dasein, that is, to a study of this entity that does not just happen to be but that also displays, in its relation to all entities (including itself), an understanding of Being that allows it to relate meaningfully to what it encounters. In seeking to analyse the ontological constitution of Dasein, Heidegger hopes to gain insight not only into Being, that is, into the givenness or intelligibility of entities in so far as they are encountered or understood, but also into the givenness of this intelligibility itself, the givenness of givenness if one will.

Here, Heidegger's **correlationism** is evident. For Heidegger Being is only in so far as there is a Dasein that relates meaningfully to entities, and Dasein is only in so far as it displays this essential relation to Being. In a similar way, the world *is* only in so far as Dasein exists, because the world is neither the sum total of entities nor their container, but the coherent milieu wherein Dasein assigns itself to a possibility of being (for example, house building) and through that assignment lights up some entities or lets them be encountered in one way rather than another. Truth also exists only in so far as Dasein is, since the uncoveredness of entities that serves as the basis for a true assertion is dependent upon Dasein's understanding of Being, which lets these entities manifest themselves. Hence, as Heidegger will say, Newton's laws were not true before Newton's discovery, but neither were they false. Rather, it is Newton's assertion of the laws of motion that made entities accessible as obeying (and as having always obeyed) these laws.

Nevertheless, Heidegger is clear that, while Dasein is the condition of the appearance or manifestation of entities, these entities are in themselves the beings that they are even when there is no Dasein. Reality, and not real things, is dependent on Dasein. This means that something can only manifest itself as real, that is, in its independence from Dasein, for a Dasein that can let the entity be encountered as what it is in itself. Furthermore, Dasein's unveiling of entities does not mean that they are merely subjective, but rather that Dasein, because it is not bound to entities but transcends them, is thrown forth or opens a world or a space of meaning in which entities are freed to be encountered. Our being-free for the manifestation of beings allows these beings to be binding for us, to be the measure of our comportments and assertions.

After *Being and Time*, Heidegger will abandon the transcendental-horizonal way of asking about the meaning of Being because it tends to represent this horizon in an objectifying way as something present that is projected by human beings. Heidegger realised that this horizon is temporal and hence includes an essentially hidden, unpresentable side. Despite this change, Heidegger's fundamental question remains the same: how to think the truth/manifestation not of entities, but of Being itself as the source of the meaningfulness (light, intelligibility) of entities. Being itself is now thought as *Ereignis*, the 'event' that appropriates the human being for Being, throws the human being into the clearing of Being and calls upon it to sustain or projectively hold open this opening. Heidegger's correlationism remains unchanged: he will say that Being needs the human while the human being belongs to Being.

HUME, DAVID

Jeffrey Bell

The philosophy of David Hume plays an important role in the argument of *After Finitude*, where the entire fourth of five chapters is devoted to what Meillassoux calls Hume's problem. Traditionally this problem is known as the problem of induction. Meillassoux refers to one of the oft-cited passages from the *Treatise*, where this problem becomes most evident – namely, the passage where Hume points out that there is nothing in the nature of the billiard balls themselves that *necessitates* where the struck ball will go once hit. There is nothing contradictory about the ball going in any of an infinite number of other possible directions. What leads us to the expectation that the ball will go where it does is that relative to the totality and set of experiences one has had with respect to billiard balls, one outcome is more likely than any of the others. If the ball were to go in an unexpected direction, then we would look for a reason to account for this. It is the totality of states of affairs that provides us with the reason that explains any given outcome.

To offer another example, if you were to encounter a random person at the store, you would think nothing of it. Given the totality of one's experiences, this happens every time you go to the store. If you encountered this person again an hour later at a completely different store, you might note the coincidence. But if such random, chance encounters were to continue you would eventually remove from consideration the explanation that they were random encounters and claim that there is another reason to explain them – namely, you are being stalked. It is only in relationship to the totality of one's experiences that one is provided with a reasonable explanation for why something is or is not the way it is.

With this Humean understanding of how we go about providing reasons for that which appears, Meillassoux is a short argumentative step away from reaching the central conclusion of *After Finitude*: to wit, the rejection of the **principle of sufficient reason** and the affirmation of the **necessity of contingency**. If the explanations in terms of necessity and contingency both rely upon a totality or set of all experiences, and if we eliminate the possibility of a totality, then we likewise do away with the capacity to provide such explanations. This is precisely what Meillassoux does. Drawing from the theory of the non-All of Georg **Cantor's set theory**, which is itself a necessary conclusion of **mathematics**, Meillassoux is led to his ultimate conclusion that the principle of sufficient reason is false and hence that only contingency itself is necessary. Nothing has a reason for being rather than not being.

Despite the importance of Hume's arguments in the build-up to Meillassoux's general conclusions, Hume's arguments themselves do not rely upon the totality or set of one's experiences, and in fact Hume's approach problematises such arguments in that the very notion of identity itself, whether of an individual or a totality of individuals, is one of the key problems and concerns of Hume's philosophy (and it has received significant attention from Hume scholars as well). In the case of the billiard balls discussed above, it is a synthesis of the mind based upon the resemblance of particular impressions that does the heavy lifting in Hume's arguments, not the relationship of these syntheses to a totality. Such syntheses, however, do not give us necessity for Hume but account for our belief in necessity, which may well be misguided. It is with Immanuel **Kant** more than Hume that the importance of a totality of syntheses becomes a problem (see Kant's antinomies of pure reason). Meillassoux's turn to Hume is a good strategic move, though it reflects Meillassoux's philosophical agenda more than it does Hume's philosophy (and perhaps that is as it should be).

HYPER-CHAOS

Robert Jackson

Hyper-chaos is one of the names for Meillassoux's primary **absolute** and is used when he wishes to convey its force or power. It resembles 'the eternal and lawless possible becoming of every law' (*AF*, 64). As Meillassoux notes, this conception of absolute is not exactly welcoming. He dubs our grasping of it a Pyrrhic victory (*AF*, 64). Unlike the traditional attributes of an absolute, hyper-chaos doesn't provide us with an orderly foundation or even an ethical standard. Since it is autonomous and indifferent anything can happen, without reason, without law, and without purpose. There is no higher law to govern its reach. Moreover, it cannot be described as anything fluid, such as flux or becoming, since this would be to misunderstand the scope of its power: even becoming is contingent when it comes to hyper-chaos. The possibility of the world emerging in complete stasis is entirely possible; as is the most frenetic degree of activity.

This seems paradoxical. For if reality is hyper-chaotic why does it not appear as such? From the vantage point of thought, causation seems stable enough, or at least stable enough to retain my experience of consistency. My fingers do not suddenly turn into wood, nor does the standard model of physics change incessantly over time, destroying the quantum framework of everything. It certainly appears that laws do not change, and we can provide recurring accurate predictions on this basis, that is, until our fallibility demands a new law to explain certain contingencies. Meillassoux's answer is to point to the consequences of the principle of **factiality**. In doing so, factiality provides an alternative to the sceptical (David **Hume**) and transcendental (Immanuel **Kant**) approaches to why thought has no knowledge of any necessary connection between certain events occurring. What Hume and Kant failed to challenge was their unquestioned positing of an unfathomable reason behind causation, and they also failed to unify contingent events with stable ones, that is, how stable events such as thought and matter emerge from such a putative hyper-chaos. If we know there is no necessary reason supporting such stability, thought need not attempt incessantly to grasp a cause for it. Rather it should accept the knowledge of an acausal absolute.

Meillassoux argues that the stable universe that we experience must be the result of hyper-chaos and that it is only by way of contingency that laws are stable. If hyper-chaos continued to emerge with frequently stable laws, it would make sense that one inferred the existence of a necessary reason. Yet, this does not disqualify the indeterminate nature of those laws when discussing the world 'in-itself' and so it would be a mistake to suggest that they are necessary. This is not to say that necessary laws are replaced by other necessary laws. Instead, hyper-chaos is defined by the lack of any totalisable grand law of necessity, apart from contingency alone, to ground ontology. Meillassoux concedes that **laws of nature** do occur within hyper-chaos, but they do not define the law of hyper-chaos, which has no law.

$$\boxed{\text{I}}$$

IDEOLOGY

Paul J. Ennis

Meillassoux links metaphysical necessity with ideology. The ideological standpoint is to assert that some state of affairs must be one way and cannot be otherwise. There are many entities that can gain credence from their association with metaphysical necessity which he defines in this context as 'the pretension of proving the existence of a necessary God ... which, in turn, leads to the upholding of the necessity of natural laws in our world or of any other kind of entity for that matter' (*IWB*, 445–6). Meillassoux's own ideological commitments are not always made clear, but a subtle undercurrent of Marxism runs throughout his work. For instance, he tells us that the **fourth World of justice** will resemble Marx's vision of a life without politics ('*a communist life*', *IWB*, 473, his emphasis).

IMMANENCE

Jeffrey Bell

As traditionally understood, immanence is how the nature of the reality of this world is characterised such that it does not depend upon anything other than this reality itself – that is, anything that transcends it. Plato's forms, for example, transcend the particular objects of this world and these objects depend upon the transcendent forms in order to be the objects they are – the form 'horseness' is the transcendent reality that determines whether or not a particular object is a horse. Aristotle's forms, by contrast, are immanent to the particular objects that embody these forms, although the dependency relationship, and hence transcendence, persists within Aristotle's thought as well. It is Spinoza who is generally considered to be the philosopher who pushed the philosophy of immanence to its most radical conclusions. In his famous statement *Deus sive Natura* (God or Nature), Spinoza is arguing that there is no transcendent reality, that nature is all there is and nothing, not even God, transcends it.

In his essay, 'The Immanence of the World Beyond', Meillassoux challenges some of the key assumptions of this traditional view of immanence. As Meillassoux states it, 'immanence is not of this world' (*IWB*, 468). On first blush, this may appear to be simply placing an immanence label on a bottle of transcendence. The reasoning behind this move, however, is that it is precisely the perspective of our biological lives in this world that places us in the context of forever thinking what is after or beyond this life. It is the perspective of finitude that leads us, ineluctably, to transcendence. The awareness of our being-towards-death as Martin **Heidegger** understood it, for example, does not result in an affirmation of immanence. Rather for Meillassoux death on this view remains that which forever eludes our grasp. In short, the recognition of our primordial finitude in Heidegger's sense draws upon a relation to that which exceeds and transcends our grasp, and hence the perspective of worldly finitude brings transcendence onto the scene.

What about Spinoza and his radical affirmation of the infinite nature of an immanent substance? For Meillassoux the answer to this question hinges upon how one understands the relationship between immanence and this life. In this context, Meillassoux argues that it is Nietzsche who truly grasps the relationship between this life and immanence when he puts forth the idea of **eternal recurrence**. The experience of eternal recurrence, Meillassoux argues, is 'not the experience of death but of immortality' (*IWB*, 468). On Meillassoux's reading this is not an immortality of a life beyond this life, a life that continues on after this life has ended, but is the continuation without end of this very life, and in all its 'prosaic' everydayness as Meillassoux puts it (*IWB*, 469). It is this attitude that is beyond the 'this-worldly' perspective in that it no longer embraces the finitude of this life but instead affirms the infinitude and absolute nature of this life and all that is. Meillassoux thus concludes, apropos Spinoza and Nietzsche, that, 'Only he who can bear the idea of this one and only life which is constantly recast in its "prosaic-ness" without any hope of escaping via the transcendent or nothingness, experiences radical immanence' (*IWB*, 469).

Meillassoux's understanding of immanence follows directly from his thesis regarding **hyper-chaos** and the **necessity of contingency** that follows from it. Key to Meillassoux's position is his rejection of the **prin-**

ciple of sufficient reason (PSR). For Spinoza, the PSR is integral, for if nature could be other than the way it is then it would be limited and determined by the modal possibility that it is not, which contradicts Spinoza's affirmation of an absolutely infinite substance – namely, God or Nature. Since all determination entails negation for Spinoza, an absolutely infinite substance cannot be other than what it is for then it becomes limited by the possibility of what it is not. Spinoza's philosophy of immanence is therefore fundamentally tied to affirming the PSR.

It is precisely the concern for substance being other than what it is that Meillassoux rejects. In fact, a pivotal consequence of the rejection of the PSR is that there is no reason at all for nature being or not being the way it is. Key to this argument is the **principle of non-contradiction**. Spinozist monism, for example, is a consequence of the law of non-contradiction in that if we propose more than one absolutely infinite substance then this would mean that this absolutely infinite substance is limited by a substance that it is not, and hence it is not absolutely infinite after all. Since this violates the law of non-contradiction the initial proposal must be false and thus there is only one absolutely infinite substance. Meillassoux also calls upon the law of non-contradiction but what supports it for him is the very possibility that each and every thing could be other than it is, and for no reason, including, somewhat paradoxically, the law of non-contradiction itself. Without the PSR, we cannot provide a rational ground for the impossibility of a contradictory being, but if we were to presuppose such a contradictory being then it would become a necessary being for it would always already entail what it is not. We could never imagine or think of a thing as not being its other, for as a contradictory entity it would always already involve its contradictory opposite. A consequence of the thesis regarding the necessity of contingency, therefore, is Meillassoux's argument for the law of non-contradiction, and one that does not rely upon the PSR, as does Spinoza.

For immanence to be beyond this world, therefore, is not for it to be a possibility other than the actuality of this life, but rather radical immanence is for life to have no reason that limits it to being or not being the life or thing that it is. It is this radical equaliser of hyper-chaos and unreason that comes in the wake of the absence of the PSR that brings us to immanence. This was precisely the core insight of Nietzsche's eternal recurrence and it is the true meaning of radical immanence according to Meillassoux.

Immanence, however, need not presuppose the radical unreason of a hyper-chaos that is the necessity that everything has no reason for being or not being. Crucial to this conclusion was Meillassoux's response to David **Hume**'s problem, whereby if we drop reference to a totality or set of possibilities, then the explanatory power of the modal distinction between necessity and contingency vanishes and we are left with radical, necessary contingency. From here Meillassoux derives the principle of non-contradiction and his understanding of radical immanence. Meillassoux's approach presupposes two key elements: first, it requires a notion of the **non-whole** that is irreducible to a determinate all or totality (or set thereof); and secondly it requires a principle of exclusive disjunction, or the law of non-contradiction and the related law of the excluded middle. These key notions provide the planks upon which Meillassoux builds his theory of immanence, **immortality**, the infinite and the **absolute**. Another option remains, however, and that is the constructivist approach as found in some contemporary mathematicians and philosophers (Deleuze belongs in this camp). A common strategy in this approach is to use infinitesimals and other related notions in order to provide for a radical PSR that provides a reason for things but not one reducible to any determinate reason for why things are or are not the things they are. This approach, likewise, will affirm a radical immanence of nature, a nature irreducible to the determinate world of this life. Hence this is in line with Meillassoux's arguments, but it will *not* affirm an immanence beyond this world if this is intended, as Meillassoux intends it, to initiate a disjunctive dualism between radical immanence and its determinate other.

IMMORTALITY

Paul O'Mahoney

Immortality as it has been conceived in mythical or metaphysical speculation is not as straightforward as might be imagined. The most unqualified form of immortality is that attributed to gods conceived of as eternal beings. Eternity implies that the deity has always existed and thus is uncreated, and is, technically, outside of time, rendering its nature, in many traditions, inaccessible to human reason. An eternal being may be distinguished from a sempiternal being, which is one created in time but potentially immortal; many archaic gods such as Dionysus, with a popular birth story, would technically be sempiternal. However, this immortality is not unqualified or unconditional. A vampire, for example, is immortal under certain conditions, but can be killed (and would not survive, for example, the total destruction of its environment). Angels are sempiternal beings that are created by God but immortal; the same goes for those promised **resurrection** and afterlife by their religions. Even in these cases, however, the immortality remains conditional: because it is granted by a superior, eternal being and creator, it can conceivably be revoked by the same. In almost every conception of immortality, the quality of deathlessness is combined with agelessness. The Cumaean Sybil in Ovid is the most prominent mythical figure granted immortality but who continued to age, having forgotten to ask for eternal youth. Early Christian theologians overcame the problem posed by the curious faithful – that many in heaven would be decrepit and old, while others remain as dependent newborns – through a novel solution stating that everybody granted resurrection would have the healthy body they had or would have had at the age of thirty-three, the age at which Christ died.

Immortality becomes important for Meillassoux in his elaboration and resolution of the **spectral dilemma**, which emphatically opposes traditional, religious visions of immortality. An essential spectre is the victim of a **death** who cannot be mourned due to its horrendous, senseless or unjust nature, and who therefore haunts the living. The mourning of such spectres would be 'essential grief', but this is impossible from either an atheist or religious position (*IWB*, 451–2). The religious position claims that life is unendurable in light of such deaths if there is no benevolent God to resurrect and compensate them; the atheist responds that such a God is whimsical and unjust to have allowed such deaths originally, and a common fate of nothingness awaiting both the ordinary and spectral dead is preferable to Him. Meillassoux thus must combine the hope in resurrection and justice for the spectres with the inexistence of God. This is done through his positing **divine inexistence**: God does not exist at all, but there is no logical reason, given the omnipotence of **hyper-chaos** and the invalidity of the **principle of sufficient reason**, that such a God might not come into being.

The immortality granted the resurrected dead would not be unqualified or final: it would constitute an eternal possibility or 'eternal eventuality', which hyper-chaos could subsequently cancel. Meillassoux coins the term 'eschaology' (*IWB*, 463), an **eschatology** in a world dominated by hyper-chaos, to describe hope for the advent of this potential **fourth World of justice** and argues that such hope must inform practical ethics and politics: if the world into which the dead were to be reborn were dismal, their resurrection would only compound and not repair the original injustice; this 'ethic of immortality' (*IWB*, 444), which makes possible essential grieving, ultimately mandates a transcendence of the political, whereby we 'love life beyond war, violence and sacrifice' (*IWB*, 473): those who desire this immortality for the dead, reborn in a world where their basic material needs are met, Meillassoux calls 'vectorial subjects', and claims their 'vectorization' equates to a 'magnetic' attraction to universal justice (*IWB*, 463).

INTELLECTUAL INTUITION

Daniel Sacilotto

In its original, Kantian formulation, intellectual intuition designates a possible apprehension of an object or entity that does not depend on sensible receptivity. For Immanuel **Kant**, this power is contrasted with the finite intuition of the human subject, for which all apprehension of being must remain submitted to the receptivity of the senses, and which thus anchors the subject on a reality which the subject did not itself produce. In contrast, the intellectual intuition attributed to God's infinite mind conveys the idea of a thought that is immediately productive of its object. Thus, unlike the human mind, God's mind is not separated from things-in-themselves; his thought of the thing produces the thing itself, and so the gap between thought and being that accounts for the subject's enclosure in the world of appearances does not obtain. In its subsequent elaboration throughout the history of **German Idealism**, intellectual intuition is postulated as required in order to ground even the subject's knowledge of itself and the objects of experience. Canonically **Fichte** proposes that the grounding principle of human knowledge consists in the intellectual intuition of the free subject itself, as necessarily grounding the identity of the agent on whose basis every knowledge is acquired. And yet, since this ground is not itself an empirical datum yielded by sensory experience, it is thereby identified as the pure practical power of the subject to identify itself as the agent of every positing, as the condition of possibility even for our apprehension of appearances.

In his own appropriation of the idea, Meillassoux attempts to wrest the thesis of intellectual intuition from its idealist and correlationist iterations, so as to adapt it for his **speculative materialism**. In the first instance, it is supposed to be coeval with our grasp of the facticity of the correlation as given, which Meillassoux then uses to derive the contingency of being itself. In a next step, intellectual intuition would be essentially connected to the rationalist thesis that, following Alain **Badiou**, proposes to reactivate the distinction between primary and secondary properties in the way of trying to think the absolute. More specifically, Meillassoux follows Badiou's ontologisation of **mathematics**, and claims that it is through mathematics that we are capable of grasping primary properties that pertain to being-in-itself, in so far as mathematical discourse thinks its objects without appeals to phenomenological givenness, and so irrespective of any experiential relation to a given subject. Put differently, mathematics thinks the absolute precisely in so far as it thinks being *qua* being, by rendering any subjective or phenomenological mediation trivial, and with it any problematic concerning the representation of being by thought. Consequentially, Meillassoux holds that mathematical discourse provides an intellectual intuition into the structure of being, and allows us to grasp the reality of an absolute no longer limited to the domain of subjective agency (as it is for idealists) or to the agency of a divine intellect (as it is for correlationists).

Fundamentally, Meillassoux must thereby tether his account of facticity, which is foundational for the proof of the principle of **factiality** and the **necessity of contingency** of all beings, to the possibility of such an intellectual intuition into the structure of being through mathematical discourse. In other words, the contingency of being that is supposed to be the result of Meillassoux's speculative proof for a materialist absolute must be compatible with the thesis that mathematics thinks being *qua* being. Already in *After Finitude*, Meillassoux announces:

We must project unreason into the thing itself, and discover in our grasp of facticity the veritable intellectual intuition of the absolute. 'Intuition', since it is well and truly in *what is* that we discover a contingency with no bounds other than itself; 'intellectual', since this contingency is nothing visible, nothing perceptible in the thing: only thought can access it as it accesses the Chaos which underlies the apparent continuities of phenomena. (*AF*, 111)

Yet, although the 'arbitrariness of the **meaningless sign**' seems to provide for Meillassoux a first clue as to how mathematics proper can think being's contingency in the desired sense, the integration of these two aspects of the speculative materialist programme remains merely a promissory note for the moment. In this respect, Ray **Brassier** has levelled the critique that Meillassoux's appeals to intellectual intuition threaten to vitiate the stringency of the materialism he proposes against the transcendental closure of correlationist philosophies (Brassier 2007: Chapter 3). According to Brassier, Meillassoux's appeals to intellectual intuition surreptitiously continue to depend on an irreducible distinction between the realm of meaning and that of being, and the transcendence of the latter with respect to the former. For Meillassoux must explain how it is that the thought that 'everything is contingent' is not itself a contingent factum, lest it fall into the contradictory position according to which even contingency is contingent.

To insist on this difference, Meillassoux must appeal to a distinction between the meaning of the statement declaring the contingency of being, and the fact of the contingency of being. Yet it is precisely this dimension of Meillassoux's discourse that, Brassier argues, delivers Meillassoux right back into the transcendental trap of postulating a gap between thought and being. Furthermore, this is a one for which the thesis of intellectual intuition seems to work as a palliative that cannot but ultimately render the contingency of being dependent on the factical determinations of thought, which is the thesis that speculative materialism has sworn to abjure. For reactivating the transcendental split between being and thought can only secure access to the former by according to the self-reflexive subject an exceptional ontological status.

IRRELIGION

Leon Niemoczynski

Irreligion is a speculative condition required for access to the divine. Irreligion's opposite is **fideism**, characteristic of a postmodern religiosity that critiques absolutes instead of speculating upon the **absolute**. In other words, against fideism, Meillassoux states that only through 'thought about the absolute, not a critique of absolutes' is access to the divine possible (*IWB*, 444). The challenge of irreligion, Meillassoux claims, is to consider an **eschatology** of **immortality**. This immortality is associated with the possible future appearance of a divine being and its **resurrection** of the dead. Hence one strives for a philosophy of **immanence** that attains not to finite knowledge, as in postmodernism, but to knowledge 'after' **finitude**, not just to the gods of the masses but to the nature of the true gods (*IWB*, 450).

In 'The Immanence of the World Beyond', Meillassoux's main target is post-Kantian transcendental (and no longer speculative) philosophy. Meillassoux claims that 'irreligiosity' ought to stand against those post-Kantian philosophers who 'prohibit the right of access' to the real or absolute in favour of a 'defense of rights to belief' about the real (*IWB*, 449). The outcome of defending 'rights to belief' over speculative access entails preserving an unthinkable transcendence that is beyond the limits of knowledge. Meillassoux claims that since the philosophy of Immanuel **Kant**, a restriction upon the rights of reason has only increased, resulting in today's postmodern anti-metaphysical philosophy, making Kant a distant forefather of postmodernism. The restriction of reason has made possible the recent Continental return to religion wherein all truths reign equally and thought or reason is left without power to 'determine with complete impunity our relationship to the absolute' (*IWB*, 450). Thus, postmodernism has secured religious fideism in place of speculation.

Meillassoux states that in its current postmodern form, religious fideism is best evidenced by the 'weak thought' of Gianni Vattimo. According to

Vattimo, the end of **metaphysics** allows a decisive return to religious concern, since 'no one can seriously argue that we can know that God does not exist' (*IWB*, 450). Here, however, Vattimo prohibits any speculative access by enabling a 'de-absolutization' of knowledge. That is, Vattimo follows Kant in placing sceptical or critical limits upon knowledge but also secures those limits with the very open-endedness of possible hermeneutical interpretation. Meillassoux claims that this move opens the floodgates for relativism as we can know nothing absolutely of God, whether God's existence or non-existence. While postmodern fideism promotes a piety concerning that which is unknown, Meillassoux claims that this is not an 'immanent' form of piety concerning what is truly possible or what *is* truly in potential, that is, the **virtual**. Meillassoux's irreligious standpoint advocates for the unbounded limits of speculation and reason, to speculate upon the absolute and its contingent conditions that may issue a future divine being. This requires a standpoint returning to the immanent, though it would be an immanence that is of a world beyond, namely the **fourth World of justice**.

KANT, IMMANUEL

Steven Shaviro

Immanuel Kant (1724–1804) is not the inventor of what Meillassoux calls **correlationism**, but he is its central and most important figure. For it is Kant's *Critique of Pure Reason* (1781) that decrees, once and for all, that, as Meillassoux puts it, 'we only ever have access to the correlation between thinking and being, and never to either term considered apart from the other' (*AF*, 5). Or in Kant's own words, 'thoughts without content are empty, intuitions without concepts are blind' (A51/B76).

Kant sought to resolve the great philosophical impasse of his day: the confrontation between rationalist philosophies derived from Leibniz, on the one hand, and the sceptical, empiricist thought of David **Hume**, on the other. On one side, there was the dogmatic claim that the world could be understood through reason alone; on the other side, the doubt that we could know anything beyond the limited data provided to us by our senses. Kant resolved the impasse by declaring that neither thought alone nor intuitions (sense-data) alone were sufficient for knowledge. Rather, Kant says, the two must always come together. He proposes a compromise, or a compact, between rational necessity and existential contingency.

For Kant, phenomena (the facts of experience) are contingent, and can only be learned through experience. To this extent, the empiricists are correct. But these facts of experience must nevertheless fit together rationally and coherently, in ways that **empiricism** itself cannot account for. For instance, phenomena always have a location in time and space, and they always follow the rules of cause and effect. As Hume pointed out, we do not ever directly experience causality itself. Rather, causality, like spatial and temporal location, is always already presupposed by whatever experiences we *do* undergo. Kant argues that, since these presuppositions do not exist in things themselves, they must be imposed upon experience by the activity of our own minds. In this sense, the rationalist followers of Leibniz are also partly correct. There is a rational ordering to the world that we experience. But the order which the rationalist philosophers attributed to the world itself in fact *only* applies to the world *as we experience it*. Things in themselves, apart from our experience of them, are radically unknowable. We can say that they exist, but we cannot say anything particular about them. As Meillassoux puts it, after Kant 'necessity is never absolute, but only ever for us' (*AF*, 31).

The outcome of Kant's great compromise is therefore double. We can have rational certainty about phenomena or about things as they exist *for us*. But the price we pay for this certainty is that we have no access whatsoever to things-in-themselves, or to things as they exist independently from us. Whenever a Kantian thinker hears a statement about the world itself, Meillassoux says, 'he will simply add – perhaps only to himself, but add it he will – something like a simple codicil, always the same one, which he will discretely append to the end of the phrase: event Y occurred x number of years before the emergence of humans – *for humans*' (*AF*, 13). There will be no getting away from this addition. After Kant, we are forever trapped within the correlational circle.

Kant describes his own thought as a **Copernican Revolution** in philosophy, a reorganisation of our very understanding of the universe. But Meillassoux suggests that Kant's Critical philosophy is rather a **Ptolemaic counter-revolution**. Recentring the universe around the human mind is much like recentring it around the Earth. Kant guarantees the objectivity and rationality of physical science only by 'revoking' all the 'non-correlational knowledge' that such science might provide (*AF*, 118). Meillassoux therefore identifies Kantian critique as a 'catastrophe' for thought, one that 'consists in renouncing every kind of absolute along with every variety of metaphysics' (*AF*, 125). Nonetheless, Meillassoux does not think that we can simply dismiss or ignore Kant. It is no longer possible 'to regress to a merely dogmatic position', such as existed in philosophy before the Kantian revolution (*AF*, 8). Kant indeed established, once and for all, 'the disqualification of every argument intended to establish the absolute necessity of an entity' (*AF*, 51). This is why Meillassoux, in his quest to discover a new sort of absolute knowledge, insists that we can only escape the correlationist circle by working through it, and pushing it to its utmost consequences. It is only by way of such a process that Meillassoux is able to establish 'the only absolute necessity available to non-dogmatic speculation – the necessity for everything that is to be a fact' – the necessity, therefore, that everything be contingent (*AF*, 79). Meillassoux does not refute Kant's correlational argument, so much as he establishes that this argument, or the correlational circle that it establishes, is itself necessarily contingent.

LARUELLE, FRANÇOIS

Anthony Paul Smith

François Laruelle (b. 1937) is a French philosopher who since the early 1980s has been developing the syntax and methods for what he claims is a new practice of philosophy. He has called this project 'non-philosophy' and most recently 'non-standard philosophy'. While the names often lead readers to confuse Laruelle's claims with those who proclaim the 'end of philosophy', Laruelle is explicit that the term 'non-philosophy' does not signify a negation of philosophy. Taking non-Euclidean geometry as his model, Laruelle holds that a completed non-philosophy would be the generalisation of philosophy just as non-Euclidean geometry is not the negation of geometry but instead broadens the practice of geometry through the selective suspension of some of the axioms underlying Euclidean geometry. Laruelle's project attempts to broaden philosophy's practice through the negation of what he calls the principle of sufficient philosophy: for whatever there is, there is a philosophy that can capture it within thought. Like non-Euclidean geometry, Laruelle carries out this negation of philosophy's principle of self-sufficiency through a change of axiom.

Whereas Laruelle claims all standard philosophies are predicated upon either thinking Being or Alterity, non-philosophy attempts to think *from* a radical identity that philosophy is unable to think *of*. This radical identity takes various names, though primarily referred to as 'the One' and 'the Real'. These names are chosen for their highly abstract character in order to signal that radical identity cannot be philosophically represented without erasing the identity by relating the One or the Real to Being or Alterity, thereby erasing the radical nature of this identity. Laruelle attempts to show how this change in axiom allows for two complimentary projects: a 'science of philosophy' and the fostering of a 'democracy (of) thought'. The first refers to the ability to treat philosophy as an object with an identity that can be described. This flows into the second, which refers to the idea that philosophy can be treated as one material equal amongst others before the Real or the One. This, for Laruelle, opens up to a more productive relationship between philosophy and science and other regimes of knowledge.

Laruelle's non-philosophy is presented by Ray **Brassier** in his *Nihil Unbound* as a corrective to Meillassoux's appeal to 'intellectual intuition' in his **speculative materialism**. Meillassoux responds to this in his contribution to the Speculative Realism event held at Goldsmiths in April of 2007 by contrasting his and Laruelle's readings of Fichte. While Laruelle described his project in its early phases as a 'transcendental realism', in recent years he has spoken of being in favour of the Real rather than realism. Meillassoux charges Laruelle precisely on this point with an inability to respond to **correlationism**. On Meillassoux's reading Laruelle's Real is merely posited by a philosopher rather than expressed in-itself. As Meillassoux claims mathematical qualities provide the in-itself (see **Cartesian in-itself**) he sees Laruelle's discursively posited Real as unable to respond to the varieties of the correlationist argument that confuses to different degrees being and thought.

LAWS OF NATURE

Fintan Neylan

Perhaps one of the better known facts about **speculative materialism** is that it conceives the laws of nature to be contingent, subject to possible change. However, what is less known is that Meillassoux conceives them as contingent *yet stable* laws. He advances such laws as a response the core question of *After Finitude*: how is the discourse of the mathematical sciences possible? Along with clarifying mathematical discourse about ancestrality, to answer this question demands an account of the stability found in the universe, for it is on the basis of this regularity that the sciences can postulate their various predictive theories.

Because the **arche-fossil** shows that the literal sense of the mathematical sciences' discourse cannot be admitted within the framework of **correlationism**, clarifying how it is possible requires we find an alternative route to that taken by philosophy influenced by the Kantian legacy. This compels one to reconceive completely the apparent law-like regularity that we find in the universe, for to reject Kant is to relinquish his nuanced critical account of why the world around us appears to be ordered. With the critical route barred, one is left to think the regularity of the universe as the result of mind-independent laws, but this is a path that has traditionally posited such laws as necessary and eternal entities. This might be a problem for Meillassoux, for one of the core tenets of *After Finitude* is that a necessary entity is not possible. But while he refers to his programme as classical, speculative materialism does not consist in a dogmatic embrace of the traditional account of eternally fixed mind-independent laws. Rather, in reformatting the account of the laws into one where they are not backed up by any necessity, factial ontology claims to offer an alternative to both the metaphysical and critical accounts of the order found in nature.

The thesis that the laws of nature, along with every other entity, are absolutely contingent occupies the first part of *After Finitude*. It rests on the argument that **contingency** is intellectual rather than phenomenal. While **factiality** holds that the laws of nature are immanent and contingent, Meillassoux still admits that it is impossible to phenomenally discern whether we exist in a world governed by necessary rules or one governed ultimately by lawless chaos. This impossibility lies in the fact that for every apparently chaotic occurrence we might discover, there may be operative a hidden law to which we have been blind. Yet despite this limitation of the empirical, it is still always conceivable that things may be otherwise. As his analysis of strong correlationism shows, this ability to conceive otherwise is not due to our finitude, but is provided to us by the fact that we can grasp contingency as the **absolute**. This ability to grasp the world in its contingency is named as the 'modicum' of the absolute which we possess. To speculate is to accede to this absolute, meaning that regardless of our empirical limits, by way of this 'modicum' we may recognise the absence of necessity in any situation. Through this speculative capacity, even apparently necessary laws can be grasped in their ontological contingency.

Having established their contingency, difficulties arise with the qualification that contingent laws may also be stable. The main obstacle posed is the thesis from probabilistic reasoning that one can allow for contingent laws or stable laws, but not both. Tackling this challenge takes up the bulk of *After Finitude's* latter half, and it is only surmounted by demonstrating that the means by which we derive this stable contingent status is beyond the scope of probability's logic.

This objection runs as follows: if the laws of nature are contingent, why have they not changed? For every moment that the laws do not alter, the fact that they are contingent seems all the less likely. Given the undeniable stability of the world around us, probabilistic reasoning states that it is far more feasible that there is a hidden necessity operative that we have yet to discover. In order to undermine this argument that some form of ontological necessity can be assumed from probability, Meillassoux takes pains to show that the logic of probability is limited to the phenomenal. Herein lies his utilisation of **set theory**. He draws upon it to show that probability cannot be used to make any ontological statement about the universe and its possibilities. This limit of probability restricts it from either advancing laws' probable necessity or disqualifying their contingency. While it is applicable to particular closed cases within the universe, his use of mathematics shows we have no grounds to make the assumption that probability can be extended to the universe and necessity in general. In relation to laws, mathematics serves two purposes in *After Finitude*, with the first being this rejection of probable necessity, including the implication that stability entails a hidden necessity. Through it Meillassoux establishes that probability can determine nothing about entities' nature in general, that is, their ontological contingency. But by his own admission, establishing this does not positively prove that the laws are stable, only that it is thus both conceivable and not unreasonable that there be contingent yet stable laws operative in the universe. Having fought off *a priori* disqualifications of the possibility of laws that are both contingent and stable, Meillassoux turns to outlining a positive account of laws by introducing a condition on mind-independent existence: if the laws of nature are to exist, they must exist as stable entities. This qualification demands that a law is not subject to flux for the duration of its existence, even though its existence is subject to the radical contingency of chaos. For as long as a law exists in a possible world, it will exist as stable, thereby maintaining a minimum amount of regularity that a science of that world would require. Yet even this qualification still does not establish their existence. This point is to be accomplished as part of his strategy of deriving what he calls **figures**, invariant truths which hold across all possible worlds. As conditions of **hyper-chaos**, these allow a non-metaphysical account of mind-independence. The stability of laws is supposed to be entailed by one such Figure, namely, the ability of mathematics to make statements that pertain to the in-itself (see **Cartesian in-itself**). Proving it would open a third route to account for stable laws: not a result of metaphysical necessity or a transcendental subject, they are guaranteed by the absolute scope of mathematics being a condition of chaos.

Demonstrating the possibility of mathematical sciences thus relies on the proof of this second purpose of mathematics; as well as enabling science's ancestral discourse, it also accounts for the contingent order found in the universe. But by Meillassoux's own admission, *After Finitude* does not accomplish this task. While it does outline various requirements for an alternate framework which accounts for the order found in the world, the derivation of mathematics' absolute scope and the framework of laws this would entail is reserved for a later work. In terms of its accomplishments, *After Finitude* opens the door for contingent laws, ones which would account for the stability of the phenomenal world; but in the absence of a proof such laws can only be as one possibility among others.

MALLARMÉ

Adam Kotsko

Stéphane Mallarmé (1842–1898) was a French poet and literary critic best known for his experiments with poetic form. Mallarmé is considered a leader of the Symbolist movement, which also included Paul Verlaine, Gérard de Nerval and Arthur Rimbaud, among others. This movement was distinguished by its embrace of free verse over against the more traditional poetic forms that dominated mainstream French poetry and by its use of evocative, indirect modes of communication. Mallarmé's own style emphasised the importance of the way the words were laid out on the page and the exploitation of the many homonyms in the French language in order to produce ambiguity. This latter quality makes his poetry exceptionally difficult to translate, and this has arguably limited his influence in the English-speaking world.

Meillassoux devotes his second book-length work, *The Number and the Siren*, to a 'decipherment' of Mallarmé's enigmatic final poem, '*Un Coup de Dés jamais n'abolira le Hasard*' ('A Throw of Dice will never abolish Chance'). As Meillassoux summarises it, '*Un Coup de Dés*' centres on the aftermath of a shipwreck, which leaves a mysterious 'Master' with one seemingly meaningless final choice: whether or not to throw a pair of dice. It is never directly revealed whether he actually does so, and he is ultimately pulled into a whirlpool. Along the way, we are treated to an enigmatic vision of a siren, who destroys the rock that presumably led to the shipwreck, along with various reflections on 'the unique Number that cannot be / another'. The poem closes with the suggestion that a new stellar constellation may, perhaps, have been set in motion by the Master's dice-throw. All of this is presented in a unique layout, with lines stretching across two facing pages, varied typography, and virtually no punctuation.

In Meillassoux's reading, Mallarmé is reflecting on the task of the poet in the wake of the 'shipwreck' of traditional poetic form occasioned by the rise of free verse. Where he breaks with most contemporary interpreters, however, is in seeing '*Un Coup de Dés*' as part of Mallarmé's attempt to create an artistic form that could found a modern ritual with all the power and meaning of the Roman Catholic mass. This project centred on the composition of a liturgical poem called 'the Book' that would be part of a numerologically structured ceremony of public reading. Many critics regard this interest as a passing phase on Mallarmé's part and would strongly dispute that it informed the composition of his great final poem. Meillassoux, however, not only claims that '*Un Coup de Dés*' is a continuation of the project of 'the Book', but that, thanks to Meillassoux's own investigation, which effectively unlocks the meaning of the poem, Mallarmé has in fact actually succeeded in an achievement that could found a new poetic religion that would be secular modernity's answer to Christianity.

The argument of *The Number and the Siren* is an interpretive tour de force that defies summary. Indeed, the book has a literary quality in itself, filled as it is with twists and turns and 'big reveals' – and so it is the rare work of literary scholarship that is vulnerable to 'spoilers'. What I would like to clarify in the remainder of this entry is the work's place in Meillassoux's overall project. On a superficial level, it seems natural that Meillassoux would be drawn to Mallarmé's meditation on contingency and chance. In his first major published work, *After Finitude: An Essay on the Necessity of Contingency*, he argues for a view of the world centred on contingency rather than necessity, that is to say, for a universe ruled by chance rather than by any supreme being or foundational laws. There is no necessary being other than contingency itself. The universe is founded not simply on chaos, but on **hyper-chaos**, a chaos so radical that it has no necessary reference to order. If our world appears to be regulated by immutable natural laws, that's just a coincidence, a state of affairs that could easily change.

What may strike readers of *After Finitude* as surprising or even disturbing are the Christian overtones of Mallarmé's project and of Meillassoux's celebration and appropriation of it. The ground for this aspect of the work was laid in *The Divine Inexistence*, sections of which have been published in Graham Harman's book on Meillassoux (*DI*). These selections, which build off of the argument for contingency found in *After Finitude*, represent an ambitious attempt to account for all of reality within Meillassoux's philosophical scheme, from matter and organic life to humanity and what might come to supersede humanity. In the latter regard, he embraces a possibility that resonates strongly with the Christian doctrine of the resurrection of the dead, involving a human figure who somehow comes into possession of divine power but gives it up after returning all those who have died to life and bestowing upon all of humanity the gift of a new immortal form of bodily existence.

For Meillassoux, Mallarmé has obviously not achieved this miraculous feat, but he could be viewed as a kind of forerunner in so far as his poetic achievement represents a successful attempt to concretely grasp the infinite. *The Number and the Siren*, then, clarifies what Meillassoux is doing in *The Divine Inexistence*. It is inaccurate to say that Meillassoux is embracing or appropriating Christianity. What he's really trying to do is much bolder and, one might say, more insane: he wants to do Christianity one better. He wants to create something more powerful than Christianity, something that would radicalise Christianity's wildest hopes – and that would deliver on them, in so far as it's based on the radical contingency of the universe rather than on the illusion of a transcendent God.

MATERIALISM

Nathan Brown

Meillassoux names his philosophical position **speculative materialism**. In *After Finitude* he offers a concise determination of this term:

Every materialism that would be speculative, and hence for which absolute reality is an *entity without thought*, must assert *both* that thought is not necessary (something can be independently of thought), and that thought can think what there must be when there is no thought. The materialism that chooses to follow the speculative path is thereby constrained to believe that it is possible to think a given reality by abstracting from the fact that we are thinking it. (*AF*, 36)

This determination includes two conditions:

1) the *materialist* must hold that 'thought is not necessary' (something can be independently of thought);

2) the *speculative* materialist must assert that 'thought can think what there must be when there is no thought'.

A materialist position thus meets an ontological criterion: the independence of being from thought. Speculation abides by an epistemological criterion: it affirms the capacity of thought to access an **absolute**. Note that these are formal criteria: they do not commit Meillassoux to a definition of 'matter', to any stance on the composition of bodies or the existence of elementary corpuscles, nor to the eliminative reduction of emotional or intellectual phenomena. They do not tether Meillassoux's philosophy to one or another model of physical reality. We can say that materialism, for Meillassoux, is a minimal, formal philosophical condition concerning the relation between being and thought.

The materialist condition of Meillassoux's itinerary does, however, have specific consequences for the relation between speculative philosophy and empirical science. The problem of how to think being's anteriority to thought – the problem of **ancestrality** – is posed to philosophy by the data of empirical science. The materialist philosopher must account for the ancestral statements of empirical science in such a way as to grant their 'literal' sense. That is, the materialist will respect the chronological anteriority of being to thought as the primary sense of an ancestral statement, rather than performing a logical inversion through which the correlation between thought and being becomes an anterior condition of any claim concerning chronological anteriority. Against **correlationism**, the materialist will hold that the chronological anteriority of being to thought is the material/generic precondition of any correlation between thought and being, including any philosophical argumentation concerning the latter. The problem for the materialist becomes that of sustaining this position in a rational and non-dogmatic fashion: upholding this position by refuting correlationism through argument rather than simply ignoring it or submitting it to various forms of *ad hominem* or institutional critique. In *After Finitude*, the heuristic burden of 'the problem of ancestrality' is to foreground the stakes of sustaining a materialist position which is at once rationalist, speculative and non-dogmatic. Meillassoux's exposition of the problem is intended to show that a rational refutation of correlationism is necessary in order to respect and account for the revisable truth claims of empirical science as a condition of philosophical reflection.

For Meillassoux, the bond between **speculation** and materialism has both ancient and modern roots. Classically, Epicureanism is 'the paradigm of all materialism' (*AF*, 36) in so far as it asserts that 'thought can access the absolute nature of all things through the notions of atoms and voice' and also that 'this nature is not necessarily correlated with an act of thought', since thought emerges through the contingent composition of atomic compounds. If Epicureanism supplies the classical paradigm of materialist philosophy, it is the speculative import of the Copernican Revolution – of modern science – that assigns to modern philosophy its materialist vocation: 'Modern science discovered for the first time thought's capacity to accede to *knowledge* of a world indifferent to thought's relation to the world' (*AF*, 118), and this 'eminently speculative character' of modern science, it's 'non-correlational mode of knowing' (*AF*, 119), should have oriented philosophy toward a speculative materialism capable of showing how thought can think what there can be when there is no thought (*AF*, 121). The task of modern philosophy is thus to make explicit the ontological and epistemological implications of scientific statements, and particularly of the use of mathematics, in those statements, to formulate physical properties and relations unavailable and irreducible to sensory manifestation. The speculative import of Galilean-Copernican physics is that 'what is mathematizable cannot be reduced to a correlate of thought' (*AF*, 117). It is this irreducibility of mathematical knowledge to correlational knowledge that speculative materialism seeks to affirm and to theorise.

Note that the recent provenance of this materialist position is Althusserian: against idealist epistemology, materialist philosophy supports the spontaneous materialism of the scientists. We can thus situate Meillassoux's materialism in a line running from Epicurus through Descartes to Althusser and Badiou: a materialist tradition whose parameters are assigned by the philosophical requirements of affirming the formally speculative import of physics, its claim to make revisable statements concerning the properties of things-in-themselves.

MATHEMATICS

Sean Dudley

Since the time of the pre-Socratics, philosophy has enjoyed an intimate relationship with mathematics. Indeed, the histories of both disciplines, when not directly intersecting, have always run parallel with one another, sharing methods and developments and exchanging questions and answers. The cause of this courtship should not be surprising when one considers that in its essence mathematics provides what philosophy seeks as its *raison d'être*: certain knowledge. However, for all the epistemic riches and gifts that the mathematician has lavished upon the philosopher, she cannot explain to him just what all this mathematical knowledge amounts to or what it is about.

Every philosopher, if not equally every mathematician, must decide how he will interpret the meanings of these often enchanting mathematical discoveries. In fact, to a large extent the history of mathematics can be read as an ongoing dispute between various groups of scholars who derive very different philosophical views from the very same mathematical findings. Platonism or nominalism? Intuitionism or logicism? Who is to adjudicate and to what criteria does one appeal in support of one's own favoured understanding? We will see that the very undecidability of the meaning of mathematical statements will play an important role in Meillassoux's speculative philosophy. To understand why Meillassoux adopts the philosophy of mathematics it will be worthwhile to rehearse briefly the history of the tradition that he is responding to.

As is largely the case within the history of **metaphysics**, philosophical interpretations of mathematical truths have gradually shifted from firebrand Platonism, the belief in the reality of numbers, to what might now be called pragmatist anti-realism, that is, the utilisation of mathematics for thinking the real without any ontological commitments about that reality in terms of number. No longer are mathematical constructions believed to put the thinker in touch with a divine realm of timeless reality but rather mathematical knowledge is widely believed to be self-contained and ultimately unrelated to the world as it is in-itself. From Plato to Galileo, from Galileo to Kant, and from Kant to David Hilbert, the ontological appetite of the mathematician has shrunk in intensity: first taking itself to rule over the Platonic heavens, then restricting itself to the bodies of the earth and stars, mathematics now finally confines itself to describing the pure and empty form of the set that many philosophers take to be a pure and therefore arbitrary construction. This repeal of jurisdiction is ironic given that it occurred simultaneously with an expanding application of mathematics to nearly every field in the sciences and the humanities from branches as far away from each other as cosmology and sociology.

This metaphysical restriction is the fallout of the work of Immanuel **Kant**, whose Critical philosophy relegated all mathematical knowledge to the spatio-temporal realm of sensible intuition and *ipso facto* relegated the sense of mathematical statements to the realm of possible anthropocentric experience. What Kant could not anticipate, however, was the extent to which new discoveries in science and mathematics, like the invention of non-Euclidean geometry and general and special relativity, for example, gave rise to new synthetic *a priori* knowledge that was nevertheless beyond the purview of possible experience, as Kant had defined it. No longer could philosophy say with a straight face that mathematics must confine itself to the kingdoms of Euclid and Newton. The pathological functions of Weierstrass's calculus, the curved manifold of Riemannian spheres, the transfinite numbers of **Cantor**'s continuum, and other counterintuitive developments pushed the Kantian from the tightrope of the transcendental back into the bleachers of dogmatism. For to claim, after the progress of the great minds of the nineteenth and twentieth centuries – such as Cantor, Dedekind, Frege, Gödel – that mathematics teaches us only about the world of possible experience is to commit what Meillassoux calls a Ptolemaic regression, rolling back the endless frontiers of epistemic potential to the near-sighted horizon of human phenomenology.

So influential has Kant's conservatism been over the last centuries of philosophical activity that it is only recently that the transcendental hangover has begun to wear off and that philosophers have had the courage to once again claim knowledge of reality outside of the life-world. It is in many respects the mathematicians who have led the way. For if one thing needs to be scrapped from the canon of wisdom and committed to the flames it is certainly the self-stultifying conviction that mathematics only treats of the objects capable of being given in sensible intuition. Far from being so limited, mathematics extends leagues and leagues beyond the bounds of sense and puts us in touch with the nothing less than the actual infinite. To see why, we'll take an example pertinent to Meillassoux's overall philosophy, Cantor's theory of transfinite numbers.

Prior to Georg Cantor, philosophy and mathematics only had the formal machinery required to deal with potential infinities and never with the actual. The potential infinite requires the positing of some nonterminating process or algorithm such that infinity is approached but never attained given an infinite amount of time. From Aristotle's treatment of Zeno's paradox to Peano's axiomatisation of arithmetic, infinity was only conceptualised as a potentiality, but never as a real entity. With Cantor's introduction of **set theory**, however, infinity was revealed to be a real mathematical entity, or at least this is the interpretation taken up by Meillassoux, which is incidentally also how Cantor himself interpreted his own work. It is only since Cantor that mathematics and philosophy alike have felt warranted to reason about the actual as opposed to merely possible infinite. Cantor's derivation can be glossed quite simply: take any set A, count its elements, and then compare this number to the number of possible groupings of these elements. This second sub-set B, will always be bigger than A even when A itself has an infinite number of elements. This means that it is possible to construct an infinite series of infinite sets, each bigger than the last though all of them exemplifying the same concept of infinitude. From this it follows that it is strictly impossible to render this series of transfinite numbers totalisable since any proposed totality will always be smaller than the set of its proper subsets.

Like his predecessor Alain **Badiou**, Meillassoux takes Cantorian set theory to have established the infinite as a concept determinate of the world in-itself and not merely, as Kant and Aristotle had held, as a regulative or guiding principle of human reason. In Meillassoux's own work, this discovery is crucial for establishing the contingency of the **laws of nature** in the face of their unwavering stability. By applying transfinite set theory to 'Hume's Problem', that is, how to explain the stability of the laws of nature once we have proven their contingency, Meillassoux shows that Kant's indirect appeal to probability is inadequate since aleatory reasoning only makes sense in the context of a totality of possibilities. However, if the absolute is comprised of an actual infinity of possible universes then our world with its short menu of stable laws is no more probable than any other possible configuration. After Cantor, it is not necessity but rather contingency that pure reason establishes as an *a priori* principle of being: the lawfulness of nature is an empirical fact capable of being overthrown at any moment by another roll of the infinitely sided dice of **hyper-chaos**.

Now, it may be objected that Meillassoux is drawing metaphysical conclusions illicitly from a branch of mathematics that has no bearing on ontology. Just as Kant saw that the discoveries of Euclidean geometry and Newtonian physics had to be anchored to the phenomenal domains of space and time, shouldn't we make sure not to cast the net of set theory too far lest we pull it back empty? What, anyway, is the proper domain of set theory? Meillassoux's answer is characteristically audacious: every domain is the proper domain of set theory. For having abstracted from all determinate content, set theory ensures that it can be validly applied over all domains that include beings or existents of any kind. Set theory describes being *qua* being. Like Kant, Meillassoux asks how mathematics is possible but unlike Kant he does not conflate this question with Kant's other thematic inquisition, concerning how experience is possible, since the possibility of mathematics is not dependent on the possibility of subjectivity. This is where Meillassoux follows the formalist project of Hilbert in the search for a foundation of mathematics in pure syntax, without content or meaning. Unlike the formalists, Meillassoux ontologises the emptiness of the set and uses it to develop a novel metaphysics of contingency on top of the mathematics of meaninglessness.

Consider the following: the set of worlds that can accommodate human life is a subset of all possible worlds mathematically describable. Thus, laws of nature and certain laws of logic necessary within human or correlationist worlds are not included within all possible worlds (for example those of hyperbolic geometry, quantum mechanics and relativity theory or even the multidimensional worlds of string theory). In other words, there are an infinite number of real worlds not experienceable by humans but still describable by mathematics. Thus, the set of correlationist worlds does not share the same particular extension as the set of mathematisable worlds though they do share at least one member, namely this world, and they are both infinite. Now consider this fact anew once we have abstracted away from any and all of the semantic content of each set. They are both infinite and they are both identical in their construction. They are identical in their respective tokenings of infinitude but nonetheless differ when compared since one is a subset of the other. As particular tokens of the same universal type (the infinite set) A and B are indistinguishable. They manifest the same conceptual intension and extend equally over an infinite number of objects. And yet, they are different iterations of the same structure in so far as they extend over different infinities.

In a strangely similar way to that in which enantiomorphs (incongruent counterparts) are conceptually identical but spatially distinct, it seems as though the infinite sets are semiotically identical but nonetheless distinct as separate iterations of the same meaningless sign. Unlike Kantian geometric incongruent counterparts, Meillassoux's reiterations do not require sensible intuition to be apprehended by the thinker but only require the **intellectual intuition** of difference itself. The only medium required to record this process of minimal differentiation is time; however, this is not a time of phenomenal experience (or becoming) but an absolute time of unprincipled pure change. Another way to look at this is to take Meillassoux to have proven, somewhat informally, the familiar dictate that existence precedes essence. This would no longer be only a trite existentialist truism but could now be offered as a necessary law of being. This it turns out is just another formulation of the principle of unreason: the only thing that is necessary is absolute contingency. In the words of Cantor himself: 'The essence of mathematics lies in its freedom.' What we get in Meillassoux is a novel form of **overturned Platonism**, one in which necessity and stability are properties of the transient phenomena of human experience and where contingency, chaos and pure differentiation are properties of the absolute which, like Cantor's transfinite set, is untotalisable but actually and not merely potentially infinite. If the essence of mathematics is its freedom then the essence of freedom is its inhumanity.

MAY-BE

Paul J. Ennis

On occasion Meillassoux evokes **Mallarmé**'s *peut-être* from the poem '*Un Coup de Dés*' ('A Throw of Dice') – a favoured poem of Meillassoux's mentor Alain **Badiou**. Ray **Brassier** translates this in 'Time without Becoming' as the 'may-be', but Robin Mackay in *The Number and the Siren* chooses the 'PERHAPS' (this is how it appears in Mallarmé's poem). Alyosha Edlebi also chooses the 'PERHAPS' in the translation of 'Badiou and Mallarmé'. The term does not appear too often, but does occur in at least two significant places. In 'The Immanence of the World Beyond' we are asked to consider the 'may-be' as a *dense possibility* (463). In this context, the 'may-be' names the intensive unification that arises when factial ontology and universal ethics are thought through the **vectorial subject** (see also *TWB*, 10–11).

MEANINGLESS SIGN

Paul J. Ennis

Meillassoux argues that the meaningless sign is the unacknowledged condition underpinning our capacity to think a mind-independent reality. This is a sign considered prior to the 'intervention of meaning' (*IRR*, 25). He takes it that the meaningless sign has the dual character of a type and its token – though he prefers to use occurrence over token. Take the example of a written sign: here we have a mark on a piece of paper that you see as a sign. You see the mark as an occurrence of the sign-type. Although I can generate many tokens, say of the letter 'a', these are all occurrences of the type 'a'. When I read the letter 'a' *as* a sign I see 'the limitlessly reproducible occurrence of an intangible sign-type' (*IRR*, 25, italics removed).

Meillassoux wants to consider these types in their 'pure state', that is non-semantically, and he introduces a technical term to reflect this: the kenotype (*IRR*, 26). The kenotype is strictly arbitrary and in formal languages '*any sensible mark*' is sufficient to perform its function (*IRR*, 27). Furthermore, on the basis of its non-semantic arbitrariness it can be 'infinitely variable' when it comes to its form (*IRR*, 29). Of especial interest is how in quantitative iteration we grasp 'identical occurrences of the same type' (*IRR*, 32). During the process of iteration the meaningless sign is both '*intemporal and non-spatialized*' as type and nonetheless 'indexed to a determinate material thing' as occurrence (*IRR*, 33). Ultimately, it is reiteration that leads us to the potential infinite and is to be considered the source of arithmetic (*IRR*, 34). Iteration allows for reiteration, which allows for augmentation, that is an arithmetical count, and this allows for the idea of number. In reiterating I take the sensible mark and do not remain with its qualitative register. I move past this such that I move beyond perception and its limits toward the intelligibility proper to the indefinite (*IRR*, 34). The meaningless sign brings us into contact with what is eternally identical in all things and that is their shared investment in absolute contingency: 'contingency is *of* such and such an empirical particularity' (*IRR*, 36). This allows one to index contingency indiscriminately and granted this I am free to posit the identity of all entities as occurrences and then engage in the differentiating process of reiteration.

Crucially the contingency of the sign does not belong to the register of the facticity of the entity in terms of its perishability. The sign can always be recoded and so can always be otherwise. Grasped as such we can begin to iterate, and reiterate, them as occurrences of a kenotype in an unlimited manner. Anything can stand in for anything else when we think the meaningless sign. The factial derivation is now presented as follows: one begins with a shift of one's 'mode of apprehension' from the semantic to the semiotic (*IRR*, 37). Here one's sense of contingency transitions from the contingency of specific entities to the eternal contingency that all things carry. Seeing this arbitrariness of entities I transform them into occurrences of kenotypes and begin to see the possibility of iteration and reiteration characteristic of the mathematical endeavour.

METAPHYSICS

Sean Dudley

Unlike other branches of philosophy, metaphysics is concerned not with this or that particular domain of inquiry but with knowledge in its broadest and most general application. Thus, the task of the metaphysician is to attain knowledge of the fundamental structure of reality or to think pure being in its **absolute** and unconditioned form. At the same time, the trial of the metaphysician is to lay hold of such knowledge without thereby contaminating it with the vagaries and vicissitudes of her conceptual framework, and deliver metaphysical truths unto the world without deforming them with the forceps of one's own epistemic apparatus. To be related to truth as midwife is to child, as Socrates says; this has always represented the metaphysician's highest aspiration. Thus, in order to do metaphysics properly one must take caution not to distort the object to be known with the tools thought employs in order to know it. This can be stated in the form of an imperative: nothing may be posited about the absolute that is itself not of the absolute.

The history of metaphysics then can be read as a cautionary tale detailing all of the ways philosophers have tried and failed to live up to this task. It is a task that has moved from being perceived as quite difficult to being seen as demonstrably impossible. For once thought contemplates its own **finitude**, it is forced to conceive of metaphysics as a fool's errand. Running with the metaphor, we might also say that the history of metaphysics can be divided into three stages: classical metaphysics, whose model is Aristotle, and which came *before* finitude; critical metaphysics, whose father is Immanuel **Kant**, and which might be called a metaphysics *of* finitude; and now, in the philosophy of Meillassoux (and perhaps for the first time) we get a glimpse of the possibility of what metaphysics might look like *after* finitude.

The key to understanding Meillassoux's relation to the task of metaphysics is to understand what in each prior stage he retains and what he rejects. While Meillassoux is openly dismissive of the lion's share of classical metaphysics, it would be a profound mistake to read him solely as a critical heir of the tradition he inherited. What Meillassoux disparages in classical metaphysics is its tendency to lapse into what is often called **onto-theology**, or the positing of necessary beings either as some first cause or deity or else as some necessary principle or law be it God, Nature or Form. What all such dogmatic entities have in common is the unlicensed order of their derivation: the movement from the apprehension of a contingent being or principle to the positing of a necessary cause and sufficient reason for the existence of such a being. Indeed, the banner of pre-critical philosophy (metaphysics before finitude) is the **principle of sufficient reason**: that everything which exists has a reason for being and for being the way it is. Following David **Hume**, Meillassoux vehemently criticises the elevation of this principle, which is everywhere at work in the concept and perception of causality, to the level of metaphysics and relegates it to realm of the psychological, that is, as one of the many contingent habits of the mind which, though indispensable as a tool of the finite understanding, must be dispensed with on the road to understanding the infinite. Sufficient reason, though it manufactures necessities, is itself the product of an entirely finite and hence contingent structure.

No one demonstrated this to a more thorough and detailed degree than did Kant, whose *Critique of Pure Reason* of 1781 augured in the age of finitude, turning metaphysics into a mere sub-discipline of the subject of human cognition, forever orbiting the latter like an ancient satellite, a monument to our hubris and a reflection of our essential and transcendental finitude. For ever since Kant, philosophy has been unable to think the absolute except as a correlate of thought (see **correlationism**), unable even to prove the existence of the thing-in-itself as noumenon apart from its appearance as phenomenon for the thinking subject. According to Meillassoux, the apparent necessity of the correlation between the phenomenal and noumenal realms, a necessity which has been affirmed for more than two centuries, can be overcome in much the same way that the principle of sufficient reason was overcome by the Humean and Kantian critique: that is, by demonstrating its essential contingency. To do this, Meillassoux retrieves from the annals of cosmological science the concept of the **arche-fossil**: the existence of a material universe predating the appearance of the thinking subject by a temporal magnitude so vast that its mere presence as a knowable fact challenges, if not openly ridicules the notion that the correlation of mind and world is itself a necessity. For though the arche-fossil is not the elusive thing-in-itself; it is a testament to the contingency of the relationship of the phenomenal to the phenomenological. In other words, being does not need to be thought.

Unearthing the possibility of the contingency of the correlate, Meillassoux believes himself entitled to affirm the necessity of not only this contingency but of contingency as such. In so doing, he retrieves the spoils of classical metaphysics though in a spectacularly inverted form: there is only one necessary principle and that is the principle of unreason. Likewise there is only one necessary being and its name is **hyper-chaos**, a being capable of bringing forth any and all possibilities without reason and without cause. No doubt Meillassoux has unearthed an absolute entirely alien to the categories and principles of the rational mind. But such an absolute, unsullied by the fingerprints of finite thought, is precisely what philosophy has always sought.

$$\boxed{\text{N}}$$

NECESSITY OF CONTINGENCY

Pete Wolfendale

It is true that thinking beings evolved on Earth, and it is also true that there are infinitely many prime numbers. Nevertheless, we can intuitively distinguish between the manner in which these statements are true using so-called modal language, for example, 'could', 'might', 'cannot', 'must', and so on. We would be inclined to agree that it might not have been the case that we evolved, and thus that, in so far as it is possible that the world could have been otherwise, the existence of human life is contingent. By contrast, we would be inclined to deny that there might have been only finite primes, and thus that, in so far as it is impossible that the world could have been otherwise, the existence of infinite primes is necessary. However, this seemingly intuitive distinction is merely the tip of the modal iceberg, beneath which lies a variety of options for understanding how we reason with modal statements (modal logic) and interpreting what they tell us about reality (modal metaphysics).

Without digging too deeply into this topic, it is necessary to introduce a few technical distinctions that help clarify the significance of Meillassoux's claims concerning the necessity of contingency. On the one hand, there are what Meillassoux calls 'real possibilities' or ways the world could possibly be in itself (see **Cartesian in-itself**). The technical name for this is alethic modality, and it is often differentiated into further kinds. For example, one can draw a distinction between logical necessity and nomological necessity, or between those truths that are invariant with respect to the laws of thought (usually including mathematics) and those truths that are invariant with respect to the **laws of nature** (usually defined by physics). This means that there can be a sense in which it is nomologically necessary that planets orbit stars even though it is logically possible that they could do otherwise. On the other hand, there are what Meillassoux calls 'possibilities of ignorance' or ways the world could possibly be as far as we know. The technical name for this is epistemic modality and it is usually relative to shared certainty within discursive contexts. For example, we might agree that JFK was actually assassinated, but disagree about whether Oswald did it, and thus be inclined to say it's necessary that someone fired the fatal shot, but that it's possible it was Oswald or a gunman on the grassy knoll. Though alethic and epistemic modals are related, they can diverge, such as when we say that Goldbach's conjecture might be true (epistemic), even though if it is true, it must be true (alethic).

Meillassoux's thesis regarding the necessity of contingency is first introduced negatively as the principle of unreason. He opposes this to the **principle of sufficient reason**, which for him is the essence of metaphysical dogmatism in so far as the claim that there is a reason for each state of affairs collapses into the claim that there is a reason for all of them. This inevitably leads to the demand of **onto-theology** for a necessary entity, for example, the God depicted by Aristotle, or a set of entities, for example, Plato's ideas; or an **absolute** capable of grounding both alethic necessity and epistemic certainty. The critical philosophy that followed from Martin **Heidegger**, for example, abandoned onto-theology at the expense of qualifying sufficient reason and adopting a **correlationism** that rejects the absolute. By contrast, Meillassoux aims to present the unqualified absence of reasons (unreason) as a post-critical absolute, thereby demonstrating the impossibility of necessary entities.

He does this by proceeding through the arguments supplied by correlationism: the circle of correlation against naive realism and the argument from facticity against absolute idealism. The former argument holds that we can only have knowledge of things as they appear for us within the correlation, never as they are in themselves. Absolute idealism responds to this challenge by denying that what is in itself is distinct from what is for us, thereby absolutising the correlation. The latter argument counters this by insisting upon the facticity of the correlation, in so far as the possibility that thought could cease to exist guarantees its distinctness from the world it thinks. Meillassoux radicalises this by claiming that the argument requires that thought's non-existence be not merely epistemically possible for us, but alethically possible in itself, thereby absolutising facticity. Furthermore, he holds that this implies a primordial power capable of completely transforming the contents of the world from one moment to the next without reason, which he names absolute time or **hyper-chaos**.

The transition from an epistemological thesis about the availability of reasons to an ontological thesis about the capacity for radical change is consolidated in its positive reformulation as the principle of **factiality**. The key to this lies in Meillassoux's subversion of correlationism's sceptical procedure, which enables one to invoke the epistemic possibility that the 'for us' differs from the in itself in any discursive context so as to undermine every claim to certainty. The general applicability of this procedure transforms the epistemic contingency it appeals to from something relative to a given discourse into something absolute. However, there is an internal limit to this applicability in so far as the procedure cannot be applied to this absolute without undermining its generality. This 'noniterability of facticity' constitutes the necessity of contingency and thereby reveals the necessary conditions of contingency. These figures of factiality are immune to correlationist scepticism in so far as they constitute the ontological structure of contingent facts.

We cannot discuss the figures that Meillassoux actually derives, namely the **principle of non-contradiction** and the necessary existence of something rather than nothing, in detail, but it is important to note that his ultimate aim is to show that logic and mathematics are factial, and thereby ground their scientific application to matters of fact. This indicates that the absolutisation of facticity hinges upon the overlap between epistemic modality and alethic modality when it comes to logical necessity, in so far as it converts the epistemological conditions of factual disagreement into the ontological structure of facts. In turn, this suggests that the inference from absolute facticity to absolute time hinges upon the gap between atemporal logical necessity and temporal nomological necessity in so far as it converts the logical possibility that things could be otherwise into the nomological possibility that things could become otherwise. The question that remains for critics of Meillassoux's thesis is thus whether or not it conflates the epistemic contingency of nomological necessity with the logical necessity of nomological contingency.

NIHILISM

Sean Dudley

In the most general sense nihilism names a simple, speculative thesis: that the order of human being, from morality, to **phenomenology**, to language, reflects nothing, not even dimly, about the order of being in-itself, taken either in the key of nature or in the key of a deeper cosmology. Nihilism is the result of reason's continual penetration beyond the order of the human into the order of non-human nature. In its most resounding tenor, nihilism ushers in the collapse of any and all transcendental philosophy whose topic, were there to be one, would be the excavation and exultation of the supposedly necessary and therefore transcendental categories of human thought as well as the phenomenological structures of first-person conscious experience that underwrite it. Since the forms of experience reflect the arbitrary and *ad hoc* morphological constraints of the human brain, there is no longer any reason to believe that how we think about and perceive the world has any relationship whatsoever to how the world really is in itself.

On this view, human cognition is a process no more or less transcendental than is perspiration or egg-laying. Our mental structure is no more necessary than the structure of our vertebrae, both simply reflecting the arborous and venal pathway of a by and large arbitrary evolutionary history of outward spreading ampliative mutation rather than the exemplification of some sort of gradual unfolding of the absolute toward a utopian 'kingdom of ends'. The human categories of possible experience, for instance as catalogued by Immanuel **Kant**, deserve no special standing above or beyond the categories enjoyed by penguins or dust-mites. Our epistemic powers provide us with a view of the world that aims not at truth but at adaptive advantage within our own ecosystem. Judged this way, it is not clear at all whether humans have been equipped by nature in any way more favourable than have the cockroach or e. coli. Like the latter, we have been armed with our own variety of experience or 'blooming, buzzing, confusion' in William James' words, and we, like any other creature, use the faculties given to us to gather energy, excrete waste and reproduce. The rest is window-dressing.

Perhaps the most damning blow nihilism lays on philosophy is the permanent foreclosure on the possibility of knowledge. In short, epistemology, the study of how we distinguish truth from falsehood, becomes annexed into the ever-expanding microscope of the empirical scientist, leaving whatever philosophers have said on the matter more or less a topic for the history of anthropology. The noble and heraldic pursuit of truth is transformed into the slow march of a slave caravan moving between the carrot and stick of lust and anxiety, different only in degree from the motivations that inform the movements of reptiles and microbial slime. It is this implosion of the old-fashioned notions of universal truth and knowledge that demote the philosopher from his former position at the head of the academy of the sciences to the basement office of the library in the role of the eccentric, broom-wielding custodian. For with truth no longer on the table, the philosopher has nothing left to do but become a kind of curator of concepts, polishing arguments here and there and helping to facilitate and expedite interdisciplinary communiqués between the sciences and humanities, mopping up any spills that happen in the hallways along the way.

But what does Meillassouxian philosophy have to say about nihilism? Any such nihilism, which yokes the frailty of man's cognitive pedigree to an external necessity, even the necessity of natural law, is itself slave to the **principle of sufficient reason**, a principle that Meillassoux explicitly rejects as pure dogma. For nihilism taken as the narrative of man's drive to extinction is itself a narrative following its own thread of ontological necessity. Once we raise the contingency of the correlation between mind and world from the level of mere possibility to the level of necessity, as Meillassoux does, we unleash an infinite nihilism powerful enough to shatter not only every concord between man and cosmos but also every discord and schism. Paradoxically, nihilism after Meillassoux becomes a principle strong enough to cradle even the most anthropocentric fantasies of man who restores in thinking the absolute contingency of necessity, the permission to believe that anything is possible.

NON-WHOLE/NON-ALL

Peter Gratton

Introduced in Lacan's Seminar XX, '*pas-tout*' – translatable as 'non-all', 'non-whole', or even 'not every' – refers to the non-totalisability or subsumability of subjects under a given universal. In Badiou's *Being and Event*, this comes to mean the non-totalisability of the universe given the outcome of **set theory**. For Meillassoux, until Cantor, what was possible was thought under a set of possibilities, even if highly improbable. In each set or **World**, there is a given range of chances. For example, for a die, the chance of rolling a one is one out of six. But what Meillassoux says is that there is no totalisable set of all possible sets or universes. As such, while within this World we have a number of possibles, the universe itself cannot be totalised in terms of its possibilities. This he refers to as 'world' (lower case) or the 'virtual', the illimitable non-Whole of possibilities of creation in **hyper-chaos**.

This non-Whole rids us of the 'frequentialist implication', as discussed in *After Finitude*. We look at the universe's apparent stability and guess that the chances would be extremely low that this universe could be stable without some eternal set of physical laws. However, Meillassoux argues that aleatory reasoning only works when you have a total number of sets from which to judge (like the six sides of a die), but given his use of set theory, there is no total set of all sets, and thus one cannot calculate any probability for this stability, even a minute one. In this way, hyper-chaos may, yes, have provided for an apparently stable universe, but it also may, at any time, give rise to a new World out of this one. For Meillassoux this has already occurred, with the physical laws changing to allow the move from the World of matter to the World of organic matter, and then to the World that allows thought, and, foreseeably, perhaps a World beyond this one, a World of justice.

OBJECT ORIENTED ONTOLOGY

Rick Elmore

Object Oriented Ontology (OOO) is a branch of speculative realism associated with the work of Graham Harman, Levi Bryant, Ian Bogost and Tim Morton. Bryant coined the term in 2009, as a corollary to Object Oriented Philosophy (OOP), a phrase Harman began using in the late 1990s to describe the trajectory of his own work (Harman 2010: 93). Although the two terms, OOO and OOP, mark different moments in the history of object oriented thought, they are today used more or less interchangeably. Despite its relative youth, OOO has a following in the fields of philosophy, media studies, ecology and cultural studies. Many of the central proponents of object oriented philosophy have long-running, influential blogs and their association with publishing companies like Zero Books and the online publisher Open Humanities Press led to the rapid release and distribution of works related to OOO.

Like all forms of speculative realism, OOO begins from the critique of **correlationism**, that is, the belief that the human–world correlate forms the central element of all philosophical investigation (Bryant et al. 2011: 19). Against correlationism, OOO contends that the cosmos is entirely made up of individual objects: 'all being is composed of objects' (Bryant 2010). The human–world relation is, from an object oriented perspective, neither unique nor fundamental, but is rather just an example of object-to-object interactions. In fact, for OOO, the universe exists as a collection of autonomous objects interacting through a process Bryant terms 'Exo-relation', a process of 'foreign relations' in which objects translate one another in terms of themselves (Bryant 2010). Morton formulates this process in his work on causality, where he describes interactions between objects as a 'sampling' in which, for example, a cup cups the table, and the table tables the cup, and a human humans the coffee, and so on (Morton 2013). Because of its central claim that reality is entirely made up of objects, OOO is a flat ontology, placing all entities in the universe on the ontologically equal footing of being equally objects. This is not to say that, for OOO, there is no difference between objects. Rather, OOO gives no ontological privilege to any particular object, a claim that strikes to the very heart of correlationism, anthropocentrism and idealism:

positions that precisely ground themselves on the ontological superiority of the human and its mind. It is this grounding of a critique of ontological privilege on the basis of an object oriented, flat ontology that distinguishes OOO from other variants of speculative realism. Of the original attendees of the now famous 2007 Goldsmith conference that inaugurated the speculative realist movement (Quentin Meillassoux, Ray Brassier, Ian Hamilton Grant, and Harman), Harman's OOO is the only position that takes objects to be the fundamental elements of the cosmos. Proponents of OOO argue that this absolute focus on objects is essential to avoid what Harman calls ontologies of 'undermining' and 'overmining'.

Ontologies of 'undermining' see objects as merely the effect of deeper more fundamental ontological forces. This includes, for example, any ontology that sees objects as constituted by their relations or by some more fundamental element such as water, air or fire, as in the ancient Greek tradition (Harman 2011b: 8–9). Ontologies of 'overmining', conversely, see objects as falsely deep abstractions of more immediate forces. This includes positions such as empiricism, where objects of experience are characterised as 'bundles of qualities' (Harman 2011b: 10–11). The problem with both these forms of ontology, from an object oriented perspective, is that they risk reestablishing the logic of ontological privilege found in correlationism.

In so far as ontologies of overmining and undermining take some entity or force to be more fundamental or immediate than objects, such ontologies relegate objects to the secondary status of mere appearances or accidents. From an OOO perspective, this risks reestablishing the logic of ontological privilege found in correlationism, since any process of abstraction is necessarily linked to processes of consciousness and, therefore, idealism. This is, in a general sense, the object oriented critique of most other forms of speculative realism, which, although akin in their rejection of correlationism, do not, at least on the OOO account, forsake correlationism entirely.

Despite the fact that the basic tenet of OOO is rather simple, requiring only that one take the cosmos to be made up entirely of objects, the positions most commonly associated with it are quite diverse, ranging from Harman's Heidegger-based insistence on the recessional character of objects to Bryant's uniquely Lacanian notion of 'a democracy of objects', as well as Bogost's video game theory inspired 'alien phenomenology' and Morton's ecologically focused concern for hyperobjects and aesthetic causality. In addition, OOO has had a number of offshoots including Object Oriented Feminism and Object Oriented Architecture.

Key texts of Object Oriented Philosophy include Harman's *Tool-Being* (2002), *Guerilla Metaphysics* (2005), and *The Quadruple Object* (2011);

Levi Bryant's *The Democracy of Objects* (2011); the edited collection *The Speculative Turn: Continental Materialism and Realism* (2011); Ian Bogost's *Alien Phenomenology* (2012); and Timothy Morton's *Realist Magic* (2013).

OBJECT ORIENTED ONTOLOGY'S CRITIQUES OF MEILLASSOUX

Rick Elmore

The critique by object oriented ontology (OOO) of **speculative materialism** asserts that Meillassoux fails to articulate a form of **correlationism** that does not ultimately fall prey to **idealism** (Harman 2011a: 124). The clearest formulation of this critique appears in Graham Harman's *Quentin Meillassoux: Philosophy in the Making* (2011). In that work, Harman contests Meillassoux's rejection of the **principle of sufficient reason**, privileging of time over space, and commitment to the concept of law (Harman 2011a: 141–58). However, Harman's primary critique, and the one shared by all proponents of OOO, concerns Meillassoux's assertion that one cannot think what is outside thought and his reliance on a notion of the 'meaningless' to ground his escape from the 'correlationist circle' (Harman 2011a: 139–40).

For Harman, Meillassoux accepts the basic truth of the correlationist position, that one cannot think what is outside of thought. This claim grounds his rejection of **realism**, Harman claims, as he contends that to think what is outside thought necessarily leads to a performative contradiction: turning what is other than thought into thought (Harman 2011a: 165). Proponents of OOO find this argument relatively weak, as, for them, the existence of any object necessarily exceeds all human thought and knowledge about it. Were this not the case, our knowledge of objects would be indistinguishable from the objects themselves, and absolute idealism would win the day (Harman 2011a: 148).

For Levi Bryant, Meillassoux's insistence on performative contradiction problematically assumes all thought to be self-reflexive (a thinking about thinking). This assumption leads to an infinite regress, since, if one cannot think something without thinking about it, then thinking becomes nothing but a thinking about thinking and so on into infinity (Bryant 2010). Hence in order for there to be any possibility of accessing a world outside thought, a possibility to which Meillassoux is committed, there must be some form of thought that is not entirely self-reflexive, and, consequently, immune to the claim of performative contradiction. Yet this is but one half of the OOO critique of Meillassoux on the issue of thought, the other having to do with his rendering of what he dubs 'meaningless'.

While committed to the importance of the human–world correlate, Harman claims, Meillassoux does not foreclose the possibility of something existing outside thought. In fact, he insists on it. This insistence comes from his rejection of the notion that the meaningful must exhaust the real. The fact that we cannot meaningfully think what is outside thought does not entail its non-existence. It is this claim that Meillassoux believes saves him from the charge of idealism, as Harman portrays it, since it shows that something exists outside thought (the meaningless) without falling into a performative contradiction (giving this outside any meaning). Proponents of OOO critique this argument on the grounds that Meillassoux cannot maintain a concept of the 'meaningless' as necessarily existing 'outside' thought (Harman 2011a: 139–40).

For OOO, it is not enough for Meillassoux to claim that something meaningless exists in order to establish that it exists 'outside thought'. One can imagine all kinds of meaningless statements that do not entail thought-independent existence, for example, 'non-white white' or 'square circle' (Harman 2011a: 140). The meaninglessness of these statements does not grant them existence as a real possibility. Hence, 'it is not simply *any meaningless statement at all* that eventually does the work of dethroning Absolute Idealism, [for Meillassoux] but a specific form of meaninglessness' (Harman 2011a: 140). For Harman, a truly meaningless statement would resist any determination of its existence. Hence, Meillassoux's argument works only by making the meaningless actually meaningful, ascribing to it the meaningful predicate of existence outside thought.

Meillassoux's response to these critiques is that any attempt to circumvent the 'correlationist circle' remains necessarily victim to 'the vicious pragmatic circle' of the performative contradiction outlined above (Harman 2011a: 164–5). For him, there is simply no ground outside the human–world correlate on which to initiate a critique of that correlate. Hence, in so far as OOO argues for the abandonment of the human–world correlate entirely, it remains, for Meillassoux, a kind of naive realism.

ONTOLOGICAL ARGUMENT

Paul O'Mahoney

An ontological argument is one which derives and demonstrates the existence of **God** using reason alone, unaided by observation. The most famous instance of the ontological argument and the most important for Meillassoux is that articulated by René **Descartes** in his *Meditations on First Philosophy* (1641). The argument has a twofold purpose in Descartes: first, the rational demonstration of the existence of God, aimed at those for whom faith in revealed scripture is not sufficient; and second, and more importantly, to furnish a guarantor of the reliability of reason and human knowledge. The Cartesian God is conceived of as the sum of all perfections. As existence is deemed superior to inexistence, existence is a perfection. A perfect being must therefore of necessity exist. As the idea of a perfect and infinite being could not have been produced by an imperfect and finite being, such as the finite thinking thing or *cogito*, nor encountered by it, the idea of such a being as God is innate: it is implanted by God in the manner of a craftsman's stamp. The idea is present innately in every person, and can be arrived at by sufficient reflection.

This perfect being has the three traditional attributes of God: omnipotence, omniscience and omnibenevolence. The last is posited as wickedness and deceit are construed as imperfections, and inimical to the nature of a perfect being. This allows Descartes to overcome the most radical hypothesis of his methodical doubt: that an evil demon, or God Himself, is deceiving Descartes at every turn. God's perfection implies that he is a non-deceiver, and this fact allows Descartes to assert that it is impossible that God Himself would actively deceive Descartes or that He would allow an evil demon to do so.

God as demonstrated by the argument functions as an **absolute**: His existence, though it can be made manifest upon reflection or demonstrated to us, is not dependent on us. The most prominent precedent to Descartes, and perhaps the first coherent articulation of the ontological argument, is that put forth by St Anselm of Canterbury in his *Proslogion* (c. 1078), where God is defined as 'that greater than which cannot be thought'. Anselm's work occasioned what remains one of the most celebrated ripostes to the argument. The Benedictine monk Gaunilo's reply 'On Behalf of the Fool' maintained that if conceiving of a perfect being implied its existence, this could be extended to a perfect island, and innumerable other entities. The objection has not been widely accepted. Perhaps the most famous twentieth-century version of the argument is that proposed by Alvin Plantinga. Kurt Gödel also offered a proof which, though logically valid, does not suffice to demonstrate the existence of God.

The most pertinent criticism of the ontological argument for Meillassoux is that offered by Kant. For Kant, existence cannot be counted as a predicate. There is no contradiction in imagining that God does not exist, and so the predicate 'exists' is merely part of an analytic judgement and adds nothing to the subject. For Meillassoux, the (Cartesian) ontological argument is the natural outcome of modern philosophy's embrace of the **principle of sufficient reason**, which, though it was articulated by Leibniz, he sees as already operative in Descartes (cf. Meditation III). It is thus the natural culmination of dogmatic metaphysics, guaranteeing, via the necessity of God, the real necessity of physical laws and beings. In rejecting the principle of sufficient reason and positing a speculative rather than metaphysical absolute, Meillassoux denies the argument's legitimacy (*AF*, 29–33; 40; 50–1; 60).

ONTO-THEOLOGY

Marie-Eve Morin

Metaphysics, according to Heidegger, seeks to answer the fundamental question, 'why are there beings rather than nothing'? This question seeks the ground for beings, yet this project of grounding splits into two. First, beings are interrogated with regard to their Being: what does it mean for an entity in general to be? At the same time, beings as a whole are brought back to a first cause or foundation, to an entity that can ground and sustain in Being what exists as a whole. As such, **metaphysics** is both ontology, the process of grounding beings *qua* beings in Being, and theology, the process of grounding the Being of what is in a highest entity, that is to say, God. In both 'branches', the ground or explanation for what exists will be transcendent, yet it will be so in different ways. Metaphysics has only one subject matter, beings, but it approaches its subject matter from two angles: according to what is universal or common, and according to what is ultimate or highest. Onto-theology is also essentially a logic: because beings are questioned with regards to their ground (*logos*, *ratio*), beings appear as what is grounded in, and as the grounding cause of, Being.

The onto-theological structure of metaphysics, according to Heidegger, is essentially related to the difference between essence and existence. Metaphysics studies beings as such and as a whole, that is, it studies beings with regards to their essence as beings and it studies the whole of beings, the world, with regards to its existence. The two are related: ontology determines the essence of the beings whose existence is explained by theology. Essence (whatness) answers the question: 'What is x'? while existence (thatness) answers the question, 'Is there an x'? While ontology lays out the essence of something in so far as it is not only a specific thing (a table or a chair) but 'a something in general', theology studies the cause of the existence of beings. This cause takes the form of a being that is itself

self-caused, i.e., the being for which existence is essential. Metaphysics assumes the precedence of beings (in the determination of their essence) and the self-evidence of Being (determined as the presence or existence of beings).

Heidegger's thesis about the onto-theological structure of metaphysics does not only say that philosophy includes ontological as well as theological considerations. The division between *metaphysica specialis* and *metaphyisca generalis* already said as much. Rather, onto-theology is characterised by the simultaneity and circularity of both ways of questioning beings. First, the 'and' between theology and ontology is not that of an addition (first this, then that) but of a doubling, a *Zwiefalt*. Second, and more importantly, ontology and theology reciprocally determine each other: each is the foundation for the other so that neither can rightfully claim to be the ultimate foundation. The determination of the Being of beings always implies the indication of the entity that best exemplifies Being and can serve as the basis for the whole of beings, sustaining them in Being. Inversely, the determination of a highest entity provides the measure for all beings and hence lies at the centre of our determination of Being (of what it means for an entity to be). It is only from an already determined idea of Being that the highest entity can be identified and the idea of Being can only be read off the entity that *is* most properly, that displays Being most perfectly.

Metaphysics as onto-theology overlooks the ontological difference as difference and instead names what is different: Being – beings, ground – what is grounded. It actualises the ontological difference, sets Being apart from beings as their ground but without being able to think the belonging-together of Being and beings in this difference. The circularity of onto-theology is the way in which this belonging-together appears within metaphysics. At the same time, this belonging-together cannot be thought within metaphysics but requires a step back into the essence of metaphysics, into the differentiation that grants a between that holds Being and beings together. It is from here, for Heidegger, that a non-metaphysical thinking of the divine, where God is not the self-caused being that brings into and sustains in existence the whole of beings, becomes possible.

OVERTURNED PLATONISM

Paul J. Ennis

On occasion Meillassoux uses the term 'overturned Platonism' to describe his intent to flip the traditional stability–becoming opposition (*CLN*,

326). In 'Potentiality and Virtuality' he tells us that we should attempt to think according to an '*inverted*, rather than *reversed* Platonism, a Platonism which would maintain that thought must free itself from the fascination for the phenomenal fixity of laws, so as to accede to a purely intelligible Chaos' (*SD*, 273). For Meillassoux the idea is that rather than assume that the world of phenomenal appearance is one of becoming and that our task is to discover the intelligible stability lying behind it through reason (*a priori*), we should revise this such that the *a priori* speaks to becoming (as chaos) and phenomenal appearance is the site of stability (fixity, consistency, etc.). The basic thrust of this inversion is influenced by Jean-René Vernes' *Critique of Aleatory Reason*.

$$\boxed{P}$$

PHENOMENOLOGY

Marie-Eve Morin

Phenomenology can be broadly defined as the study or science of phenomena. As Heidegger points out in the introduction to *Being and Time*, unlike other sciences such as biology or sociology, the name 'phenomenology' does not name a specific realm of objects to be studied, such as living things or social things, but is a purely methodological concept. *Phenomenon* names that which shows itself in itself and *logos* originally means letting something be seen. Putting both together, phenomenology means, 'to let that which shows itself be seen from itself in the very way in which it shows itself from itself' (Heidegger 1962: §7), without any reference to a subject matter.

Husserlian phenomenology arises out of critique of both psychologism and representationalism. Psychologism assumes that because all truths are achieved by a conscious subject, then all truths are necessarily dependent on factual conditions of thought. For example, the law of non-contradiction does not say objectively that something cannot be both A and not A, but rather that it is not possible for us subjectively to think both A and not A. For Husserl, this is a category mistake. When I say that 2+2=4, I say nothing about counting, even though the truth of the result 4 can only be achieved through an act of counting. The puzzle of phenomenology is how subjectively individuated acts of consciousness can give rise to objectivity, that is, to something that is or is true independently from consciousness.

Objectivity is for Husserl an achievement (*Leistung*) of subjective consciousness. The second target of phenomenology is representationalist theories of outer perception. For Husserl, when I perceive a house, for example, I am not in contact with mental representations that would veil or distort the real house; rather, I see the house itself. This house is of course given to me from a specific perspective, in a specific lighting, and so on, that is, it is given to me through what Husserl will call an adumbration or a series of adumbrations (*Abschattungen*). Yet, this mode of givenness reveals the house itself; it is not some third thing that stands between me and the house and mediates my relation to it. If the mode of givenness were different, for example, if the house were given absolutely, all at once, from no standpoint, then the house would be thought as Idea but not perceived. Of course, the house can be perceived more or less well, but this is something I can figure out by perceiving more of the house, that is, by doing more of the same, not by accessing something other than the perceived house.

In its Husserlian form, phenomenology studies what appears to consciousness as it appears and only in so far as it appears, trying to bracket all assumptions, including philosophical and scientific theories. This is the meaning of the Husserlian motto 'back to the things themselves'. The 'things' (*Sachen*) of phenomenology are not to be understood as physical or material things. In fact, their ontological status cannot be presumed but will have to be attested phenomenologically, that is, attested by the way the 'thing' shows itself. Another way of defining phenomenology is to say that it studies intentional life. Consciousness for Husserl is defined by intentionality: to be conscious is always to be conscious of or to 'intend' something. It should be noted that intentionality does not require volition or 'intention' in the normal sense of the word; rather volitional, explicitly intentional conscious acts are one type of intentionality. If consciousness is defined as intentionality, it means that consciousness is not a thing such as a blank slate or a box, but a movement or an arrow. Hence the question of how consciousness can reach out of itself in order to 'hit' an object makes no sense for the phenomenologist.

The method of phenomenology for Husserl consists first of a suspension of our natural attitude, called the *epoché*. The natural attitude is the way in which we are normally conscious of or engage in the world, and it forms the basis for the all sciences, including psychology. In this attitude, we are focused on what is given (numbers, tomatoes, people, and so forth) and overlook the mode of appearance or givenness of these things. Because consciousness is a movement toward objects, we tend to overlook the intentional relation between consciousness and what is given. To study objects in their givenness we need to put out of play the object-pull, refrain from following through with the 'arrow' that consciousness is. Thanks to this suspension, we are led back and hence gain access to a forgotten or overlooked dimension, that is, the consciousness–world relation. This is the phenomenological reduction. Reduction here does not mean that something has been removed, that is, that the object has been lost, but rather that one is 'led back to' (*re-ducere* in Latin). In the reduction, I still have the whole of my consciousness with everything that is presented in it. Furthermore, what is presented is still presented as real, as illusion, as ideal, and so on, but instead of being interested in what is presented (what is it? is it real?), I suspend my judgement so that I can focus on how it is presented as this or that, as real or illusory, and so on. Hence, we cannot say that, because of the phenomenological reduction, the phenomenologist does not have access to or disregards 'reality' (or real things). Rather, 'being-real' now means 'being given to consciousness in a certain way'.

The field of study uncovered by the phenomenological reduction consists of two interrelated poles, the noetic or act pole and the noematic or object pole. Phenomenology studies the correlation between these two poles, for example, how a perceived object gives itself in a perceiving, how a modification of the perceiving into an imagining changes some features of the perceived (it is not an imagined object but a perceived one) but not others (it is still 'the same' blue house, and so on). At this point, the phenomenologist also needs to perform an eidetic reduction. This is the reduction that leads from particular facts to essences. This is achieved through imaginary variations: I vary the perception until it is not a perception anymore so as to uncover the essential features of the perceiving–perceived correlation, and so on. Finally Husserl thinks that the phenomenological reduction if correctly and radically performed will necessarily lead to a transcendental reduction because consciousness (the dimension uncovered by the phenomenological reduction) cannot itself be a worldly thing that appears to consciousness. Such a circularity would lead us to transcendental realism and we would be committing the same mistake as psychologism.

POTENTIALITY

Leon Niemoczynski

Meillassoux is careful to distinguish between two cases of being: the potential and the **virtual**. Similar to how Deleuze's ontology hinges on a distinction between the virtual and the actual, Meillassoux's ontology of contingency requires a fine distinction between virtuality as involving a realm of unpredictable hyper-chaotic creation, and potentiality as a concept involving a realm of probabilistic, though predictable within odds, chance.

In the article 'Potentiality and Virtuality', after refashioning David **Hume**'s problem concerning the lack of causal connection between events, which asserts a radical contingency refusing inductively established laws subject to probability, Meillassoux focuses on the issue of why probabilistic reasoning is said to be an option even though the laws of nature themselves are subject to radical contingency. Meillassoux states that a reasonable probabilistic chain of inference to law cannot take place due to the fact that it is impossible to establish a numerical calculation that could cover a total set of possible cases in which the calculation could take place. If probabilistic reasoning considering chance were to be justified in terms of wagering what may happen via established laws, it would need to determine a set of possible universes within which a probability calculation could occur.

Traditionally, this meant that there is a sum total of possible worlds where the set of all possible worlds would constitute a finite number from which one could draw a probable case. However, as Meillassoux points out, short of anyone other than Leibniz's God, no one has ever surveyed that sum total of possible worlds. Meillassoux's argument concerning the untotalisable nature of worlds stems from his engagement with Cantorian **set theory** (see Georg **Cantor**). According to Cantor, infinities are multiple as it is possible for there to be an infinite number of multiple sets, each with varying cardinalities. Therefore, it is impossible to foreclose sets of infinite multiples given that a set of all sets would involve contradiction. As Meillassoux points out, the Cantorian 'revolution consists in having demonstrated that infinities can be differentiated, that is that one can think the equality or inequality of two infinites ... whatever infinity is considered, *an infinity of superior cardinality* (a larger infinity) *necessarily exists*' (*PV*, 66). Because there is no reason to choose one infinite over another, as a closed set, there is no mean by which any number can probabilistically be employed against a specific set. Reason cannot rely on an absolute totality of possible cases, as any singular 'totality' would be one closed set among an innumerable order of other sets. Thus probabilistic reasoning, given this infinite number of sets of infinity, would not make sense.

When a supposed law is considered to be determined from an ordered, pre-given set of possibilities, Meillassoux states that we have fixed becoming such that we can speak of a potential for some event to occur given a number of other fixed cases that determine the probability of that event occurring. On the other hand, by 'detotalising' the possible as a result of 'liberating time from all legal subordination' (*PV*, 71), it is possible to speak of a deeper sense of the potential that is not subject to finite totalisation and determination. This is the virtual. In sum, for Meillassoux '*potentialities* are the non-actualized cases of an indexed set of possibilities under the condition of a given law' whereas *the virtual*, supported by the Cantorian decision to refuse totalising the thinkable, delineates the irruption *ex nihilo* of **hyper-chaos**, that is, a **creation** *ex nihilo* (*PV*, 71–2).

PRIMARY AND SECONDARY QUALITIES

Francis Halsall

The opening sentences of *After Finitude* are an audacious declaration that the theory of primary and secondary qualities will be rehabilitated. Hence Meillassoux revisits an old philosophical theme that had become, he claims, seemingly obsolete. This is his way back into a speculative metaphysics that reconsiders the relation between consciousness and the **absolute**. In short, primary qualities are those which objects actually have; secondary qualities are produced in experience. They are utterly distinct from each other. Secondary qualities are those features of the phenomenal realm by which it is present to consciousness. They are sensible for us and are not the necessary features of objects. The secondary qualities of an object do not exist in things themselves; rather, they emerge from the *relation* of consciousness to objects. The primary qualities of an object, in distinction, are autonomous from sensible qualities. They are not part of the relation of consciousness to objects but those elements of objects which can be expressed mathematically.

The terms were most famously coined by Locke, although Meillassoux identifies a significant pre-emption in René **Descartes'** discussions of sensations, such as pain, originating in a subject's relation to an object and not in the object itself. By returning to a well-worn philosophical topic Meillassoux's intention is to challenge the transcendental tradition of post-Kantian philosophy. Hence, he wishes to sidestep both Kantian arguments regarding the un-knowability of the noumenal world of things-in-themselves and phenomenological attempts to negotiate these arguments by returning to the primacy of objects in perception and moving from these to analysis of noematic and noetic content. These philosophical moves create a problem which is exemplified for Meillassoux in the correlationist position, namely how the primary qualities of the world-in-itself can be represented without them subsequently becoming available 'for us'. Meillassoux finds the philosophical route to 'de-subjectivated nature' in mathematics which is universal and objective. Hence, 'what is mathematizable cannot be reduced to a correlate of thought' (*AF*, 117)

Thus, Meillassoux seeks to isolate primary qualities from experience in order to establish the primary object of his speculative metaphysical project. Primary qualities are independent of thought yet available to it through the abstractions of mathematics. The in-itself is mathematisable; hence it not only exists but can also be demonstrated to exist independently of consciousness. Meillassoux's argument is framed by the rhetorical flourish whereby he self-consciously returns to a topic supposedly discredited by contemporary philosophy. He claims that this allows him to return to a 'pre-critical' or pre-Kantian metaphysics which lets him step outside of the legacy of 'correlationist' philosophy. This is, in effect, Cartesian in so far as Meillassoux is attempting to restore thought's access to reality though mathematics. To do so requires two assertions regarding the primary qualities of objects: first, that they are logically consistent, that is, they are subject to the **principle of non-contradiction**, and second, that they are contingent, that is, they could be otherwise. In short, mathematics is the route to his ontology.

PRINCIPLE OF NON-CONTRADICTION

Raphaël Millière

Whether contradictions can exist or not in the world has been an important philosophical issue since Aristotle, if not Heraclitus. Naturally, it also occupies a central place in Meillassoux's work, since the ontological principle of non-contradiction is the first of the non-trivial **figures** he intends to deduce from the apodictic principle of factuality. Though this proof appears in *After Finitude* (67–71), Meillassoux's earliest treatment of the principle of non-contradiction is to be found in his PhD thesis, *L'Inexistence divine* (excerpts of which appear in *DI*, 128–71). Interestingly, it is also his lengthiest examination of this issue, although it comes from an unpublished academic work. Meillassoux intends to publish a revised and expanded version of *L'Inexistence divine*, which he has been working on for more than a decade. Since this *opus magnum* still remains unpublished, we will focus on the original version, which is in line with his shorter development of non-contradiction found in *After Finitude*. It is however possible that Meillassoux will revise part of his position on the matter in forthcoming publications, since we may consider he hasn't yet given his definitive thesis on this central theme.

Meillassoux's main thesis on contradiction is the following: it is impossible that there are contradictions in the world, because necessarily everything is contingent (principle of **factiality**), and a contradictory being would have to be necessary. We shall not discuss the former thesis, since we will focus on the demonstration of the latter, which, as will become clear, is not immune to criticism. Meillassoux's central claim is that a contradictory entity would be immutable and necessary, since there would be no 'alterity' for it to change: it would have simultaneously every property and its opposite, would be existent and non-existent, and thus could not change or cease to exist. Therefore, such a hypothetical entity would be a necessary being, which is impossible if we grant factiality:

Non-contradiction is therefore an eternal truth because it states that if something is, it is determined, and that being determined means being actual as a reality among other equally possible realities. Nothing can be what it is not, because nothing can exhaust, as long as it exists, the universe of possibility. (*DI2*, 155)

This argument is not entirely clear nor is it unproblematic: why couldn't there be local contradictions in contingent objects, such as a round square? The extensive discussion of this issue in *L'Inexistence divine* casts some light on Meillassoux's answer. In classical logic, if a contradiction is true, anything is true. As medieval logicians put it, *ex falso sequitur quodlibet*, that is, 'from falsity anything follows'. This well-known characteristic of classical propositional logic appears in the truth-table of material implication: $P \rightarrow Q$ is always true if P is false.

Thus a 'local' contradiction (P & ¬P) would entail the truth of any formula, including all contradictions. This so-called 'principle of explosion' has been, at least for some people, a major problem in logic for several centuries, and the recent invention of a non-classical branch of logic called 'paraconsistent' logic, in which some contradictions are true (without entailing the truth of anything) was mainly intended as a solution to it. Interestingly, Meillassoux discusses the relevance of a paraconsistent approach to his problem, but ultimately dismisses such an approach on the basis that it does not deal with genuine contradiction but only with apparent ones, giving credit to Quine's statement that non-classical logics 'only change the subject' (Quine 1986: 81).

The author of *L'Inexistence divine* tells a small story, the 'tale of the zebra', to explain the alleged misconception of the friend of paraconsistence: he is like an explorer discovering an exotic animal – which happens to be a zebra – and coming to believe it exhibits an authentic worldly contradiction because it is both black and white. Obviously, the description of a zebra as black and white can only be misinterpreted as a contradiction, while it merely means that the animal is striped. Meillassoux implies that each time a philosopher claims to have found a genuine contradiction, what he really talks about is only the 'diversity' of determinations (that is, local properties, like the zebra's blackness and whiteness). A real contradiction would involve a white-*and*-not-white zebra, or, for that matter, an animal both dead *and* alive, like Schrödinger's cat. As Meillassoux puts it, the 'defender of real pseudo-contradiction . . . mistakes the infinite specifiability [*précisabilité*] of the world for its contradictory nature' (*DI2*, 152).

However the idea that real contradictions exist in the world is not as absurd as it seems; it has indeed its promoters, called 'dialetheists'. Dialetheism is the metaphysical counterpart of paraconsistent logic; it is the real target of Meillassoux's argument, since a formal calculus, whether classical or non-classical, does not involve any ontological commitment by itself. The 'tale of the zebra' is supposed to exhibit a fundamental misconception of dialetheism, showing that so-called 'true contradictions' are not *bona fide* contradictions. But what exactly justifies such a statement? Graham Priest, one of the notable defenders of dialetheism, has shown at length that his view is coherent and deals with genuine contradictions. For example, Priest (1987) includes a lot of interesting applications of dialetheism to metaphysical issues about change, motion and time. He claims that 'there are some sentences . . . α, such that both α and ¬α are true' and concludes that 'if some contradictions are true, then the world must be such as to make this the case . . . In this sense, the world is contradictory' (Priest 1987: 299). Elsewhere, he even tells a story of his invention about a contradictory object, a box described as 'really empty and occupied at the same time' (Priest 2005: 127). Suppose there can be such a thing as a box both empty and full: it does not follow from this 'local' contradiction either that the whole world is contradictory or that the box is a necessary being – it may well cease to exist. Even a contradictory object having *all* properties at the same time (a 'maximal contradiction') would still be subject to change, since it could still lose one of its properties.

Therefore Meillassoux's argument against dialetheism seems flawed: not only is he is unable to show why dialetheism only deals with 'pseudo-contradictions', but he also fails to justify the claim that a real contradiction would entail the existence of a necessary being. While the reason for this mistake remains unclear in *After Finitude*, a close examination of *L'Inexistence divine* shows that it probably comes from a misunderstanding of the real meaning of the classical 'principle of explosion' – which is a formal law of (some) logical systems and has no bearing on metaphysical issues.

PRINCIPLE OF SUFFICIENT REASON

Sergey Sistiaga

The principle of sufficient reason (PSR) was first stated explicitly by Leibniz (*Monadology*, §31), but was implicitly at work from the very beginning of philosophy. It says that everything has a reason why it is, as it is, rather than otherwise. As such it is the central principle of **rationalism**, stating that everything admits theoretically of an explanation, is potentially intelligible, and that the structure of being must be fundamentally rational. Rigorously applied, as in Spinoza, it entails necessitarianism. This means everything happens with metaphysical necessity and leads to the postulation of a first cause or *causa sui* that had no previous cause, which is supposed to end the infinite regress of reason/explanations/grounds by means of a self-explanatory and self-grounding necessary entity. These extreme consequences lead various philosophers to soften its consequences. In Leibniz, God has the free choice of all possible worlds. Some have condemned the PSR as unjustified metaphysical speculation, as David **Hume**, Immanuel **Kant** and their post-metaphysical followers did.

Meillassoux explicitly rejects the PSR on philosophical grounds as 'absolutely false' (*AF*, 53, 60, 71), but sometimes hints at political motives, where he claims an incompatibility between the PSR and the critique of ideology (*AF*, 33–4). Proceeding from Leibniz's distinction of two independent fundamental principles (*Monadology*, §31; *AF*, 71), the PSR and the **principle of non-contradiction** (PNC), we find that Meillassoux's rejection of the PSR is based on two different historically very influential arguments. Meillassoux uses a controversial Cartesian argument, which today falls under the name of the conceivability argument, where one concludes real possibility out of logical conceivability (Descartes, Meditation VI). With Hume, Meillassoux argues that since the denial of the PSR implies no contradiction, it is conceivable and therefore possible that the PSR could be wrong, because the latter is not a necessary truth or tautology. In addition Meillassoux generalises Kant's critique of the ontological argument into the thesis that every proof for a necessarily existing entity is impossible. In extrapolating from the impossibility to prove a necessary entity to the strong claim that no such entity could exist, Meillassoux thinks the PSR cannot be maintained anymore because no self-explanatory entity could stop the infinite regress of reasons (*AF*, 30–3).

Meillassoux's own argument is based on the Cartesian dualism between thought and being, transformed through Berkeley and Kant into the thesis that Meillassoux terms **correlationism**, which says that thought can never access being in-itself, because then being would just be being for-us, because thinking always turns the unthought into thought via the correlationist circle (see **Cartesian in-itself**; René **Descartes**).

His rejection of necessary entities and the structure of the correlationist circle, which does not allow us to think any de-correlated entity that could be the hidden reason of this very structure, preclude the possibility of absolutising the correlation itself. Having excluded all external and internal reasons for the correlation's existence, Meillassoux concludes the facticity or groundlessness of the correlation. Rejecting with the PSR brute and unexplainable facts, Meillassoux turns the only remaining fact that doesn't fall prey to correlationism into an explanatory **absolute**, the facticity of the correlation. If facticity is necessary, which he dubs factiality, then the PSR as a metaphysical absolute is false, because its opposite, the principle of unreason, a speculative absolute, is true (*AF*, 50–60).

To counter the obvious objection, that this move would only render thought's inability to think the absolute into an 'absolute inability' (*AF*, 52), Meillassoux argues that only by assuming ontological facticity in the first place is one able to make sense of the distinction between the in-itself and the for-us. Since for being to be different from thought it needs to have the potential of being-other than it actually is for us, since otherwise thought could think being in-itself. The possibility to think the dualist basics of correlationism implies for Meillassoux that every epistemic possibility has to be a real possibility, otherwise correlationism itself would become unthinkable. In holding that everything that can be thought can become real, Meillassoux denies against Leibniz the complementarity of the PNC with the PSR, by turning the former against the latter.

To use the PNC to deny the PSR is no problem, because so far nobody has come up with a demonstration that the PSR is a necessary truth whose denial would involve a contradiction. Nonetheless, it could seem that Meillassoux's argument for his principle of unreason is itself threatened by a set of structurally similar contradictions. On several occasions Meillassoux denies the premise, which as in the case of correlationism is indispensable for his argumentation, in the conclusion of his argument. He argues from the truth of correlationism to its falsity, from dualism to monism, from the non-absolute to the absolute of the non-All, which may in-itself be a contradiction. In all cases his conclusions contradict their premises. Indeed, trying to convert correlationist dualism into an absolute monism of unreason may well be an impossible task, as the absolute cannot by definition be fundamentally divided in itself. Seen from this angle it is not surprising, as Brassier observes, that Meillassoux never gets rid of his initial dualism of thinking and being (Brassier 2007: 85–94).

Ultimately, the idea of the whole project, to derive an absolute from a dualist premise, could be said to be inconsistent from the start since an absolute can by definition only be some type of monism. Therefore, by necessity, one of the terms of the correlation has no place. Either one reduces reality to thought or vice versa, and in any case, the argumentation via the facticity of the correlation against the PSR would be impossible even to conceive. Rather than an assault on the PSR, Meillassoux's philosophy might be seen as a radical re-interpretation of it under a dualist premise, because to argue rationally against the PSR means to presuppose it already in its most general form. It is not so much the content of the PSR that is in question, but more the form this principle can take and whether or not, then, it is primary or secondary to the PNC.

PTOLEMAIC COUNTER-REVOLUTION

Francis Halsall

The Ptolemaic counter-revolution appears in Chapter 5 of *After Finitude* to name the philosophical response to the **Copernican Revolution** in science. Meillassoux recognises that the Copernican revolution has two meanings: a 'literal and genuine' sense from which modern science emerges; and a metaphorical use in philosophy. In this second sense it is often used to name the transcendental turn to **correlationism** taken by philosophy from Kant onwards. Meillassoux's decision to call this second sense the Ptolemaic counter-revolution is rhetorical as it suggests the tradition he ultimately wants to oppose is retrogressive. Meillassoux recognises that the Copernican revolution in science does not refer to astronomical modelling but rather the theoretical awareness, developed also by Galileo and René **Descartes**, that fundamental features of nature can be described mathematically. Hence the world, by virtue of its mathematisation, is separable from human consciousness and is not reducible to being a correlate of thought.

This Copernican-Galilean revolution leads to 'the decentring of thought relative to the world within the process of knowledge' (*AF*, 115). This creates the 'catastrophe' that science replaces **metaphysics** as the 'guarantor' of knowledge, namely that simultaneous to the scientific positing of a world independent to thought comes the realisation that the claims of science are naive and secondary to philosophical thought for they cannot guarantee their own truth. This, Meillassoux claims, is the violent contradiction at the heart of the 'schism' of modernity: that whilst science allows for the possibility of a mind-independent reality, philosophy insists that thought about that reality in-itself is impossible.

Within philosophy the use of the Copernican Revolution as a metaphor originated from a comment in the second preface to *The Critique of Pure Reason* (1787) where Immanuel **Kant** proposes to do for metaphysics what Copernicus had done for cosmology, namely effect a sudden revolution leading to a paradigm shift. In *On the Revolutions of the Heavenly Spheres* (1543) Copernicus proposed a heliocentric system that reversed the commonly accepted Ptolemaic geocentric model of the universe. Kant states that whereas previously it had been assumed that knowledge conforms to its objects he will develop a metaphysics that begins from the supposition that objects conform to knowledge. From this emerges the transcendental turn that modifies metaphysical questions directed toward things-in-themselves, knowledge of which is claimed to be impossible, into questions of how knowledge of the world of appearances is possible.

Meillassoux recognises the shortcomings of this metaphor by claiming that it gives rise to the paradox that its meaning is the opposite of what was intended, as it positions the observing subject at the centre of an epistemological system. In terms of their use in philosophical discourse both the **Copernican Revolution** and the Ptolemaic counter-revolution should be acknowledged as metaphors and rhetorical devices rather than cosmological or epistemological models. Kant's metaphor is less puzzling and certainly not paradoxical, if it is recognised as not predicated on positioning humans at the centre of the cosmos but rather in identifying that the movement of the universe is relative to the subject's perception of it and not the movement of objects around the subject. This is, ultimately, not as antithetical as it first appears to Meillassoux's project of focusing philosophical attention back onto the world itself and his attempts to reverse the 'catastrophe' of the anthropocentrism of the transcendental tradition.

RATIONALISM

Daniel Sacilotto

Rationalism is first thematised in distinction to empiricism in the context of the modern philosophical enquiries about the connection between mind and world. Thus understood, the germinal rationalisms attributed to René **Descartes**, Leibniz and Spinoza would be contrasted with the empiricisms developed paradigmatically by Locke, Berkeley, and David **Hume**. The crucial point of divergence between these thinkers concerns the relative priority each side would accord to either thought or experience in accounting for the link between mind and world. Thus while the rationalists generally ground our knowledge of the world on the conceptual means endowed to us, typically the 'primary properties' studied by mathematics, the empiricists would contest the fundamental status assigned to conceptually mediated thought and emphasise that knowledge has to begin in experience. So the narrative goes, short of securing our knowledge of the world, empiricists would then mobilise the resources of sceptical doubt farther than Descartes himself, calling into question the possibility of thought's access to the **Cartesian in-itself** as well as the necessity accorded to natural law. Even the essence of those primary properties studied by mathematics, according to Berkeley, lies in our perception of them; even the laws of nature, according to Hume, lie in our mere inductive habits. To save rationalism from the sceptical doubts raised by empiricism, while reckoning the constitutive link to experience, Immanuel **Kant** had thus to delimit thought's cognitive powers to the realm of appearances, resulting in weak **correlationism**, which Meillassoux argues leads the way for absolute idealism.

In its contemporary appropriation by Meillassoux, following Alain **Badiou**, rationalism becomes not so much opposed to modern empiricisms or to the weak correlationist doubts concerning the knowability of the in-itself. It addresses itself rather to the anti-realist positions exemplified by strong correlationism, subjectalism, and even the idealism with which it entered into complicity. Meillassoux's rationalism must be then understood as complimentary to his **materialism**, in the integral pursuit to attest our capacity to think the absolute. Thus while the exemplary strong correlationist, the Heideggerian phenomenologist (see Martin **Heidegger**), insists on the radical divorce between rational cognition and the pre-cognitive experience of being as such, Meillassoux dispels the reification of experience and the anthropocentric prison it builds so as to recover a properly discursive, even dialectical, access to the absolute. Similarly, resisting **idealism** and the 'transcendental empiricisms' proposed by vitalist subjectalists of which Bergson and Deleuze would be paradigms, and rather than disseminating thought into being or reifying the creative power of life ubiquitously in the material, Meillassoux's rationalism seeks to defend the radical autonomy of being with respect to thought and its conditions.

But how? First, Meillassoux's 'speculative method' proposes to overcome the impasses of correlationism and idealism by unravelling tacit assumptions in the former that ultimately yield a form of access to the in-itself. This is the dialectical procedure that unfolds as a sort of informal 'proof' or 'derivation' of the principle of **factiality** and its consequences. Second, following Descartes' lead, Meillassoux proposes to rehabilitate the rationalist distinction between **primary and secondary qualities**, once again identifying the former with what we think of being-in-itself through mathematical discourse (*AF*, 109). Appropriating Badiou's ontologisation of mathematics, **speculative materialism** thus defies the circumscription of thought to appearances and experience by avowing the stringency of formal discourse as it renders inoperative the empirical and phenomenological vocabularies on whose basis the correlationists, subjectalists and idealists conflated thought and being or limited the latter to the former in an inescapable circle. Still, Meillassoux merely anticipates the corresponding proof that would testify to mathematics' ontological status in his own programme. For to say that mathematics endows us with a direct or intuitive access to being without further ado would be simply to revert to the modern rationalist, that is, pre-Kantian, appeals to dianoetic intuition by merely postulating rather than arguing for a privileged access to the real through formal discourse. Antipathy to phenomenological piety can therefore not be a sufficient ground for ignoring the mediation of experience on whose basis the empiricist raises sceptical doubts. Merely trivialising or disavowing sensible affection, Meillassoux would obviate rather than resolve the question of how experience and causal receptivity mediates our epistemic grip and ontological belonging to the world as such.

REALISM

Lee Braver

If any question is distinctly philosophical, surely it is the question, 'what is reality?' The standard answer, so much a default position that it can sound rather odd when explicitly stated, is that reality is just out there, regardless of us – mind-independent, to use the technical term. The particularities of our beliefs, language, concepts and so on are to have no impact on the existence or nature of the world beyond trivial instances of our actually doing things to it of course. Any properties introduced by the mind are, at best, a second-rate reality essentially tainted by subjectivity such as secondary qualities or aesthetic values.

While mind-independence is generally taken to be its core component, realism tends to bring other ideas in its wake. Truth, for instance, is usually taken to be a form of correspondence: we must capture the world the way it really is or the way it is anyway, as Bernard Williams has said. Even sceptics agree on this definition of knowledge, only concluding that it is impossible. Certain ideas about the mind also fit into this view: for us to be capable of capturing reality, the mind must be able to remain still, merely reflecting the world like an untroubled mirror or a blank piece of paper. Some have attributed a certain determinacy to reality in the form of bivalence: every claim about the world either is or is not true, regardless of our ability to ascertain this.

Some form of realism has been tacitly assumed throughout the vast majority of the history of philosophy, with disputes mainly concerning which entities form the paradigms of reality – the realest reality, if you will: Forms, particular individuals, God, quantitatively measurable substances, noumena, and so on. It was Immanuel **Kant** who constructed the first coherent, thorough alternative to realism with his **Copernican Revolution**. Because the mind actively organises experience, necessarily introducing certain forms and structures into it, he argues that we can never capture or even encounter reality as it is in-itself, what he called noumena. Instead, we can only experience and know the world for-us, as our faculties have shaped it, phenomena. Meillassoux calls this view **correlationism** because it shifts attention from studying reality in-itself to studying reality in relation to us. He believes that Continental philosophy has largely taken this Kantian approach for granted. It has almost consistently operated on the view that we can only talk about the world as it presents itself to us, in the ways that we talk about it. This idea, sometimes called anti-realism, has displaced realism as the default, almost self-evident philosophical view during the last two centuries of Continental thought.

Analytic philosophy in many ways arose from its rejection. Its founders, Frege, Moore and Russell, all vehemently reject **idealism**, whether in its Kantian, German, or British varieties. They return to a pre-Kantian realism where we could achieve unmediated contact with the realist real, which took the form of logic for Frege and Russell. By the mid-twentieth century, however, analytic resistance to this 'naive' realism took hold, with philosophers such as the later Wittgenstein, Quine, Goodman, Davidson, Putnam and Dummett all pushing back to varying degrees and in various forms.

Anti-realism or correlationism maintained its dominance in Continental philosophy, on the other hand, through the end of the twentieth century. In his later work, Heidegger insists that being only is in relation to human beings, for Foucault the historical forms various phenomena take exhausts their reality, and Derrida (in)famously claims that 'there is nothing outside the text', that is, that all of our experience and encounters with the world are essentially mediated by language and other contextual features.

Perhaps the most interesting and important feature of the movement known as speculative realism, with which Meillassoux has been associated, is its attempt to turn the page on Continental anti-realism without retreating to a pre-Kantian naivety. Speculative realists want to be able to talk about the world itself but by going through Kant rather than ignoring him. Meillassoux raises two arguments against correlationism in *After Finitude*, his anti-anti-realist manifesto, a fairly simple, straightforward argument, and a rather complex one.

The complex argument, which I will only gesture at here, performs a conceptual judo flip on the correlational. Meillassoux claims that even the assertion of correlationism commits one to claims about reality as it is outside of or independent of its connection with us, namely, its radical contingency. The simpler argument raises a scientific common-sense objection. When a correlationist hears a scientist talking about events that took place before humans existed and hence outside of any correlation with us – in what Meillassoux calls 'ancestral time' – the correlationist translates such claims into a more sophisticated version. Instead of the naively realist claim, 'Dinosaurs roamed the Earth 4,000,000 years ago', the scientist really means that, 'According to our way of computing such things, in terms of our form of temporality, in keeping with evidence that has surfaced within our experience, we posit that dinosaurs roamed the Earth 4,000,000 years ago, for us.' What initially appeared to be about the world turns out to be about our present positing, hence remaining within its connection to us.

Meillassoux argues that this correlationist translation does not simply make it more sophisticated, but actually changes the meaning; indeed, it contradicts the most relevant feature of the claim. If we are to preserve the actual meaning of the claim, we must retain the common sense or naive reading of such ancestral claims: they really are about the world as it was before, and so independently of, us. Science does not go gently into that correlationist reading so, unless we wish to reject vast swathes of science, we must make our peace with its overt commitment to realism and so must give up correlationism.

RESURRECTION

Leon Niemoczynski

In Meillassoux's divinology the dead must be bodily resurrected in order for the most absurd conditions of **death** to be surpassed. According to Meillassoux an absurd death is a death where the living have departed under unjust conditions: odious deaths, premature deaths, deaths of children. A bodily resurrection is instituted by the divine being who may or may not be produced under **hyper-chaos**. Resurrection may occur within a **fourth World of justice**, a World preceded by the World of life, the World of matter, and the World of thought.

In 'Spectral Dilemma' Meillassoux sets out to argue that spectres, the dead who have suffered horrible deaths, have suffered injustice due to the fact that there is no reason to think why such an atrocious event could occur; that is to say, those who have suffered such terrible deaths seemed to not deserve such a terrible fate (*SD*, 262). Because an all good, all loving God could not permit such deaths or has chosen not to stop them, the theist cannot come to terms with the unjust nature of these deaths and the corresponding spectres they have left behind. Likewise, the atheist, who refuses the existence of **God**, cannot hope for justice for the departed if there is no God to eventually bring justice about (see **atheism/theism**). Meillassoux's resolution, arguing for the non-existence of God but hoping that God may one day come to be, entails that this thought of the future God 'allows me to hope for something other than the death of the departed' (*IWB*, 459).

Such an event, an advent where the dead are resurrected so that the wrongs of past deaths are righted in the ability to live again, seems improbable. However Meillassoux maintains that in the advent of a fourth World conditions may be such that physical laws will be able to permit the renewal of past human bodies. As Meillassoux states, 'The event in question is really possible, eternally contingent, forever uncontrollable, and completely improbablizable' (*IWB*, 458).

The fourth World of justice is a World where an ultimate being can act as a guarantor of universal equality, where equality stands for any being who is 'aware of the absoluteness of contingence, knows his own contingency . . . and thereby arrives all at once at both a cognitive and tragic dimension, which gives him his insurmountable worth' (*DI*, 290). Justice is the symbol of universality because it renders possible the surpassing of even the most absurd conditions of death in the new World. In the new World of justice there would still be the possibility of death, since a necessary existence is impossible, but immortality would be involved by the ability to indefinitely prolong death, for reinstituted bodies would no longer be subject to biological laws and forced to die according to the **laws of nature** that govern our current World.

S

SCIENCE

Robert S. Gall

Science and a particular understanding of science lie at the heart of Meillassoux's philosophical project. Meillassoux sees his task and the task of philosophy as completing the **Copernican Revolution** in science. He thinks that revolution calls for eliminating any consideration of the subject within the process of knowledge; science has the last word about what it says. This makes Meillassoux suspicious of post-Kantian critiques of science, which he does not address specifically but characterises generally as claiming 'that science harbours a meaning other than the one delivered by science itself' (*AF*, 119). This is why in *After Finitude* Meillassoux undertakes an analysis of certain kinds of scientific statements, which he calls ancestral statements, in an effort to undermine the coherence of all Kantian and post-Kantian philosophies and their corresponding philosophies of science. That analysis reveals a philosophy of science that dovetails with his own rationalist philosophy that seeks to explain how science is able to give a description of the world uncontaminated by experience.

Meillassoux notes that science routinely makes statements about the state of the universe prior to the existence of human beings, indeed, prior to the existence of any life on earth. For example, scientists claim that the accretion of the earth occurred roughly 4.56 billion years ago and took place over the course of tens of millions of years, occupying a certain volume in space that varied through time. Meillassoux argues that Kantian and post-Kantian philosophy, which he calls **correlationism**, cannot make any sense of such a claim. Since correlationism binds together thinking and being, correlationism must say the ancestral statement is only true *after* the emergence of thinking, even though it refers to a situation *prior* to the emergence of thinking. That, Meillassoux says, does not make any sense. This leaves only one alternative: 'the realist meaning of the ancestral statement *is its ultimate meaning*', that is, '*an ancestral statement only has sense if its literal sense is also its ultimate sense*' (*AF*, 14, 17, his emphases).

From this we can see that Meillassoux's philosophy of science falls under the heading of what is known as scientific realism. Generally, scientific realism is composed of three commitments. First, it holds that the world studied by the sciences exists independently of any mind. Meillassoux refers to this mind-independent world as the 'absolute', drawing on the original meaning of *absolutus* as severance to indicate a being that is separate from and non-relative to human beings. Thus he sometimes characterises his philosophical project as once more taking up the thought of the absolute. Second, as emphasised by Meillassoux in the quote above, scientific realism is committed to a literal interpretation of scientific claims about the world. In Meillassoux's particular brand of realism, given his commitment to a Galilean-Cartesian mathematisation of nature, this literal sense is mathematical. Thus his thesis is that

all those aspects of the object that can be formulated in mathematical terms can be meaningfully conceived as properties of the object in itself. All those aspects of the object that can give rise to a mathematical thought (to a formula or to digitalisation) rather than to a perception or sensation can be meaningfully turned into properties of the thing not only as it is with me, but also as it is without me. (*AF*, 3, his emphasis)

(This emphasis on mathematics shows the influence of Meillassoux's teacher Alain **Badiou**.) Finally, scientific realism holds that our best scientific theories give true or approximately true descriptions of observable and unobservable aspects of the mind-independent world. So, recognising that scientific theory is falsifiable, Meillassoux is not so naive as to think that a current scientific description, e.g., of an ancestral event, is the last word on what happened prior to life on earth. Nonetheless, he notes that it makes sense to suppose that the current scientific description about events is true so long as it has not been supplanted by another scientific theory. Thus Meillassoux holds that referents of scientific statements can be posited as real (mind-independent) once they are established by science at a given stage of its development.

Meillassoux's analysis and views on science might be contested on two fronts. First, a number of problems arise from the sweeping, abstract nature of his criticism of post-Kantian philosophy and philosophy of science. For instance, much of what Meillassoux has to say about the inability of post-Kantian philosophy to make sense of scientific statements depends upon the extent to which all post-Kantian philosophy can be labelled correlationist. It is not clear that this characterisation is apt for all post-Kantian philosophies, and certainly not all post-Kantian philosophy would accept such a label. In addition, Meillassoux does not address specific post-Kantian philosophies of science and their criticisms of scientific knowledge. This is especially problematic in so far as some of these philosophies – those of Heidegger and Foucault are prominent examples – are critical of the ways in which calculation dominates the contemporary world. These direct challenges to Meillassoux's emphasis on the mathematisation of nature are not addressed in any specific way by Meillassoux.

Another set of issues cluster around Meillassoux's insistence on equating science with quantitative and formal discourse, that is, mathematical discourse. This seems reductive at best, since most natural and social science – past and present – is not completely reducible to mathematical reasoning. By Meillassoux's account of science, it would seem that the results of scientific experiment in scientific fields in which methods, objects and data are not exhaustively mathematised would be denied any material/realist ontological status – a strange, anti-empirical conclusion. In short, it could be argued that Meillassoux's emphasis on quantitative and formal discourse in science does not appreciate the historical or current diversity of science and the richness of scientific knowledge.

SET THEORY

Sebastian Purcell

Set theory is a branch of **mathematics** that studies sets, or collections of objects defined exclusively by their membership in that collection. Because almost every mathematical notion can be defined in terms of sets, set theory, in conjunction with predicate calculus, is understood to provide the most basic foundation for mathematical investigation. Historically, this area of mathematics was developed in the 1870s by Georg **Cantor**, who produced the modern account of sets in order to settle questions of number theory in relation to real numbers. In doing so he also established the existence of different sizes or cardinalities of infinity, which serve as the foundation for contemporary number theory. For Meillassoux, set theory is significant because it expresses the most fundamental aspects of ontology in-itself, or reality independent of human consciousness, since he identifies the in-itself with whatever can be formulated in mathematical terms.

In its initial 'naive' formulation, set theory understands sets to be any sort of well-defined collection, whether real or imaginary. The collections of all trees or all unicorns are equally sets. The things that are *in* the sets are called either the set's elements or its members, and the symbol ϵ is used to denote the binary predicate '... *is a member of*...'. Thus, for example, if a is a member of set X, then this would be denoted 'a ϵ X'. There are two common ways to name or denote a set. The simplest way is to use brace notation. So, for example, the set {1, 3, 5, 7} is the set containing just the members 1, 3, 5 and 7. This method of notation, however, suffers from limitations: it can only name finite sets, and sets whose members we know specifically. An alternative way of naming sets that avoids these problems takes recourse to definition by abstraction. This method defines sets by means of a predicate. For example, one could take the predicate '... is a cat' and define the set of all (and only) cats by writing: '{x | x is a cat}', which can be read in English as 'the set of all x such that x is a cat'.

In order to know whether two sets are the same, one needs what philosophers call a principle of identity. In set theory, identity is specified through the principle of extensionality, which maintains that two sets are the same if and only if they share the same members. The binary predicate '=' is used to signify that two sets are the same. Thus, for example, the set X of all even prime numbers, and the set Y which contains the sum of 1 and 1 share the same members, namely {2}. Thus set X = Y.

The empty set (alternatively: null set, or void set) is a set with empty or null extension. For example, there is no set that satisfies the predicate 'x ≠ x'. This set then is null and may be symbolised either by empty braces, {}, or with the symbol Ø. Because any two sets that share the same members are the same sets (principle of extensionality), and because any empty set shares the same members (namely none), all empty sets are the same, which is to say there is only one empty set.

The reason there is a distinction between so-called naive set theory and axiomatic set theory is that if one takes the definition of sets by abstraction to be the only way of defining sets, as Cantor and Frege did, then one is bound to run into self-contradictory paradoxes. Perhaps most famously, Bertrand Russell in a letter to Frege pointed out that using this definition it was possible to formulate the predicate 'x is not a member of x'. One may then ask whether the set of all 'x that are not members of themselves' is a member of its own set or not. The answer, infamously, is that such a set would be a member of itself if and only if it is not a member of itself, which is a clear contradiction. In order to avoid this and related paradoxes, axiomatic versions of set theory were developed that would exclude the possibility of ever encountering such self-contradictory sets. The most standard form is the one formulated from insights by Zermelo and Fraenkel, and includes the axiom of choice (abbreviated ZFC). Its basic idea is to restrict the available universe of sets to what can be constructed consistently, so that paradoxes are not resolved, but avoided. This is done by ensuring that one can only apply rules to make sets out of existing sets, and that the only two sets one is given in axioms are the empty set and the smallest sized infinity.

Using these basic axioms and an operation to produce more sets out of the two existing sets, John von Neumann produced what is now called the set-theoretical hierarchy, abbreviated V, which begins with Ø and 'builds up' indefinitely. What is particularly important for speculative ontology is that V is not itself a set of all sets (in which case it would it run into the problem of Russell's paradox) but a construction. It thus provides a vision of the universe that is well-defined, but incomplete.

SPECTRAL DILEMMA

Leon Niemoczynski

Meillassoux's spectral dilemma pits the injustice of 'terrible deaths' ('odious' deaths, the deaths of children, violent deaths) against the existence or non-existence of God (*SD*, 262). Meillassoux's solution to the dilemma does not appeal to theism ('God exists') nor does it reject God absolutely in a form of atheism ('God does not exist'). Meillassoux formulates a third position which he calls 'divinology' – a position that features **divine inexistence** (*l'Inexistence divine*), a 'virtual God', who is not culpable for the injustice of deaths which have occurred in the past due to the fact that it did not exist during the time of those deaths, but who may come to be at some point in the future in order to create a new world where the dead are resurrected and past injustices absolved (*SD*, 275). This would be a world where our 'rational ends' and 'universal aspirations' involving truth, beauty and justice are finally met (*DI*, 218).

In his article 'Spectral Dilemma' Meillassoux identifies spectres, that is, those dead who have not been properly mourned and therefore who haunt us. Meillassoux is here referring to not only the terrible mass deaths of the twentieth century – Auschwitz and genocide, world wars, atomic destruction – but to the senseless and premature deaths throughout all of history: children, innocents, and deaths with which we cannot come to terms. Properly mourning these deaths means forming a bond where we would be able to live in a 'non-morbid' relation with the departed (*SD*, 263). Meillassoux asks whether or not it would be possible on the traditional alternatives of theism and atheism to face properly the sorts of deaths that have befallen those who have died without 'life hearing their complaints' (*SD*, 262). A spectral dilemma becomes apparent: one is either to believe in the existence of God or not believe in the existence of God given the injustice of these terrible deaths throughout all of history. (It is also possible of course to 'not believe' in an existing God in the sense that one simply 'revolts' against God, thus choosing not to follow God. But this is more of a matter of disbanding faith in God rather than outright denying God's existence.)

Both of the traditional alternatives, theism and atheism, lead to despair according to Meillassoux. Without God's existence, the atheist cannot hope for any redemption for the dead as there is no God and no afterlife. Life becomes an absurdity where it is impossible to bring justice for the departed. On the other hand, a theist posits God and believes in an afterlife where there may be justice in the next world. Yet this God has allowed these terrible deaths to occur despite being able to stop them. But why would a beneficent, omnipotent God allow the injustice of such odious deaths to occur in the first place? The traditional answer to the problem of evil is that the sufferings of life and the reality of death are a mystery, or that they contribute to a greater good, or that they are self-inflicted. For Meillassoux these alternatives are 'perverse' (*SD*, 264). But Meillassoux also states that both the theist's position and atheist's position are unsatisfactory. The theist enters into despair upon having hope for the dead with a God who has allowed unjust deaths to take place; the atheist enters into despair believing that another life is impossible and that there is no God to offer the dead a chance to live again. Cynicism and sadness result. Only the third option – believing in a God that does not exist now but someday may exist – makes sense. God is not held blameworthy for the injustice associated with terrible deaths and a resurrection of the dead is possible.

Regarding the third option, one may legitimately hope for the appearance of a divine being given the nature of the radically contingent ground or **hyper-chaos** responsible for issuing any event. The details of how a divine being may emerge and the sort of the future world of justice that is to be brought about with its emergence are developed in Meillassoux's dissertation *L'Inexistence divine* (*The Divine Inexistence*). According to Meillassoux's thesis of radical contingency, a contingency responsible for whatever appears in the world, because there is nothing preventing the emergence of a future divine being there is no reason why a virtual God could not appear in the future. Thus human beings cannot be prohibited from hoping for it. As Meillassoux writes, a 'contingent effect of Chaos', God can 'once more be desirable' (*SD*, 275).

SPECULATION

Steven Shaviro

Meillassoux defines his own speculative philosophy in opposition both to classical **metaphysics** and to modern critical and relativist thought. Speculation seeks to discover an **absolute** through the exercise of pure reason alone. This was the metaphysical project of the great 'pre-critical' thinkers, from René **Descartes** through Leibniz, who claimed to deduce the necessity of an '*absolute* outside', one that 'was not relative to us' (*AF*, 7). But all such metaphysical speculation was put to an end by Immanuel **Kant**, who questions the limits of thought and seeks to draw the boundary beyond which thought is unable to go. Kant turns thought back upon itself, and denies that thought can ever get beyond or outside itself. We can only know things in the world, Kant says, in so far as they exist *for us*; we cannot know anything about how these things might exist for themselves, without us and apart from the ways that we think of them. Any attempt to go beyond the limits of thought is sheer arbitrary **dogmatism**: metaphysical statements that spin out the empty forms of rationality, without any actual content to which these forms might apply. In this way, Kant de-absolutises thought, and outlaws speculation.

For Meillassoux, Kant succeeds in 'refuting every proof that would presume to demonstrate the absolute necessity of a determinate entity', whether that entity be God or something else (*AF*, 32). In this way, Kant outlaws speculative metaphysics. And Western philosophy since Kant has largely repeated this dismissal. There is a clear line, for instance, from Kant's rejection of the **ontological proof** of God's existence to Heidegger's rejection of all forms of **onto-theology**. Meillassoux does not seek to overturn such arguments. Rather, he seeks to open the way to *another form of speculation*, one that is not dogmatic or metaphysical: 'We must uncover an absolute necessity that does not reinstate any form of absolutely necessary entity' (*AF*, 34). Indeed, Meillassoux concedes that 'all metaphysics is "speculative" by definition' (*AF*, 34). But he denies the inverse of this proposition: 'our problem consists in demonstrating, conversely, that not all speculation is metaphysical, and not every absolute is dogmatic' (*AF*, 34).

Meillassoux's speculative project therefore leads him 'to develop an idea whose elaboration and defence require a novel kind of argumentation' (*AF*, 76). It is only in this way that he can posit 'an absolute without an absolute entity' (*AF*, 34). Meillassoux finds his absolute in the seemingly oxymoronic form of 'a reason emancipated from the principle of reason – a *speculative form of the rational* that would no longer be a *metaphysical reason*' (*AF*, 77). Meillassoux seeks to discover an absolute necessity that does not posit that anything in particular is necessary; and he finds this precisely in the claim that everything is *necessarily* non-necessary, or contingent. In this way, Meillassoux succeeds in, as it were, squaring the circle; he achieves 'an *absolutizing* thought that would not be *absolutist*' (*AF*, 34). He obeys the letter of Kant's ban on speculation, while circumventing its spirit. He restores the rights of speculation, without thereby lapsing into metaphysical dogmatism.

SPECULATIVE MATERIALISM

Ben Woodard

Speculative materialism names the proper response, according to Meillassoux, to the widespread anti-realism of philosophy following the progressively tighter **correlationism** between thinking and being. This deabsolutisation amounts to the prohibition of thinking the **absolute** (or anything for that matter) in a place in which there is no thought (*AF*, 36). Furthermore, this deabsolutisation applies not only to the limits of our knowledge but to the relational model as such (*AF*, 37). As Meillassoux argues it is not merely that our knowledge's relation to the world is ontologised but that this relation is crystallised as facticity. Given that Meillassoux wishes to think an absolute, a world without thought (*AF*, 28), he constructs speculative materialism to combat the devils of correlationism and other pernicious forms of idealism, by transforming the logic of strong correlationism from within. Why the conjunction of the terms speculative and materialism?

For Meillassoux the term **speculative** names the spirit of the original and properly scientific Copernican turn whereby the conservative structures of thought were challenged at base. **Kant**'s absorption of this lesson, according to Meillassoux, necessitated a reversal of the reversal, a **Ptolemaic counter-revolution** in which knowledge is protected from those claims which would potentially mark its frailty (*AF*, 119). Philosophically adapted, speculation is that form of thinking which makes any claims to an absolute (*AF*, 34). However, Meillassoux claims that a particular form of speculation is desirable in order to avoid both dogmatic and metaphysical speculation. While dogmatic speculation assumes an absolute entity or set of entities (*AF*, 78), metaphysical speculation, which Meillassoux aligns with Kant, asserts that the absolute exists as things-in-themselves and can be described as forms or necessary properties (*AF*, 76). In opposition to these forms Meillassoux argues that a properly non-dogmatic and non-metaphysical form of speculation must assert that the absolute is the very structure of facticity (that we can purportedly claim that things are a particularly way through description and not foundation) (*AF*, 39). As a further step, Meillassoux then applies speculation to the structure of facticity itself and arises at **factiality**, namely that facticity is not factual (*AF*, 80).

The upshot of this formulation of speculation is that Meillassoux is able to argue that contingency and contingency alone is necessary but that this contingency leaves **derivation** intact as a means of making existential statements such as 'There is X'. Following this, Meillassoux asserts that such a lean articulation of speculation allows one to explain manifest existential stability in a world without necessity (*AF*, 101) but not necessarily without mathematically coherent and therefore noetically derivable structure. Hence the speculative philosopher is the one who simply states that the transition is possible (*AF*, 56).

Only following this exposition of the speculative can we attempt to fuse speculation with materialism. For Meillassoux, the figure who represents the form of materialism he wishes to endorse is Epicurus, whose materialism simply states that thought can access the nature of things through the construction of concepts such as atom, swerve and void (*AF*, 36). This form of materialism, however, would still remain too metaphysical for Meillassoux as it would state that particular entities are necessary. Meillassoux argues that **materialism** is simply the thesis in which we assert that there is a–subjective matter (*AF*, 38). Whereas Meillassoux engages in impressive mental acrobatics to arrive at his formulation of speculation, his conception of matter is largely an assertion that matter does not necessitate thinking, that thinking is an eventual accident which occurred after the formation of matter. This formation functions as a primordial ontological order in a positive sense and a lifeless mass to which we return in a negative sense.

In so many words, speculative materialism names the form of thinking by which thought can propel itself outward, deriving the mathematical structure of ontology speculatively in conjunction with the materialist constraint that matter is the contingent demonstration of such order. It is for these reasons that toward the end of *After Finitude*, Meillassoux reiterates that speculative materialism is his self-description of the most desirable form of philosophy in the wake of idealism's long and errant reign (*AF*, 121).

SPECULATIVE REALISM

Rick Elmore

Speculative Realism (SR) is a broad term encompassing an array of philosophical positions all of which share a general resistance to what Quentin Meillassoux calls **correlationism**, the belief that the human–world correlate forms the central element of philosophical investigation

(Bryant et al. 2011: 3). Ray Brassier coined the term in 2007 as the title of a workshop held at Goldsmiths College. This workshop brought together Quentin Meillassoux, Ray Brassier, Ian Hamilton Grant and Graham Harman, thinkers that have, in many ways, become representative of SR. In addition, SR is intimately tied to a number of online communities and open access publishing, which have contributed to the rapid distribution of SR related works (Bryant et al. 2011: 6–7). Although SR is not a homogeneous philosophical 'school', a brief review of the work of the original Goldsmiths attendees gives one a sense of its philosophical terrain.

Meillassoux is often credited with catalysing SR with his notion of correlationism (Harman 2011a: vii). In addition, he is the only thinker from the original Goldsmiths conference that does not abandon the 'correlationist circle' outright. Rather, Meillassoux's work attempts to radicalise the correlationist project from within, showing that one can have a rational, mathematical basis for the existence of things outside of human thought (see **Cartesian in-itself**). It is on the basis of this claim that Meillassoux argues for the **necessity of contingency**, sketching the contours of a world in which anything is possible including the resurrection of the dead and the reign of pure justice (Bryant et al. 2011: 8).

Graham Harman's **object oriented ontology** is perhaps the best-known school of thought within the SR universe. In connection with the work of Levi Bryant, Ian Bogost and Tim Morton, Harman develops a realism based on the inherent inaccessibility of all objects, suggesting a flat ontological universe in which objects interact only indirectly by translating one another (Bryant et al. 2011: 8). Ray **Brassier**'s 'transcendental nihilism' takes the positive project of the Enlightenment to be the destruction of meaning (Bryant et al. 2011: 7). For Brassier, the realist assertion that there is a world independent of the human mind leads to the nihilist's conviction that such a world would be necessarily 'indifferent to our existence and oblivious to the "values" and "meanings" which we would drape over it in order to make it more hospitable' (Brassier 2007: xi). Hence, nihilism is a speculative project aimed at undermining all that might make humans feel at home or important in the universe.

Ian Hamilton Grant's work returns to the nature philosophy of Schelling in order to provide a transcendental and ontological foundation for science (Bryant et al. 2011: 7). Grant takes seriously the insights of natural science, particularly physics, as a means to push philosophy to 'redefine the transcendental and the conditions of thinking in the wake of a thoroughgoing naturalism' (see Iain Hamilton Grant, http://naught-thought.wordpress.com, 6 September 2012). Hence, his work sketches a dark reserve of pure 'productivity' that undergirds and produces the phenomenal world (Bryant et al. 2011: 7).

In addition to the authors listed above, SR has been shaped by the work of thinkers as diverse as Bruno Latour, Alfred North Whitehead, François Laruelle, Slavoj Žižek, Alain Badiou, Manuel DeLanda and Isabel Stengers to name but a few (Bryant et al. 2011: 2). This diversity of approaches explains both the influence of SR in fields such as ecology, queer theory, political theory, feminism and architecture, as well as the difficulty of defining SR in a strict sense. On this second point, there has been a growing dissatisfaction with the term SR, on the grounds that it fails to capture these different and often oppositional approaches. Hence today, SR is becoming more of a historical term, marking the turn in twenty-first-century philosophy toward questions of realism.

SUBJECTALISM

Daniel Sacilotto

For Meillassoux, the term subjectalism designates one of the two basic kinds of absolutism, and is introduced to clarify the distinctions between **materialism**, idealism and **correlationism** as characterised in *After Finitude*. In essence, subjectalist philosophers hold that it is possible for thought to access the absolute, at the price of identifying this absolute with some dimension of subjective existence itself. According to Meillassoux, these absolutisms do not dispute the closure of thought upon itself, but rather go on to identify thought, or an aspect of thought, as the very absolute that is within our grasp. Rather than seeing the correlation as the sign of an epistemic impasse, the subjectalist sees the correlation as an ontological fact. Historically and in spite of substantive differences in their specific contents, the variety of positions associated with subjectalism rest on a fundamental agreement 'that, after Berkeley, there could be no question of returning to the totally a-subjective reality of Epicurean materialism' (*IRR*, 3). But, unlike correlationism, which simply forecloses the possibility of **metaphysics** in the name of an investigation of the epistemic, existential, historical or discursive conditions for thought, the subjectalist wishes to preserve the speculative ambition of philosophy, by marking subjective mediation as part of reality, that is, by absolutising thought and so the correlation as such, either in its totality or partially.

To avoid confusion, however, some terminological remarks are in order. In *After Finitude*, Meillassoux had used the term correlationism more broadly to include both positions that de-absolutise thought through the correlation, and those that absolutise the correlation itself. Refining his position, however, it is only the former that is now to be squarely identified with correlationism, while the latter comprises the variety of positions advancing a post-Berkeleyan subjectalist metaphysics. The salient exemplar that Meillassoux used to illustrate what he now calls subjectalism in *After Finitude* was idealism, and particularly the absolute idealism attributed to G.W.F. **Hegel**, according to which the correlation of thought and being through the Concept (and thus reason) was identified with the absolute itself. Although the absolutising of the correlation remains an invariant feature in all its forms, in its most recent elaboration, subjectalism acquires an amplified scope to target a variety of positions that absolutise different aspects of thinking: 'Sensation was absolutized (Maupertius' and Diderot's hylozoism), as was reason (Hegelian idealism), freedom (the Schelling of 1809), perception (Bergson and the image in itself, in the first chapter of *Matter and Memory*), will (Schopenhauer), wills in their mutual conflict (Nietzsche's will to power), the self in its initial germ state (Deleuze's "larval selves" in *Difference and Repetition*), etc.' (*IRR*, 3).

In short, subjectalism would be the genus of which every variety of idealism, vitalism or hylozoism would be a species. Even if vitalism and hylozoism perceived themselves on occasion in sharp antagonism to idealism proper, Meillassoux notes, in rejecting materialism, they ultimately resemble each other in so far as they see no other alternative than to subjectivise matter, and so inscribe subjective mediation as necessarily implicated in the world. Similarly, every variant of subjectalism which sets itself against its counterparts will usually question the privilege accorded to a certain aspect of subjective life, only then to reify a different aspect of it. Taken together, subjectalism and correlationism designate what Meillassoux now proposes to call the era of correlation (*IRR*, 3).

Consequentially, Meillassoux's own speculative materialism would be set against not only naive materialism, idealism and correlationism, as *After Finitude* overtly suggests. It proposes to advance an absolutist alternative that is neither naive/dogmatic materialist, correlationist, nor subjectalist. It would have to be absolutist without thereby being dogmatic and yet insisting on the possibility an a-subjective reality. This is precisely the purported import of Meillassoux's speculative hypothesis through the thesis of **factiality**.

We should note that, under Meillassoux's strictures, absolutism is therefore not synonymous with **realism**, at least as the latter term is commonly used in the literature. Canonically, a position will be called realist if it upholds the existence or knowability of something which is independent of thought altogether. In Meillassoux's terminology, it is rather materialism, in both its dogmatic and speculative variants, which seems to be closer to the meaning of realism proper, in its 'classical' sense in so far as it designates 'every thought acceding to an absolute that is at once external to thought and void of all subjectivity' (*IRR*, 2). Absolutism, in turn, designates more broadly any position where one claims not just that some X is merely epistemically relative to thought, but is ontologically in-itself. However, this term is broad enough to cover both dogmatic and speculative materialist views for which the absolute is a-subjective, as well as those subjectalist views according to which the absolute is the subjective itself, or an aspect thereof. Thus, for instance, even Graham Harman's **object oriented ontology**, which proclaims to be realist in so far as it claims to speak of non-human relations, is, Meillassoux argues, in truth subjectalist since, like its vitalist and hylozoist predecessors, it continues to conceive the absolute by analogy to the aspects of thought, specifically in Harman's account, the account of intentional mediation and withdrawal that he adapts from Heidegger and Husserl.

That said, while materialism usually designates either a naturalist thesis according to which scientific description provides the lever for metaphysical insight, or in its Marxist historical form as coeval with the becoming of socio-economic relations of production, as Meillassoux uses it it simply designates any non-subjectalist realist position. Adapting Badiou's own rationalist Platonism in taking mathematical discourse to be the lever for metaphysical insight, Meillassoux's own speculative materialism overtly positions itself against naturalism, as he claims that the laws of science and the latter's description of the world remain subject to the absolute contingency of **hyper-chaos** (*IRR*, 11).

SYMBOL

Fintan Neylan

Rejecting traditional ideas of what philosophy should be, for example, a handmaiden of the sciences, Meillassoux conceives philosophy as that through which we can orient ourselves toward the universal. In his view, the philosopher is tasked with explicating the universal in a system where it can have coherence in the face of sophistries, religious obscurantism, and the despair of existing in a cold world.

This task is accomplished by means of the symbol, Meillassoux's name for that in which the philosopher situates the universal as real. There is, however, a problem with such orientation: the universal does not immanently exist, so one can either conceive it as part of some transcendent realm, or deny its existence altogether. As transcendent foundationalism is ruled out for Meillassoux, it would seem the philosopher must orientate herself to something which does not exist. Factial ontology provides a further option: the possible universal. Here the universal can be conceived as a value which may be realised, thus existing as a real possibility, but one which is *not presently* actual. This is known as symbolisation: the act of representing a universal value as a real possibility in order to give a philosophical account of the world, but without committing to the existence of the transcendental. For humans, the universal is manifest as justice. Symbolisation constitutes what Meillassoux calls a rational guarantee of this universal: despite the fact that justice does not currently exist, it is guaranteed as a possibility to which the philosopher can rationally assent and thus orientate herself.

A value may serve as a symbol: a rationally demonstrable possible truth concerning the immanent world. Because of this possibility for values, Meillassoux rejects the idea that they are but useful linguistic constructions with no ontological traction. The importance of the discourse of value is that it expresses the universal. This is distinguished from the discourse of being, which discloses the impersonal world we find around us. In symbolisation, the philosopher performs what Meillassoux calls an immanent inscription of a value in being, an elaboration of the world in which a universal value (justice) has coherence as a possibility. The inscribed value, for example the symbol, serves as an ontological link between the universal and being. Philosophy consists in the discovery of an ontological link through symbolisation, for it serves as a bond upon which any theoretical account between being and value is tenable. The symbol, as a link, is thus the cornerstone of any philosophy.

The history of thought is read as a series of divisions and reunifications of these two discourses. In these divisions the current system of values which explicates the universal becomes untenable and is forsaken. These displacements come in light of a radical shift in thinking, such as the supplanting of myths in favour of mathematical concepts' ability to explain the world. Though these new conceptual discourses open up an original way to envision existence, they are devoid of the universal. Born from this original schism between mathematical concepts and myths in Ancient Greece, philosophy's task is to engage in a reunification of the two discourses of value and being through a new symbolisation. In the destruction of a symbol by a new discourse of being, philosophy must reinscribe the universal back into the world, giving it a renewed rational coherence without attempting to disavow or reverse the content of the new discourse.

Meillassoux reads in the history of thought numerous attempts to reinstall the universal, but only what he calls the factial symbolisation can fully guarantee the universal as immanently possible, and bring the two discourses back into alignment. Gathered under three headings (the Cosmological, the Naturalist, and the Historical symbol) these types all aimed to place the universal as justice in **immanence**, but relied on some form of metaphysical necessity. In their orientation to the universal, the admission of metaphysics placed justice beyond the reach of any possible immanent actualisation, fixing it instead as transcendental. Properly speaking, they were attempts at symbolisation, as they could not meet the requirement of pure immanence.

Factial symbolisation is different because justice is conceived in a non-metaphysical manner. The symbol for Meillassoux is a universal value (justice) inscribed not as established actuality, but as a real possibility. A factial symbol is a link which allows one to fully acknowledge the current world as a brutal and cold one, while still rationally assenting that the very same world harbours the possibility of becoming a better one.

T

THING-IN-ITSELF/THINGS-IN-THEMSELVES

See **Kant, Immanuel** and **Cartesian in-itself**.

TIME

Michael Austin

Meillassoux discusses time in two different ways: in terms of chronology (past, present, and future) and in terms of time-itself. The former appears most prominently when discussing **advent, ancestrality** or the futural **God**. The latter is closely connected to his conceptions of **virtuality, contingency**, and **hyper-chaos**. Meillassoux's conception of time requires a basic retelling of important historical precedents, since his own work operates within the tradition, while also attempting to invert and radicalise it. The most significant figure in this respect is Plato, specifically his distinction between the eternal (the forms outside of time) and the temporal world of becoming and decay. The distinction between eternal and temporal finds common cause with the theology of the Middle Ages, where the eternal forms are replaced or superseded by God, and the shifting world of becoming becomes the realm of creation. Both Platonic and Christian conceptions of time are grounded on a beginning, an event of creation out of the eternal, while Neo-Platonism and its Christian heirs add to this a return to the eternal through contemplation or death.

Immanuel **Kant's** 'Transcendental Aesthetic' is a watershed for philosophical conceptions of time, transforming the exterior, eschatological and theological conception of time of the Middle Ages into the Modern conception of subjective duration and the rhythm of thought. Conceptions of time are radicalised from here, taken to their critical extremes in Anglo-American debates concerning the reality of time and their subjective extremes in Heidegger and, most importantly for Meillassoux, Bergson. While Kant maintains that space and time are coextensive and equiprimordial, both beyond empiricism and the basis for rationality, Bergson's 'superior empiricism' (through the method of intuition) radicalises Kant by removing space from the equation, determining it to be a derivative idea and not, as Kant claimed, immediately given to consciousness. It is time alone, understood as pure duration, that is the ground of conscious thought. Meillassoux's basic challenge is to invert or Platonise Bergson's *durée*, leading to a time outside of universal laws, to an eternal time of pure contingency and absolute chaos.

There are then essentially two modes of time at work in Meillassoux, that of worldly time and that of absolute time. When he speaks for instance of the **arche-fossil** or ancestrality, this is intra-worldly time, since it is still governed by our physics. Underlying this chronological time, however, is the possibility of another time, or perhaps better put, a time of other possibilities. Time, thus, is capable of transgressing its own laws; it is the indeterminate *par excellence*. Time-itself, in opposition to the flow of past to present, is the absolute power of contingency, the capacity for being-otherwise at the heart of Meillassoux's ontology, and the source of all change. When novelty irrupts within the cosmos, it is an irruption of time-itself. It is not the case however that time-itself for Meillassoux is equal to Platonic forms, containing all possibilities and pre-existing the world. Rather, time *is* the capacity to bring forth situations that were precisely *not* contained in the past. While our perception of time remains tied to various strata (the emergence of matter, life and thought for instance), such stratification, when viewed through the rational grasping of contingency, reveals time as the creator and destroyer of all, a power only understood when there is precisely no continuity between past and present. In order for there to be novelty in the advent of thought, there must be not only the principle of contingency, but an excess already at work within the universe, or else all would remain static and unchanged.

This power to destroy what once was and to create *ex nihilo* is time-itself. Pure time contains nothing, no past and no future. It is neither beholden to what once was, nor is it determined by a goal. Time is pure chaos and absolute illegality.

UNIVERSAL

Fintan Neylan

In Meillassoux's view, the task of the philosopher is explicate the universal in a system where it can have coherence in the face of sophistries, religious obscurantism, and the despair of existing in a cold world. As committing to the universal is traditionally seen as either admitting a form of **metaphysics**, or accepting ourselves as within a subject conditioned world, the presence of the universal seems to go against Meillassoux's ontology. However, his conception of the factial offers another option: the **virtual** universal. Unlike a metaphysical universal or one bound up with the transcendence of a subject, through factial ontology the universal can be conceived as that which *may* be realised at any moment, but one which is *not presently* actual. Given the world's disenchantment, the philosopher must accomplish her task by finding the *possibility* of the universal in a universe void of it. She discovers this possibility as the **symbol** and thus builds a philosophical account of the world around it. Whereas previous philosophers situated it in transcendence, the factial placement of it in the virtual allows Meillassoux's philosopher to rationally assent and orientate herself to the universal, while not committing to its current existence.

In their orientation to it, the universal is manifest to humans as justice. Meillassoux maintains this has been the case for all of philosophy: no matter how it is phrased, the explication of the universal throughout history has always been that of justice. In his system, the realisation of the universal would thus be the emergence of a just world. This manifestation of an eternal possibility of universal justice is part of Meillassoux's prioritisation of the ethical. Its status as a virtual possibility serves to underwrite just acts in the present world of pain *as just*, rendering the concept of ethical action both meaningful and rational. For even if it is not realised, through the factial humans may orientate themselves to the universal: this allows them to fully acknowledge the current world as a brutal and cold one, while still rationally assenting that the very same world harbours the possibility of becoming a universally just one.

VECTORIAL SUBJECT

Peter Gratton

Meillassoux argues that there has not been just the world as we currently see it, but previous worlds of matter and organic matter. The current world of thought is one given over to painful injustices. This leads Meillassoux to posit the **spectral dilemma**: if I believe in an existing, personal **God**, then I make that God responsible for the evils of the world, including the deaths of children and massacres of whole peoples. But if I don't believe in that God, then I affirm a hellish existence in which those who have died in horrible ways have no chance for redemption. Given the vicissitudes of **hyper-chaos**, Meillassoux argues that we cannot foreclose the coming of a **fourth World of justice**, one in which a God comes to be who resurrects the dead and oversees a communist-like community of equals. The vectorial subject is also the eschatological subject who sees her way past the spectral dilemma, acknowledging that while God does not exist *now*, that does not mean God will not come to exist. 'Magnetically attracted by the vector of the emancipation to come', the vectorial subject works *in this world* without the despair that weighs down so many others (*IWB*, 463). Filled with rational hope for a world that is not yet real, but foreseeable, the 'militant universalist', the vectorial subject, is led not by an ideal but by a possible world of equality to come (*IWB*, 465).

The vectorial subject, however, faces a second challenge more difficult than the spectral dilemma, namely a true **nihilism** in which she does not wish the immortality of the world to come, since it could be unending creative ineptitude or dissolving loves, and so on. The vectorial subject would also face the end of the meaning of her existence: she comes forward in the name of equality and emancipation to come, but if it arrives, then her meaning as a subject dissolves. Transcending this nihilism means thus seeing that we must at some point transcend politics, the brutal and costly ways in which the work for equality occurs. Having faced these two tests, the vectorial subject moves past potential hatred for existence, as in the spectral dilemma, and a hate for her fellow beings, as in the test of nihilism.

VERNES, JEAN-RENÉ

Peter Gratton

Vernes' *Critique of Aleatory Reason* (1982) provides a key resource for Meillassoux's argument against the 'frequentialist implication'. The frequentialist implication goes as follows: if the **laws of nature** could change without reason, since they are not necessary given **hyper-chaos**, they would do so frequently. But since the laws do not evidently do so – the world appears stable after all – the laws '*cannot* change for no reason ... they are necessary' (*AF*, 94). Vernes' text is important for Meillassoux as he identifies the 'probabilistic reasoning' behind the claim, since the idea is that it would be extremely improbable without necessary laws that we would have stability in the universe. But, as Meillassoux asks, what warrants the 'claim that the constancy of experience opens onto genuine necessity, whereas the *a priori* does not open onto veritable contingency?' (*AF*, 95). Meillassoux uses the example of a set of dice, where we take it that *a priori* one side of the dice are to come up more than any other. From this we calculate the probability that, say, snake eyes (two one's) can occur one out of thirty-six throws, and if you were getting snake eyes several times in a row, you are being had by a set of loaded dice.

Now, Vernes' takes this to a cosmic level and millions of chances, all of which we assume are equal, concerning the contingencies of the universe, where we remain getting the same outcome (a stable world). We assume, then, that we have a 'loaded' universe, that is, a set of laws that *cause* it necessarily to be stable. Meillassoux believes David **Hume** and Immanuel **Kant** take it for granted 'that the necessity of the laws is self-evident', just like someone who thinks they are more than unlucky on a bad night at the casino and blames the craps dealer. But Hume and Kant have merely extended this probabilistic thinking to the universe as a whole, or better, construct this universe as one among a total set of conceivable universes, and then think the changes of this stable universe against that 'universe of all universes' and consider it highly improbable that this universe would be a stable one: 'the nub of the argument consists in registering the immense numerical gap between those possibilities that are conceivable and those that are actually experienced' (*AF*, 97). Yet, the whole consideration of chance requires stable physical laws: the dice remaining the same during the throw and so on.

Having found the presupposition for the thinking of necessary physical laws, Meillassoux can then move to critique what is at the heart of it: that that universe is a 'whole' (see **non-whole/non-all**) from which a (yes, extremely high) number of probabilities follow. Wedding Vernes account to Georg **Cantor**, however, Meillassoux argues 'that we have no grounds for maintaining the conceivable is *necessarily* totalizable' given the teachings of **set theory** regarding the transfinite (*AF*, 103). Since there is no total of all possible 'sets', the universe cannot be amenable to aleatory reasoning, since there is no 'whole' from which to deduce any probabilities, as one can do with a die (where there are a total of six faces). This is the improbable though rational turn Meillassoux makes in *After Finitude* given Vernes' critique of aleatory reasoning.

VIRTUAL, THE

Michael Austin

In order to understand Meillassoux's use of the term 'the virtual' the concept must be understood in the context of twentieth-century French thought as employed by Bergson, and the term must be differentiated from both the actual and the potential. First and foremost, the virtual is not opposed to the real, as in the phrase 'virtual reality', but to the actual. The virtual and the actual are logically and necessarily opposed, while also being necessarily connected and coming into being simultaneously. The virtual is as real as the actual and grants us a glimpse of the possibilities of actualisation. The prototypical case of virtuality for Bergson is that of memory, which is real but not actual, yet affects us 'as if' it were actual. Memory is a capacity of matter for Bergson, the carrying forward of the past into the present, a display of the fluidity of time.

While it seems in some cases that Bergson will speak of the virtual as something of a reservoir of potentiality from which the actual emerges and argue that the virtual and actual are synonyms for process and product, nevertheless the virtual does not pre-exist the actual. Nor should we believe that the virtual is the target of 'true' ontology, while the actual is determined to be illusory or somehow false once its conditionality is grasped. The virtual is an emergent product of the actual, granting the observer insight into the power and possibilities of becoming. For Meillassoux, the virtual maintains this capacity for knowledge, as the epistemological arm of *After Finitude*'s ontology of **hyper-chaos**, and *L'Inexistence divine*'s **advent**. While **potentiality** defines the realm of possibilities concerning intra-worldly affairs, that is to say, possibilities under a given set of laws, the virtual is the realm in which all laws or sets of laws are possible. For example, while certain actions are possible given the law of gravity, Meillassoux maintains that it is possible for new laws to take its place, that is, for a new **World** to come into being. The example given by Meillassoux in 'Potentiality and Virtuality' is helpful here: while the roll of a die presents us with six intra-worldly possibilities, that is to say, given the six-sided nature of a standard die all sides are equally probable, the virtual nature of the die is infinite; the die could burst into flames, melt on impact, or present us with *A Tale of Two Cities*; while none of these results are as probable as the numeric sides, all are equally *possible* given the contingent nature of reality. The virtual is the index of the possible, or to state it even stronger, the virtual is the infinite set of all possibilities. Virtuality is the possibility for total universal ungrounding, the power and potentiality for creation and annihilation at the heart of time itself.

VITALISM

Rodrigo Nunes

For Meillassoux, 'only the materialist absolutizes the pure non-subjective – the pure and simple *death*, with neither consciousness nor life, without any subjectivity whatsoever, that is represented by the state of inorganic matter – that is to say, matter anterior to and independent of every subject and all life' (*IRR*, 6, his emphasis). It follows that vitalism, as he understands it, is inherently anti-materialistic: it absolutises the correlation through the hypostasis of some vital term (Nature, Will, Memory, Habit, Life...), thus ascribing human and/or organic traits to the inorganic/ non-human. Ironically, this is often done in the name of de-centring the human, which makes vitalism into a 'humanism-in-denial' (*IRR*, 5).

Vitalism falls under the general heading of **subjectalism**, meaning all those positions that absolutise the correlation. While **correlationism** proper absolutises facticity, subjectalism 'may select from among various forms of subjectivity, but it is invariably characterized by the fact that it hypostatizes some mental, sentient, or vital term' (*AF*, 37). The term therefore encompasses both the absolutisation of the subject that *After Finitude* also calls 'speculative idealism' (Fichte, Hegel) and vitalism; and 'even in those cases where the vitalist hypostatization of the correlation (as in Nietzsche or Deleuze) is explicitly identified with a critique of "the subject" or of "metaphysics"', it is still equivalent to speculative idealism in understanding that nothing can be 'unless it is in some form of relation-to-the-world', and that this proposition is not merely relative to our knowledge, but absolute (*AF*, 37).

For Meillassoux, the 'critical force' of the term lies precisely in putting 'into *the same camp* ... currents that claim to be radically opposed', and which are ultimately in 'the camp of Berkeley himself' (*IRR*, 6, his emphasis). Yet the possibility of collapsing the two appears to depend on the equivocity of his idea of 'de-subjectivized matter' (*IRR*, 6). We can understand the phrase 'de-subjectivized matter' in two ways: as referring to matter in itself, taken in abstraction from any correlation or human mediation of any kind (mental, sensible, etc.); or to matter as devoid of anthropomorphic traits, or any continuity with human or subjective life. The two, which respond to an *idealist* and a *vitalist* subjectivisation of matter respectively, are not synonymous. Meillassoux suggests that vitalism, 'even if not always in full consciousness', accepts the idealist principle that 'we always experience subjectivity as a necessary, and hence eternal, principle', and thus that 'thought thinks thought as the absolute' (*IRR*, 8). Yet he does not support the claim, and it is unclear that he can.

It is one thing, as idealisms from Berkeley to **phenomenology** have done, to take as a starting point that Being is only accessible to us as subjectively mediated, and thus reduce the question of Being (in–itself) into that of givenness or appearing (for–us). It is another to start by refusing pre-eminence to the subject in order to think a Being in which it is included, not as exception, but in some sort of continuity, as the likes of Deleuze and Whitehead have done. The latter can no doubt be criticised for engaging in imaginary anthropomorphising projections, to the extent that they ascribe to Being elements that would be 'proper' to human subjectivity. Yet that is done *precisely* by overstepping the boundaries of the reduction of philosophical enquiry to subjectivity or to the conditions of appearing; if anything, vitalist subjectivisation seems to run counter to idealist subjectivisation.

Conversely, showing that matter is thinkable outside of subjective mediation (not 'subjective' in the idealist sense) does not in and of itself say anything about whether it is 'devoid of all subjectivity' (*IRR*, 2) in the anti-vitalist sense. Obviously, I must be able to think or know matter as it is in itself so as to assert that it is discontinuous with life/subjectivity; but I cannot deduce this discontinuity from the mere fact that matter is thinkable or knowable in-itself. Here, Meillassoux merely begs the question: what evidence does he have that the continuities between Being and subject asserted by vitalism are erroneous projections of the 'properly' subjective, and not in Being itself? The failure to establish what he assumes is indirectly acknowledged: '*If we posit* that the inorganic real is non-sentient, we ... save ourselves the very complex task of adding to matter a very problematic sentient capacity' (*IRR*, 14, my emphasis). Yet not only is his preferred alternative (**creation** *ex nihilo*) hardly less problematic, the statement's conditionality ('if we posit') raises the question of whether **speculative materialism** can really differentiate itself from the 'postulative, hypothetical' nature of 'hyperphysics' (*IRR*, 13–14).

WORLD

Peter Gratton

For Meillassoux the World (*Monde*) (with a capital letter) is a given universe of particular laws, which he also calls 'orders' (*ordres*). These Worlds were created *ex nihilo*. The utter contingency of **hyper-chaos** means the appearance of these Worlds can occur without reason. That is, each World comes about as an 'effect' unexplainable from a given previous World. Meillassoux argues that there have been at least *three* different Worlds:

So far there seem to have been three [Worlds] of irreducible facts: matter (reducible to what can be theorized in physico-mathematical terms), life (understood more specifically as a set of terms, that is, affections, sensations, qualitative perceptions, etc., which cannot be reduced to material processes), and finally thought (understood as a capacity to arrive at the 'intelligible contents' bearers of eternity, and which as such is not reducible to any other terms). (*IWB*, 461)

Meillassoux will use the word 'world' (*monde*) (lower-case 'w') to designate the 'non-Whole' of what is. He's a bit unclear on what this means: 'Worlds arise suddenly from the world, and if these have a right to a majestic capital letter for the first time, it is because there is more in the World than in the world, since there is more in what ensues than there is in the origin (more in the "effect" than in the "cause")' (*DI*, 189). This suggests that Meillassoux thinks of the 'world' as the factial or the virtual, the hyper-chaos that gives rise to new Worlds. As he notes, the laws of any one World provide no reason to think that they will continue:

Laws have no reason to be constant, and nothing entails that they will not contain new constants in the future. Such cases of advent [*surgissement*] ... can be divided into three *orders* [that is, Worlds] that mark the essential ruptures of becoming:

matter, *life*, and *thought*. *Each* of these three *appears* [my emphasis] as a Universe that cannot be *qualitatively* reduced to *anything* [my emphasis] that preceded it. (*DI2*, 284; *DI*, 187)

Finally, the 'intra-Worldly' (*intra-Mondaine*): what occurs and is possible within a determinant World. For example, in a World in which life exists, evolution of new species can occur; in a World where thought is available, we can witness creative invention. Describing the intra-worldly and the facts of this World falls to science, as Meillassoux makes clear in his argument from the ancestral. However, it is the task of speculative philosophy to describe what may be, that is, the possibilities opened up by the hyper-chaos of the world, one possibility of which is a coming **God** impossible in this World but rationally foreseeable coming to us as a **fourth World of justice**.

Bibliography

BIBLIOGRAPHY OF WORKS OTHER THAN BY MEILLASSOUX

Badiou, Alain (2007), *Being and Event*, trans. Oliver Feltham, London: Continuum.

Brassier, Ray (2007), *Nihil Unbound: Enlightenment and Extinction*, London: Palgrave Macmillan.

Brassier, Ray (2008) 'The View from Nowhere', *Identities: Journal for Politics, Gender, and Culture*, 8:2, pp. 7–23.

Brassier, Ray (2011), 'Concepts and Objects', in *The Speculative Turn*, ed. Levi Bryant, Nick Snricek, and Graham Harman, Melbourne: re.press.

Bryant, Levi R. (2010), 'Lexicon of Onticology', *Larval Subjects* (blog), <http://larvalsubjects.wordpress.com/2010/05/22/a-lexicon-of-onticology> (accessed 1 September 2013).

Fichte, J.G. (1982), *The Science of Knowledge*, ed. Peter Heath and John Lachs, Cambridge: Cambridge University Press.

Grant, Iain Hamilton (2006), *Philosophies of Nature after Schelling*, London: Continuum.

Hallett, Michael (1986), *Cantorian Set Theory and Limitation of Size*, Oxford: Clarendon.

Harman, Graham (2010), *Toward Speculative Realism: Essays and Lectures*, Winchester: Zero Books.

Harman, Graham (2011), *The Quadruple Object*, Winchester: Zero Books.

Heidegger, Martin (1962), *Being and Time*, trans. John Macquarrie and Edward Robinson, New York: Harper & Row.

Heidegger, Martin (1969), *Identity and Difference*, trans. Joan Stambaugh, New York: Harper & Row.

Heidegger, Martin (1973), *The End of Philosophy*, trans. Joan Stambaugh, New York: Harper & Row.

Heidegger, Martin (1982), *Nietzsche IV: Nihilism*, ed. David F. Krell, trans. Frank A. Capuzzi, New York: Harper & Row.

Husserl, Edmund (1965), *Phenomenology and the Crisis of Philosophy*, New York: Harper.

Husserl, Edmund (1981), *Husserl: Shorter Works*, Notre Dame: University of Notre Dame Press.

Husserl, Edmund (1983), *Ideas Pertaining to a Pure Phenomenology and to a Phenomenological Philosophy, First Book: General Introduction to a Pure Phenomenology*, trans. F. Kersten, The Hague: Martinus Nijhoff.

Lewis, David (1998), *Papers in Philosophical Logic*, Cambridge: Cambridge University Press.

Livingston, Paul (2012), *The Politics of Logic: Badiou, Wittgenstein, and the Consequences of Formalism*, London: Routledge.

Moore, A.W. (2001), *The Infinite*, London: Routledge.

Morton, Timothy (2013), *Realist Magic: Objects, Ontology, and Causality*, London: Open Humanities Press.

Nietzsche, Friedrich (1954), *The Portable Nietzsche*, ed. Walter Kaufmann, New York: Viking.

Nietzsche, Friedrich (1974), *The Gay Science*, trans. Walter Kaufmann, New York: Random House.

Priest, Graham (1987), *In Contradiction: A Study of the Transconsistent*, The Hague: Martinus Nijhoff.

Priest, Graham (2005), *Towards Non-Being*, Oxford: Oxford University Press.

Quine, W.V.O. (1986), *Philosophy of Logic*, Cambridge, MA: Harvard University Press.

Vernes, Jean-René (1982), *Critique de la raison aléatoire, ou Descartes contre Kant*, Paris: Aubier.

Zahavi, Dan (2003), *Husserl's Phenomenology*, Stanford: Stanford University Press.

SECONDARY LITERATURE

Ayache, Elie (2010), *The Blank Swan: The End of Probability*, United Kingdom: Wiley.

Brassier, Ray (2007), 'The Enigma of Realism: On Quentin Meillassoux's *After Finitude*', in Robin Mackay (ed.), *Collapse Volume II: Speculative Realism*, Oxford: Urbanomic, pp. 55–81.

Brown, Nathan (2011), 'The Speculative and the Specific', in Bryant et al. (eds), *The Speculative Turn*, pp. 142–63.

Bryant, Levi, Nick Srnicek and Graham Harman (2011) (eds), *The Speculative Turn: Continental Materialism and Realism*, Melbourne: re.press.

Burns, Michael O'Neill (2010), 'The Hope of Speculative Materialism', in Anthony Paul Smith and Daniel Whistler (eds), *After the Postsecular and Postmodern: New Essays in Continental Philosophy of Religion*, Newcastle: Cambridge Scholars Publishing, pp. 316–34.

Corby, James (2013), 'Style is the Man: Meillassoux, Heidegger, and Finitude', in Ivan Callus, James Corby and Gloria Lauri-Lucente (eds), *Style in Theory: Between Literature and Philosophy*, London: Bloomsbury Academic, pp. 163–86.

Critchley, Simon (2009), 'Back to the Great Outdoors: Review of Quentin Meillassoux, *After Finitude: An Essay on the Nature of Contingency*', *Times Literary Supplement*, February 28.

Crockett, Clayton (2011), 'Review of Quentin Meillassoux: *After Finitude* and Graham Harman, *Quentin Meillassoux* ', *International Journal for Philosophy of Religion* (2012), 71:3, pp. 251–5.

Cutler, Anna and Iain Mackenzie (2011), 'Critique as a Practice of Learning: Beyond Indifference with Meillassoux, towards Deleuze', *Pli*, 22, pp. 88–109.

Delancey, Craig (2012), '*After Finitude: An Essay on the Necessity of Contingency*, by Quentin Meillassoux', *The European Legacy*, 17:3, pp. 403–4.

Ennis, Paul J. (2011a), *Continental Realism*, Winchester: Zero Books.

Ennis, Paul J. (2011b), 'The Transcendental Core of Correlationism', *Cosmos and History*, 7:1, pp. 37–48.

Galloway, Alexander R. (2013) 'The Poverty of Philosophy: Realism and Post-Fordism', *Critical Inquiry*, 39:2, pp. 347–66.

Gironi, Fabio (2011), 'Meillassoux's Speculative Philosophy of Science: Contingency and Mathematics', *Pli*, 22, pp. 25–60.

Gironi, Fabio (2012), 'Assessing the French Atheistic Turn', *Speculations: Journal of Speculative Realism* (2012), 3, pp. 473–490.

Gratton, Peter (2009), 'After the Subject: Meillassoux's Ontology of "What May Be"', *Pli*, 20, pp. 55–80.

Gratton, Peter (2009), 'Quentin Meillassoux, *After Finitude: An Essay on the Necessity of Finitude*', *Philosophy in Review*, 29:6, pp. 427–9.

Gratton, Peter (2012), 'Meillassoux's Speculative Politics', *Analecta Hermeneutica*, 4, pp. 1–14.

Gratton, Peter (2014), *Speculative Realism: Problems and Prospects*, London: Bloomsbury Press.

Hägglund, Martin (2011), 'Radical Atheist Materialism: A Critique of Meillassoux', in Bryant et al. (eds), *The Speculative Turn*, pp. 114–29.

Hallward, Peter (2011), 'Anything is Possible: A Reading of Quentin Meillassoux's *After Finitude*', in Bryant et al. (eds), *The Speculative Turn*, pp. 130–41.

Harman, Graham (2007), 'Quentin Meillassoux: A New French Philosopher', *Philosophy Today* (2007), 51:1, pp. 104–17.

Harman, Graham (2011a), *Quentin Meillassoux: Philosophy in the Making*, Edinburgh: Edinburgh University Press.

Harman, Graham (2011b), 'Meillassoux's Virtual Future', *Continent*, 1:2, pp. 78–91.

Johnston, Adrian (2009), 'The World Before Worlds: Quentin Meillassoux and Alain Badiou's Anti-Kantian Transcendentalism', *Contemporary French Civilization*, 33:1, pp. 73–99.

Johnston, Adrian (2011), 'Hume's Revenge, À Dieu, Meillassoux?', in Bryant et al. (eds), *The Speculative Turn*, pp. 92–113.

Morelle, Louis (2012), 'Speculative Realism: After Finitude, and Beyond?', *Speculations: Journal of Speculative Realism*, 3, pp. 241–72.

Moshe, Josef (2011), 'Correlationism Reconsidered: On the "Possibility of Ignorance" in Meillassoux', *Speculations: Journal of Speculative Realism*, 2, pp. 187–206.

O'Mahoney, Paul (2013), 'Hume's Correlationism: On Meillassoux, Necessity and Belief', *Journal of French and Francophone Philosophy*, XXI, pp. 132–60.

O'Sullivan, Simon (2012), *On the Production of Subjectivity: Five Diagrams of the Finite-Infinite Relation*, Basingstoke: Palgrave.

Padui, Raoni (2011), 'Realism, Anti-Realism, and Materialism', *Angelaki*, 16:2, pp. 89–101.

Purcell, L. Sebastian (2010), 'After Hermeneutics?', *Symposium*, 14:2, pp. 160–79.

Riera, Gabriel, (2008), 'Review of Quentin Meillassoux, *After Finitude: An Essay on the Necessity of Contingency*', *Notre Dame Philosophical Reviews*, 10, no pagination.

Roffe, Jon (2012), 'Time and Ground', *Angelaki*, 17:1, pp. 57–67.

Saldanha, Arun J.J. (2009), 'Back to the Great Outdoors: Speculative Realism as Philosophy of Science', *Cosmos and History*, 5:2, pp. 304–21.

Smith, Anthony Paul (2011), 'A Stumbling Block to the Jews and Folly to the Greeks: Non-Philosophy and Philosophy's Absolutes', *Analecta Hermeneutica*, 3, pp. 1–16.

Thorne, Christian (2012), 'Outward Bound: On Quentin Meillassoux's *After Finitude*', *Speculations: Journal of Speculative Realism*, 3, pp. 273–89.

Toscano, Alberto (2011), 'Against Speculation, or, A Critique of the Critique of Critique: A Remark on Quentin Meillassoux's After Finitude (After Colletti)', in Bryant et al. (eds), *The Speculative Turn*, pp. 84–91.

Van Houdt, John (2011), 'The Necessity of Contingency or Contingent Necessity: Meillassoux, Hegel, and the Subject', *Cosmos and History*, 7:1, pp. 128–41.

Watkin, Christopher (2011), *Difficult Atheism: Post-Theological Thinking in Alain Badiou, Jean-Luc Nancy and Quentin Meillassoux*, Edinburgh: Edinburgh University Press.

Žižek, Slavoj (2012), *Less Than Nothing: Hegel and the Shadow of Dialectical Materialism*, London and New York: Verso (Interlude 5).

Notes on Contributors

Jeffrey Bell is Professor of Philosophy at Southeastern Louisiana University. He is the author of several books and numerous articles, including *Deleuze's Hume* (2009) and *Philosophy at the Edge of Chaos* (2006). Jeff is currently working on two manuscripts: a critical introduction and guide to Deleuze and Guattari's *What is Philosophy?* and *Truth and Relevance: An Essay on Metaphysics*. When not immersed in philosophical texts, Jeff and his wife are busy with raising two wonderful daughters.

Lee Braver is Associate Professor of Philosophy at the University of South Florida. He is the author of *A Thing of This World: A History of Continental Anti-Realism* (2007), *Heidegger's Later Writings: A Reader's Guide* (2009), *Groundless Grounds: A Study of Wittgenstein and Heidegger* (2012), *Heidegger: Thinking of Being* (2014), and editor of *Division III of Being and Time: Heidegger's Unanswered Question of Being* (forthcoming), as well as number of articles and book chapters.

Nathan Brown is an Assistant Professor in the Department of English and the Program in Critical Theory at UC Davis. His first book, *The Limits of Fabrication: Materials Science and Materialist Poetics*, is forthcoming with Northwestern University Press. With Petar Milat, he is the editor of *The Art of the Concept* (2013), a special issue of *Frakcija: Performing Arts Journal*. He is currently finishing a book manuscript titled *Absent Blue Wax: Rationalist Empiricism in Contemporary French Philosophy* while beginning a research project on the problem of measure in modern science, philosophy and poetry. His articles have appeared in journals such as *Radical Philosophy*, *Qui Parle*, *Parallax*, and *Mute*.

Levi R. Bryant is a Professor of Philosophy at Collin College. He is the author of *Difference and Givenness: Deleuze's Transcendental Empiricism and the Ontology of Immanence* (2008), *The Democracy of Objects*, *Onto-Cartography: An Ontology of Machines and Media* (2014), and co-edited *The Speculative Turn: Continental Materialism and Realism* (2011), with Nick Srnicek and Graham Harman. He has written widely on speculative realism as well as contemporary French philosophy.

Sean Dudley is a graduate of Simon Fraser University in the Department of Philosophy where he is currently studying metaphysics, free will and morality. Sean blogs regularly at hochestepunkt.wordpress.com.

Rick Elmore received his PhD in Philosophy from DePaul University in 2011. He works primarily in the areas of contemporary French philosophy and Critical Theory with a focus on ecology, violence and animal studies. Rick is currently a visiting Faculty Fellow at Colby College and is writing, with Peter Gratton, a manuscript entitled *The New Derrida*.

Daw-Nay Evans is Assistant Professor of Philosophy at Lake Forest College in Lake Forest, Illinois. He has published in such journals as the *Journal of the History of Philosophy*, *Philosophy and Literature*, *The Classical Review*, *The Philosophers' Magazine*, and *The Journal of Nietzsche Studies*.

Robert S. Gall is an independent scholar who has taught at a variety of colleges and universities in the United States. He is the author of *Beyond Theism and Atheism: Heidegger's Significance for Religious Thinking* (1987) and numerous articles on philosophy of religion and contemporary European philosophy.

Fabio Gironi recently completed his PhD at Cardiff University, with a dissertation on Alain Badiou's ontology and analytic philosophy of science, and is an editor of the journal *Speculations: Journal of Speculative Realism*. His research interests include comparative approaches to the philosophy of science and its history, neo-Kantian epistemology and the study of conceptual creativity.

Francis Halsall is a Lecturer in the History/Theory of Modern & Contemporary Art at National College of Art and Design, Dublin, where he is director (with Declan Long) of MA Art in the Contemporary World (www.acw.ie). In 2014 he will be visiting Critical Studies Fellow at Cranbrook School of Art and Design. His research practice is situated across three main areas: The history, theory and practice of modern and contemporary art; Philosophical aesthetics; and Systems-Thinking. Publications include the books *Systems of Art* (2008) and the edited volume *Rediscovering Aesthetics* (2009). Recent work, ideas and publication details can be found at www.alittletagend.blogspot.com.

Robert Jackson is a PhD student at Lancaster University. His research incorporates computational art, computer science, art theory and speculative realism. He is the author of several essays and a forthcoming publication with Zero Books, *BioShock: Decision, Forced Choice, Propaganda*. Robert is also an associate editor of *Speculations*, an independent peer-reviewed journal dedicated to speculative realism and he writes regularly for the digital arts collective Furtherfield.org as well as the Chicago-based art blog Bad-At-Sports.org.

Adrian Johnston is a Professor in the Department of Philosophy at the University of New Mexico at Albuquerque and a faculty member of the Emory Psychoanalytic Institute in Atlanta. He is the author of *Time Driven: Metapsychology and the Splitting of the Drive* (2005), *Žižek's Ontology: A Transcendental Materialist Theory of Subjectivity* (2008), *Badiou, Žižek, and Political Transformations: The Cadence of Change* (2009), *Prolegomena to Any Future Materialism, Volume One: The Outcome of Contemporary French Philosophy* (2013), and *Adventures in Transcendental Materialism: Dialogues with Contemporary Thinkers* (2014). He is the co-author, with Catherine Malabou, of *Self and Emotional Life: Philosophy, Psychoanalysis, and Neuroscience* (2013). With Todd McGowan and Slavoj Žižek, he is a co-editor of the book series *Diaeresis* at Northwestern University Press.

Adam Kotsko is Assistant Professor of Humanities at Shimer College in Chicago. He is the author of *Žižek and Theology* (2008), *Politics of Redemption: The Social Logic of Salvation* (2010), *Awkwardness* (2010), and *Why We Love Sociopaths: A Guide to Late Capitalist Television* (2012), and the translator of several works by Giorgio Agamben. He blogs at *An und für sich* (itself.wordpress.com).

Paul Livingston is Associate Professor of Philosophy at the University of New Mexico. He works on phenomenology, philosophy of mind, philosophy of language and the history of twentieth-century philosophy, among other topics. He has published three books: *Philosophical History and the Problem of Consciousness* (2004), *Philosophy and the Vision of Language* (2008) and *The Politics of Logic: Badiou, Wittgenstein, and the Consequences of Formalism* (2012). He is currently finishing a book on Heidegger, tentatively titled *The Logic of Being: Heidegger, Truth, and Time*.

Sean J. McGrath is a graduate of the University of Toronto specialising in phenomenology, metaphysics and psychoanalysis, and a native of Newfoundland, where he currently works as an Associate Professor of Philosophy. His first major work was on the early Heidegger and Medieval Philosophy, *Phenomenology for the Godforsaken* (2006). He was a Humboldt fellow at the Universities of Bonn and Freiburg from 2008 to 2011. The product of that research is his *The Dark Ground of Spirit: Schelling and the Unconscious* (2012). He is currently working on a book on Western spirituality and a major study of the contemporary relevance of Schelling's Philosophy of Revelation.

Paul O'Mahoney completed a PhD in Philosophy at University College Dublin, focusing on the work of Jean Baudrillard and postmodernity. He has published a number of articles on Baudrillard, as well as on Plato, Descartes, Nietzsche, Leo Strauss, James Joyce, Jacques Derrida and Samuel Beckett. His article 'Hume's Correlationism: On Meillassoux, Necessity and Belief' appeared in *Journal of French and Francophone Philosophy*, 21:1 (2013).

Raphaël Millière is a graduate student at the École Normale Supérieure in Paris. In 2011 he created a weekly workshop of contemporary metaphysics and ontology where he discusses with other graduate students and invited professors important metaphysical issues drawing from both the analytic and the Continental tradition. He has since given in a few papers and talks including a critical assessment of Meillassoux's thesis from a logical standpoint.

Marie-Eve Morin is Associate Professor of Philosophy at the University of Alberta. She received her PhD from the University of Freiburg, Germany, with a dissertation on the concept of community in Jacques Derrida and Jean-Luc Nancy. She is the author of *Jean-Luc Nancy* (2012) and co-editor, with Peter Gratton, of *Jean-Luc Nancy and Plural Thinking: Expositions of World, Ontology, Politics, and Sense* (2012).

Leon Niemoczynski teaches in the Department of Philosophy at Immaculata University near Philadelphia, Pennsylvania. He specialises in both the American and Continental philosophical traditions, and his interests include the philosophy of religion, the philosophy of nature, logic and metaphysics, aesthetics, German Idealism, environmental philosophy and philosophical ecology.

Fintan Neylan is an independent researcher currently living in Dublin. He studied philosophy at University College Dublin and is a co-founder of the Dublin Unit for Speculative Thought.

Christopher Norris is Distinguished Research Professor in Philosophy at the University of Cardiff, Wales. He has written more than thirty books on aspects of philosophy and literary theory, among them *Badiou's* Being and Event: *A Reader's Guide* (2009) and *Derrida, Badiou and the Formal Imperative* (2012). His most recent publications are *Philosophy Outside-In: A Critique of Academic Reason* (2013) and *The Cardinal's Dog* (2013), a collection of verse-essays on philosophical, musical and literary themes.

Rodrigo Nunes is a Lecturer in Modern and Contemporary Philosophy at PUC-Rio, Rio de Janeiro, Brazil. He coordinates a countrywide research group on the intersections between contemporary ontology, science and politics called Materialismos (http://materialismos.tk), and is a member of the editorial collective of Turbulence (http://turbulence.org.uk).

Sebastian Purcell is Assistant Professor of Philosophy at SUNY Cortland. He has published numerous articles on moral and political philosophy, Latin American philosophy, and contemporary Continental philosophy. In this last domain, his interests concern the ways in which recent developments in non-classical logic might open new possibilities for speculative ontology.

Daniel Sacilotto is a doctoral student in the Comparative Literature department at UCLA.

Steven Shaviro is the DeRoy Professor of English at Wayne State University. He is the author of *Connected, Or, What It Means to Live in the Network Society* (2003), *Without Criteria: Kant, Whitehead, Deleuze, and Aesthetics* (2009), and *The Universe of Things: Whitehead in the Light of Speculative Realism* (2014).

Devin Zane Shaw teaches in both the Department of Philosophy and the Department of Visual Arts at the University of Ottawa. He is currently writing a book on Jacques Rancière and philosophy, which is a loose sequel to his *Freedom and Nature in Schelling's Philosophy of Art* (2012).

Sergey Sistiaga studied philosophy at the University of Freiburg and the Sorbonne, Paris. He translated Graham Harman's 'On Vicarious Causation' into German. His areas of research are metaphysics, rationalism, philosophy of science and nihilism.

Christina Smerick is Associate Professor of Religion and Philosophy and the Chair of the Philosophy and Religion department at Greenville College. She is also Shapiro Chair of Jewish-Christian Studies. Her most recent publication is 'Bodies, Communities, Faith: Christian Legacies in Jean-Luc Nancy', in *Analecta Hermeneutica*, 4 (2012).

Anthony Paul Smith is an Assistant Professor in the Department of Religion at La Salle University. He is the author of *A Non-Philosophical Theory of Nature: Ecologies of Thought* (2013) and the translator of numerous works by François Laruelle including *Principles of Non-Philosophy* and *Future Christ: A Lesson in Heresy*.

Pete Wolfendale is an independent scholar with a PhD in philosophy from the University of Warwick. His work focuses on the methodology of metaphysics and the structure of rationality, and the relation between the two, for which he draws from a cross-traditional set of influences including Kant, Hegel, Heidegger, Deleuze, Quine, Sellars and Brandom. This work can be viewed on his long-running philosophy blog http://deontologistics.wordpress.com.

Ben Woodard is a PhD student at the Centre for Theory and Criticism at the University of Western Ontario. He is currently writing his dissertation on the connection between speculative physics and the intuition of space in the work of F.W.J von Schelling. He has published two short monographs, *Slime Dynamics: Generation, Mutation, and the Creep of Life* (2012) and *On an Ungrounded Earth: Towards a New Geophilosophy* (2013).

Bart Zantvoort is an IRC Government of Ireland Postgraduate Scholar at University College Dublin, currently working on his doctoral thesis on inertia and resistance to change in complex structures. Current research interests include German Idealism, particularly Hegel, early Frankfurt school Critical Theory, twentieth-century French philosophy, and systems theory.